RICH IS BETTER

By the Same Author

WINNING BY NEGOTIATION

RICH IS BETTER

How Women Can Bridge the Gap
Between Wanting and Having It All:
Financially, Emotionally, Professionally

Tessa Albert Warschaw, Ph.D.

ISBN 0-9630298-0-0

First paperback edition, 1991.

1 2 3 4 5 6 7 8 9

For my mother and sister Harriet,
Women of abundance who, without reservation,
Share their "Riches"

To Helen — another
sister on the path —
lucky me

Blessings,
Lisa

ACKNOWLEDGEMENTS

We all have "significant others," and most significant to me and to the realization of this book is Sheila Weller—perceptive, insightful, and generous. Her commitment to this project has been invaluable.

To my editor, Loretta Barrett, who shares my vision that women can break away from the *poverty mentality*. I am respectful of her courage to support this project with its complex vision of pragmatism and idealism. Appreciation to Felecia Abbadessa for her competent assistance.

To Elaine Markson, my literary agent and friend, who lovingly shepherded this book and never stopped believing in it—and in me. To Geri Thoma, who also shared this belief and watched it grow with a keen critical eye. And to Raymond Bongiovanni, always helpful . . . thanks.

To Dr. Dee Barlow for invaluable professional insights and Dr. Dick Varnes for sharing his own experiences and expertise.

I am particularly grateful to Dr. Lee Gardenswartz and Dr. Susanna Hoffman for their generosity of ideas, support, and love.

I remain indebted to the men and women who are my clients—and continue to be my teachers.

To the many anonymous "Comers and Havers" and professional men and women who have given so freely of their time, knowledge and experiences.

I am pleased to have worked with Russell Pearson as my financial consultant to this project.

My deepest appreciation to Lester Levenson and Virginia Lloyd of the Sedona Institute, who gave me the gift of the Sedona Method. They have greatly influenced my beliefs and ideas, "beyond money."

I am fortunate to receive "wise counsel" from a creative "kitchen cabinet" which includes Fred Siegel, Howard Siegel, Julia Chang, Robert Resnick and Andrew Watkins. I am profoundly grateful to Don Marts of Mitsui Manufacturers Bank for his continuing commitment to my work.

For loving support, a special thank-you to my old and new friends: Ernie Castaldo, Francis Hill, Bonnie Collins, Stuart Schwartz, Stephen Black, Henry Steern, Cynthia and Marty Deutsch, Maureen Benun, Judi Hochman, Paul Moran, Jane Collins Snowday, Behnam Nateghi, Maya and Jeff Haddow, Gail and David Stone, Mollie Gregory, Phyllis Touchie Specht, Chet Specht, Norma DeSofi, and Sandy Carter. And, of course, Andrea Szmyt.

And to those who epitomize the best of networking: Sandy Burke,

Sandy Gabin, Marjorie Kouns, Cecilia Moy, Brenda Ratcliff, Lyn Salzburg, Marie Sibilla, Karen Weinberg, Ann Bauer.

To all children who pull red wagons, I send my love.

My heart is filled with love and gratitude to my family, who have always been a source of inspiration and strength on whichever coast I happened to land. To the women of my family: Shelli, Mindy, Lora Dean; and to the men: Loren, Jeff, Tim—my love to you all. To the youngest of the clan, Adam and Jaclyn, who fill me with love and laughter. And of course to P.J. and Ted, wherever you both may be—know that you continue to nourish me with loving memories.

unconscious decision to live an unfulfilled life—financially, emotionally, creatively or physically. That subsequent starvation in one aspect of her functioning is thrusting the rest of her life into a lopsided arrangement of compensations, defenses and resignments, making it all the harder for her to get what she really needs and wants—be that intimacy or independence, success in work, comfort in love or sturdiness in self-esteem.

- The Poverty Mentality is the means by which negative emotions directly lead to a negative balance sheet of dollars and cents.
- The Poverty Mentality is a woman's keeping herself in Less— a state of neediness, denial and unhappiness. She may do this by remaining in a bad love relationship (or not letting herself see that a flawed one can be improved); by sabotaging herself in such a way that she stays stuck in economic deprivation; by making it financially, only to punish herself afterward; or by becoming so driven in her work life that she starves herself in terms of friendship, love and play.
- The Poverty Mentality is a woman's assumption that she can't have it all: that she must somehow be punished for her accomplishments or good fortune; that for any advance, achievement or triumph in either the personal or the professional sphere there must be a corresponding loss in the other.
- The Poverty Mentality, for some women, manifests itself in the feeling that there exists a ceiling to the understanding they can attain in the worlds of finance and power that govern their existence; that it is futile to try to take control of big chunks of their lives. For others, it takes a more metaphorical form: the deep-seated fear of separateness from mate and family that ends up stifling their attempts to find any creative release on their own. For still others, it is the opposite side of that coin: a terror that intimacy with another person will threaten the freedom and self-hood they have struggled so gamely to achieve.

Women who have the Poverty Mentality can be divided into two groups. There are those I call the *Comers.* These are women, young and not so young, who are on their way up, who haven't yet "arrived." Their fight to break out of the Poverty Mentality consists largely of learning to change their ways of assuming and expecting and going for so they'll be able to raise their incomes and their levels of professional satisfaction and success.

INTRODUCTION

Poverty, Fulfillment, Abundance . . . and You

All day long—in my therapy practice, in the seminars I run, at lunches, dinners and cocktail parties—I find myself listening to women talk about their lives. Some are executives with six-figure incomes and power to burn whose names regularly appear in Hollywood trade papers. Others are housewives who've never held a paying job. Many fill up the points on the continuum in between. But one theme keeps popping up in all of their talk like a running stitch through a very long piece of cloth. And that theme is *deprivation.*

For as earnestly as many of these women subscribe to the ethic of fulfillment, and as vital as they are in most ways, in some pocket of their lives they are wanting. They may feel financially strapped, emotionally undernourished, frustrated in their careers—or powerless to choose and change in one or all three of these areas.

Some women are so in touch with their deprivation they can analyze it for hours on end. Others are so removed from theirs that only their nervous laughter, tight voices and distracted hand motions betray the true state of affairs beneath their superficially self-assured banter. Some apologize for and belittle their complaint, backing into disclosure with "Maybe I'm being impatient, but . . ." and "I'm basically a happy person, except. . . ." Others wrap their dissatisfaction in the bright flag of feminist rhetoric, self-actualization jargon, psychoanalytic theory.

But, however, they exhibit it, each woman is suffering from what I have come to call *the Poverty Mentality: the conscious or*

V: Beyond Money

Contents

Other women are those I call the *Havers*. They do have money and power, to one extent or another. But the cost of it all has proved high; the rewards, hollow. They are still unfulfilled. I spend an equal amount of attention in this book to each of these two groups of women.

Whichever group you belong to, you will probably find at least a part of your life in one of the many examples in this book. You may be:

- Joyce, who since her divorce three years ago has chosen to sink almost all of her time and energy into her work as a travel agent—but who, in that process, has lost touch with her need for the very spontaneity and leisure her field represents; who goes to parties to "develop contacts," dates men for their "potential" and hasn't taken a trip of her own without her briefcase in two years.

Or you may be:

- Ruth, whose apparel-industry job is as demanding as her husband's patent-law practice but who hasn't found a way of negotiating with her husband to share the job of household management and parenting that has been left solely to her.

- Eileen, who could well be a talented architect—or so say the professionals at the architectural firm where she works as a secretary. But who still has it in her head that she'll be married someday and that will take care of her future.

- Fran, who, despite her status and salary as a senior editor at a publishing house, still spends Saturdays and Sundays washing her own laundry and doing housework in an apartment whose scruffy furniture reflects not the success she is today but the scrambling, abashed assistant she was years ago.

- Caitlin, who is dependent on her attorney, accountant, business manager, realtor, stockbroker and auto mechanic to tell her what's happening with the money and possessions she's earned all by herself.

- Monica, who chooses men technically "appropriate" (they have money, power, charm) and "available" (they are not married) but who are so emotionally closed—so loathe to commitment— that one after another her futures with these Good Catches turn to dust, handily absolving her from any blame for avoiding intimacy.

- Pam, who is dragging her heels toward the promotion she knows she can have because it will raise her income and job title above that of her mate's. Won't this, she fears, threaten him and damage their relationship?

■ Audrey, a political science Ph.D. who has remained at a middle-level job in a large research institute during the same three years that a former coworker, a man with only a master's degree, made two job switches that advanced him in money, status and responsibility.

Finally, you may be:

■ Gwen, wife and mother of two, who keeps saying she is going to go back to school to finish the art history curriculum that so perfectly squares with her avocation of weekly gallery- and museum-going—but who never gets around to doing it.

But wait, I hear you protesting. Don't men have a Poverty Mentality, too? Certainly! And, in most cases, in a worse form than women's. For many men, career, money and winning (against someone else) have often meant everything. They gave little attention to the rewards and prerogatives of being good fathers, husbands, lovers and friends. But what is exciting about these times we live in is that, ever since the sixties, that old traditional male system of narrow rewards has proven more and more bankrupt. Men are opening up to new gratifications and ways of being —with no small assist from the women in their lives.

Women have already changed. And while we hardly need to be told this, a few statistics really drive home the distance between today and the fifties with startling clarity: As of 1981 (the most recent year for which statistics are available), two-income marriages accounted for 62 percent—three fifths—of all American marriages. The "typical" American family—working father, stay-at-home mother, one or more children—has plummeted from 70 percent of the U.S. population thirty years ago to 15 percent today. In 1978, for the first time in history, more women than men were admitted to American institutions of higher learning. Women now occupy one quarter of managerial and administrative jobs in private industry in the United States—compared with almost none ten years ago. In the late fifties, public opinion analyst Daniel Yankelovich surveyed women in their teens and early twenties to find that 100 percent of them assumed they would marry and have children. In a 1982 survey conducted by *Mademoiselle* magazine, only 23 percent of similar-aged women believed that marriage and children were an essential part of life—but 45 percent said that work was.

"Fulfillment." We use that term a lot. Perhaps because our notion and practice of fulfillment has changed so greatly (and perhaps, too, because the climate of economic scarcity we're living in now is forcing us all to turn for gratification to our only truly expandable commodity: ourselves), women today are vigorously consumed with the issue of fulfillment, with the juggling necessary to "have it all": work and love, intimacy and independence. Laid end to end, the number of articles written on this subject in the last five years alone could probably pave a road from New York to Brazil.

Yet the "answers" they provide aren't giving us enough. Clearly what is for men a not impossible balance is for women still a complex and elusive ideal. And the quest for fulfillment is not merely for narcissistic reasons, as is commonly supposed; it's often a matter of sheer survival. Caught in transitional times—with new responsibilities and yearnings but without a changed society in which the day-to-day details of the old ones are shared—today's women do face boggling scheduling and prioritizing problems.

What's more, they often face these problems alone. Single-family households headed by women outnumber those headed by men by nine to one. Seventy-five percent of divorced mothers in America are receiving only a part of the child support owed them —if they're receiving any at all.

Undoubtedly political action is needed to reverse these unhappy facts. Yet another, more personal kind of action is needed as well. For even if it is fair to blame a government of a "system" for inequities that reverberate on individual lives, such blame puts the power to change those inequities in other people's hands.

You can only feel in control of your life if the power to change things is in your own two hands.

This book is aimed at getting women to delve inside themselves to realize the psychological power they have always had; to understand the stumbling blocks they erect against the full use of that power; to learn how to undo those blocks and how, with specific strategies and techniques, to take action not just to correct the problem but to enrich their lives.

This book is also aimed at teaching you how to enlist the men in your life to help you. For, far from being the Enemy, the men in your life whether they're lovers or business associates, are your greatest untapped asset. All of my work is directed at encouraging collaboration, and my best results have come from helping my clients to understand that their partners are truly that: potential assistants, allies and facilitators, not adversaries. In fact, only the limits of length have kept me from writing this book as much about men as about women. I believe that human emotional problems transcend gender—and that their solutions are utterly based on respect for and love of the opposite sex.

Too many women don't know how to negotiate for what they want and need from even those men most intimate with them. For this reason, Part II of this book is devoted to showing couples how they can very specifically, and sensitively, break through and reverse some of the greatest, and most painful, rituals of Poverty Mentality that keep them down together today. (Currently unpartnered women who wish to form loving and equal relationships can learn a great deal from this, too. And the dynamics that so often bring couples to financial and emotional poverty are not an exclusively male-female phenomenon. This part is just as apt for same-sex couples.)

By enlisting the men in her life to help her break out of her own Poverty Mentality, a woman can also show these men how to break out of their own. This is true particularly in marriage and living-together relationships. Over years of counselling both women and men, separately and together, I've watched many stale and constricted marriages swivel around over time to equity and vibrance. Wives crawled out from under their husbands' shadows (and economic grips) to become functioning professionals and vital personalities in their own right; husbands—once taciturn and work-obsessed—learned to relax and tune in to their families' emotional and domestic needs.

Many couples today have progressed past the classic male-female role fossilization. Still problems remain. However equal they may be on the job, most women still assume much more responsibility than their mates for the running of the home. This is time-consuming and energy-draining. Worse, it often serves to nip career incentive in the bud. ("How can I volunteer for that new project?" a city-planning trainee laments. "It'll mean working ten instead of eight hours a day. Who'll take care of the kids?")

Then too, the fear of outpacing their husbands and lovers in income and status is still pervasive in women. Even if they've intellectually gotten past the fear that their men will be diminished or emasculated by their achievements, these women often feel it's unfair to hog the game: to get credit not only for succeeding in the female realm but also for outshining their mates in the *only* realm in which this society allows a man to prove his worth. ("If I don't make partner," said an associate lawyer married to an insurance-industry junior executive, "I'll still be considered to have done damn well for a woman in business today—and I've been a good mother, which gives me another whole set of Brownie points. But to the outside world, Jim's points come only from his track record at work. He's been a good father? 'Well, so what?' says the world.")

On the face of it—given the moment in time and the imperfect world that we live in—such reasoning is not entirely irrational. (One recent study of a wide cross section of American couples* found that many men are still very uncomfortable when their wives make more money than they do.) But this thinking is also very destructive, often serving to trigger an automatic slowdown or backtrack mechanism in many an otherwise promising career. The terrible buildup of resentment this process inevitably fosters in the woman can be lethal to the very marriage she intended it to protect. Therefore, it's a no-win bind for both partners.

In Chapter 7 ("Breaking the No-Win Bind") I will give you a program for tackling and solving this obstinate problem, just as in Chapter 6 ("Brand-New Poverty Games Couples Play"), we will explore several other emotional and economic conundrums that the half-opened door to equality has left men and women in. You will learn how to lift yourself out of these, too. In Chapter 9 (Divorce As Positive As Possible) we will take on the shocking epidemic of nonsupport-paying ex-husbands. I will show you not only how you can set up your own divorce so that you will not be a victim of this, but how you and the man you are separating from can achieve what so many men, women and lawyers think is a contradiction in terms: the Divorce That's As Positive As Possible.

And in Chapter 8, "Making Peace with the Nurturance Gap" (one of my favorite parts of the book), we will leap from negative to positive—and study how men and women can honor—and help

* Philip Blumstein and Pepper Schwartz, *American Couples,* William Morrow, 1983.

fill—each other's needs for the real staff of life, emotional nurturance.

But before that, in chapters 1 through 5 (Part I), we will explore something else that this syndrome illustrates: the four concepts that comprise a woman's Poverty Mentality. For the woman who is backing down on her career for the "sake" of a man—as well as the woman who has turned down a demanding work project because she alone "must" take care of the house and kids—is actually suffering less from an injust system or an imbalanced marriage than from a series of subtle yet profound internal bluffs and blocks. These are:

1. *Ambivalence*, which translates into the question, "What do I really want?"
2. *Undeservingness*, or, "Am I entitled to try for what I want?"
3. *Vacant Hope*, meaning, "Do I really expect to be able to get what I want?"
4. *Guilt As A Smoke Screen*, which means, "I'm going to fall back on easy self-blame and the facade of selflessness to avoid the question, 'If I do risk and try for it, what love and comfort will I lose?' "

Though they're presented here as separate concepts, ambivalence, undeservingness, vacant hope and guilt are really intricately interlocked, nourishing and reinforcing each other within a woman's psyche. Sometimes I visualize them as a diagram of the four protons perpetually encircling and bouncing off each other inside the atom—or as dominoes propped up against each other: when one is flicked, all four collapse.

In a moment, we'll take a long look at these concepts and how they operate in your life, but the crucial thing to know now is that they may all result in paralysis. Breaking out of Poverty Mentality depends, more than anything else, on risking change and taking action. Throughout this book you will see dozens of examples of women whose changes in habits, routines and responses (sometimes small, seemingly arbitrary changes) have begun to jolt them out of negative patterns and assumptions they've lived with all their lives.

I helped these women by devising exercises for them. As my clients in psychotherapy, they've made lists and kept charts, graphs and diaries to unearth their styles of self-sabotage, to probe their fantasies and dreams. I've taught them to brainstorm for the hidden possibilities in their lives—and then to make agendas, write negotiating scripts, even practice lines of dialogue to transform those possibilities into action. Because these assignments have worked so well for them, I've adapted them and in some cases reproduced them throughout this book for you.

I think of myself as a pragmatist, a problem solver. So we're not going to reach all the way back to your early childhood to mull over the roots of your self-esteem. And no sentence in this book begins, "Because men were conditioned, as little boys, to aggress and achieve and women, as little girls, to be pleasing and helpless. . . ." You already know all of that. It's fresh territory I want to explore—it's your present and future, not your past, that I care about.

Women, it's often said, are afraid of success and of money. This is simply untrue. Women *love* money. They relish the fruits of success as much as any man. The trouble comes in the distance between the desire for money and success, and its realization. It is here in the operational midrange that women get tangled up.

Women say, "I deserve to be successful!" and "Damn it, I should get a raise!"—but they don't know how to pull those plums off the tree. Even when they get past being ambushed by guilt and fear of loss, and past the fear that they'll be "found out" as frauds; even when they stop needing an emergency to know that they're "it" (the one person in control of their destiny)—even when women get past all these roadblocks which we discuss in Part I, there are still practical things to learn.

Part IV addresses these practical matters: how to own up to, bring out and make happily operational your appetite for having more (Chapter 10, "Lust Is Not a Dirty Word"); how to demystify the people who stand between you and your money, and how to take control of that realm yourself (Chapter 12, "Demystifying the Moneylords"); how to draft an actual plan that will really get you from the point you're at now in your bankbook and career to the point you want to be at one year from now (Chapter 11, "Tailor-Making Your Agenda for Abundance: The One-Year Time Line for Real Results"); and how to get all the help you need from others to implement your plan, on time, while keeping up a full, happy home front as well (Chapter 13, "Interindependence: Negotiating for Help").

Does this sound suspiciously like "having it all"? Well, in fact, it is. A few words are in order now on this recently maligned phrase. In the late seventies, the bugle call "You can have it all!" began to feel a little tyrannical and accusatory. Women who during the first flush of the women's movement had felt inspired by that exhortation now turned confused and began to feel wanting and more than a little breathless against the media-foisted image of the dynamo executive who was also a doting mother, sparkling hostess, dashing Ferrari racer, soothing helpmate, gourmet cook and crack fly fisherman.

We were right to be cynical about that fictional Superwoman. The immediate rejoinder "You can't have it all!" (with its implied second sentence, "So don't feel inadequate if you don't") was valuable reassurance to all those women, fresh from the old conditioning, who felt pressured by that impossible ideal.

But we've progressed way beyond all that now. Most women have seen through that old cookie-cutter model of "liberated" fulfillment and have traded in the naïve excesses of infant feminism for a more mature, considered view. Women have found their own individual, nuanced, authentic versions of fulfillment. These versions—these dreams and goals—come from the heart, not from magazine articles; from life experience, not from TV commercials. This thought-through "all" that is wanted is well within reach. Many have taken very real steps toward it. And those who have achieved it are not the frantic jugglers that the received wisdom of six or eight years ago would have us believe; they are happy women.†

So it not only is time to stop feeling embarrassed for wanting it all. It's time to go after the clear possibility of having it all—and finding delight in the having.

Having it all doesn't take magic. It doesn't take luck. And it certainly doesn't take duplicity or manipulation. I believe I have found what it does take, step by step—and, in as clear and comprehensive, as specific and as loving a way as I know how, I have written this book to tell you.

---

† Dr. Grace Baruch of Wellesley College, author, with her colleague, Dr. Rosalind Barnett, of *Lifeprints: New Patterns of Love and Work* (New American Library), is one of many who have found that "the greatest sense of well-being is among women who have high-level jobs, are mothers and are married. Juggling these multiple roles does not stress women."

And with this book, I hope I can add to the vital dialogue—the quest—that we women have been so energetically pursuing for three and a half decades.

During these years, we have departed radically from traditional ideas about female roles and happiness, discovered new discontents in the terms of that rebellion have returned to redefine and to synthesize the best of both worlds:

In the fifties, women were in the thrall of the Feminine Mystique,‡ blithely discarding the prerogatives of their college degrees for almost violently serene wife-and-motherhood with their gray-flannel-suited men.

In the sixties, the sexual revolution and a spirited, hedonistic antimaterialism (the latter, the luxury of an indulgently healthy economy) crushed those white-picket-fence values to the ground.

In the seventies, feminism entered mainstream life—and reversed a good number of the edicts of the sixties. (Now women shouldn't drop out, wear long skirts and bake bread on communes; instead they should don business suits and join the upwardly mobile careerists.)

The self-actualization movements that led the seventies to be called the Me Decade neatly buried the rest of the Sixties Think: "Love Power" turned to the power of the well-looked-after Number One; tribalism gave way to narcissism; personal growth, not communal good, was the ideal.

Finally, at the beginning of the second half of the eighties, we have the hindsight (and perhaps the sage weariness) to see that none of the past decades' strident, unilateral "answers" were really complete or satisfying in themselves. All those ideas of fulfillment were constrictive and limited and mutually exclusive, based on wiping out what went before, rooted in either/or. What we want now is to go beyond either/or to and/and/and—past mere fulfillment—the filling up to capacity—to what I call *expansive abundance:* the art of living a life that never loses spiritual and ethical meaning for all its material conquests; the art of adding richness to others, indeed to the very planet, while at the same time acquiring and achieving. (I devote the last chapter of the book—Part V, "Beyond Money"—to a discussion of this inspiring living-style.)

‡ Betty Friedan's wonderful phrase and revolutionary book.

Women now want a nonexploitative, redefined sense of belonging (to mate, children, friends, community) and at the same time the wide-open chance to succeed and to flower in personal identity and career. We want to expand our options to encompass both halves of the pie.

And the good news is: We can do it.

I have found, in working creatively with my clients, that women's lives—men's lives, too—need not be impoverished in terms of career, money or relationship. We are worthy of the wholeness that we dream our lives to be—and capable of engineering it. Since we are going to spend several hundred pages learning how to do so, let me borrow eleven words to preface the trip.

The title of this book, *Rich Is Better,* is the tail end of a remark first made by comedian Joe E. Louis, later picked up by the great singers Sophie Tucker and Ella Fitzgerald (in which order is always debated). The line, in its entirety, goes: "I've been rich, and I've been poor, and rich is better." The beauty and the humor and the almost poetic quality of that line are not just in its sublime understatement of the obvious but in its wry assumption that being rich and being poor are *absolutely equally available choices that anyone can make;* that it is no more complicated or difficult to be rich than to be poor. The assumption is supposed to be ironic.

But, do you know something?

It's really not ironic at all. It is—as you will discover through these pages—literally true.

RICH IS BETTER

1

DO YOU HAVE THE POVERTY MENTALITY?

CHAPTER 1

Feeling to Attitude to Behavior: The Crucial Circuit

A young sportswear buyer plans to take two business school courses—capital investment and importing—so she can open her own store someday. Yet when her husband's law firm tells him they're sending him to Alaska during that same three months to help on an oil-company suit, she finds herself planning immediately her cold-weather wardrobe.

Because she says her main commitment is to the serious novel she's been working on, off and on, for several years, a talented writer goes from one low-paying short-term job to the next—while her less gifted friends are making advances in editorial and advertising careers.

After her promotion, a market researcher in a division of a large company goes to the office party—and has one gin and tonic too many to be in perfectly top form when the visiting company sales director comes over to congratulate her and to talk projected demographics.

During an early-morning long-distance phone call to her boyfriend from a location-scouting trip, a film assistant producer senses that an innocent wisecrack she made may have hit him the wrong way. She thinks about it until noon, when she grabs the first available pay phone, calls him at his office to make sure he's not upset with her—and finds that he doesn't even remember the remark and is puzzled by her clearly unnecessary act of making two calls in five hours.

Real life, I often tell my clients, takes place in the unconscious. And these four women are examples of that fact. Each one might give you a perfectly sound, unblinking account of what she believes she is doing—preparing to open a store someday; conducting her life as a serious writer; jumping into a new promotion with confidence; allaying her guilt over possibly hurting the man she cares about. But her actual behavior subtly or glaringly tells us something else.

Looking at these examples, we can see that the potential result of each of these women's behaviors was less money—either directly (the first two women) or indirectly—through the self-sabotage of a job (the third woman) or the parlaying of valuable work-time energy elsewhere (the fourth).

In each case, the woman's behavior is the manifestation of an attitude that stems from a feeling she is only dimly aware of, if she's aware of it at all. These feelings are, respectively, ambivalence, vacant hope, undeservingness and guilt as a smoke screen for fear of separation and grief over loss.

My years as a therapist have shown me that, more than any other force, these four syndromes work powerfully together to steer women's lives off their positive courses and right into the Poverty Mentality.

In a moment we will explore each of these feelings in the detail they deserve. But for now let me briefly say:

- *Ambivalence* is the oscillation between two different, often mutually exclusive goals—or the holding of contradictory emotions toward the same thing.
- *Undeservingness* is the feeling that you're not good enough or capable enough to go after and get what you want. It can also be the dismissal of some goal as inappropriate to you—before that goal has a chance to become a conscious consideration.
- *Vacant hope* is a term I've coined for indulgence in the act of hoping without hope's positive, motivating content. It's longing for something you don't really expect to get—or feigning a desire or aspiration (even to yourself) in order to justify and perpetuate stasis in your life.
- *Guilt as a Smoke Screen* is the use of an easily available re-

sponse to disguise one that's harder to find and to face. It occurs when the independent action that would be appropriate for you at this time frightens you. You're afraid that by pursuing that action, you'll lose closeness, connection and love. So you foment guilt or an exaggerated sense of duty to another person as an unconscious alibi to forgo that threatening independence.

All of these are feelings, and though we use that word incessantly these days, we rarely stop to think about what a feeling really is.

A feeling is what you say to yourself about the state of your psyche and its relation to the world at a given point in time. A feeling is the first switch on what can be pictured as an electrical circuit that goes on to include two other switches. That first switch sets in motion the second (which is attitude) and the second sets in motion the third (behavior). Of these three, feelings are the most diffuse, passive and unexhibited—which is to say they're hardest to pinpoint, they don't *do* anything in and of themselves and they're often not apparent to others.

Because I see our emotional lives not as static and fixed but as fluid and ever changing, I find it easiest to visualize feelings by referring to them as stuck motion. What do I mean by this? Imagine yourself as a film projectionist who's watching a movie of an hour of your life, frame by frame. Now suddenly stop the machine, freeze and blow up one single frame for scrutiny.

When we experience a feeling—anger, elation, distrust, melancholy, apprehensiveness, whatever—that is just what we are doing: involuntarily halting, pausing over and magnifying one discrete unit of sensation out of the rushing stream of many; letting that one sensation suffuse us and assume enough dominance over the others to define our mood for even the briefest period of time.

And if that period of time is not brief but protracted, then enough energy is conducted to throw the next switch on the circuit: attitude.

An attitude is the middle stage on the continuum. It is less diffuse, passive and unexhibited than a feeling, but not as concrete, active or expressed as a behavior. If a feeling is what you say to yourself about the state of your psyche and its relation to the world at a given point in time, an attitude is what you project, often inadvertently, to others about that same state. Attitude might be visualized as the slightly clouded windowpane through which those who interact with you can glimpse at the feeling inside.

And no more than glimpse they do, for attitude is subtle. It radiates, hints at, suggests. It colors and informs what you do and say to others. An attitude is what used to be called in the late sixties and early seventies your "vibrations." It is a constellation of subarticulate beliefs and thoughts—an undercurrent, a posture, a predisposition to act.

And when that predisposition meets provoking or stimulating circumstances, enough energy is conducted to throw the next switch on the emotional circuit: behavior.

Behavior is the third and last stage on the circuit—the most concrete, active and exhibited of the three. Behavior is attitude ripened to manifestation. What was simply paused over in feeling, then implied by attitude, is now expressed in a physical or verbal way.

The four women described at the beginning of this chapter all exhibit behavior that was ripened from attitude that stemmed, respectively from the four feelings I've discussed as being critical to the Poverty Mentality. Doing this is common. I've done it myself. Several years ago, for example, I was faced with the question, Should I actively expand my business of running seminars or not? For nine years, people had sought me out to set up workshops and programs on negotiation; I hadn't needed to print up a single brochure. Now, if I wanted to expand, I had to make it happen.

And having to make it happen on this larger scale would mean taking time away from my private therapy practice and from my writing, both meaningful parts of my life. I wanted the expanded seminar schedule and the writing and the private practice. I wanted to travel and to stay home. What I was feeling, in a word, was ambivalence. My attitude, during those initial weeks of sorting out my plans, was indecisiveness. And the behavior that sprang from the attitude that grew from the feeling was this: flying first-class on planes to set up the seminars, I'd meet fascinating people who implicitly or explicitly offered themselves to me as valuable contacts—and then I'd lose their business cards!

That "accidental" or unconscious behavior was self-sabotaging, and as soon as I saw it in myself, I sat down and traced it back along its emotional circuitry to the "culprit" stem feeling, ambivalence.

After analyzing my situation, I resolved the ambivalence by deciding to go for the expanded seminar schedule on a trial basis. If, after six months, I was happy with the extra traveling and the shift in priorities, I would wholeheartedly continue to expand.

That's just what happened: as I took on more seminars, I was able to make organizational changes in my life at home to minimize the sacrifice to my writing and my therapy practice. Robbed of its reason to be, my ambivalence collapsed. The uncertainty ceased. And, of course, I stopped losing those business cards.

Although the form of ambivalence that afflicted me here was rather limited, other forms are not. Neither are most forms of the feelings of undeservingness, vacant hope, and—as I abbreviate it —guilt/grief/loss. Over years of sensing my clients' feelings, picking up on their attitudes, and witnessing their behavior and its results, I have devised a chart of the emotional circuitry that comprises the Poverty Mentality. (See Table 1.) All roads, you will notice, lead to the same dead-end place: stasis and self-destructiveness.

There's a way to reverse all of this, but in order to find it we must first of all know what we're dealing with.

So let's explore each stem feeling.

Table 1

THE POVERTY MENTALITY

The FEELING Is	The ATTITUDE Is	The BEHAVIOR Is
Ambivalence	Indecisiveness Uncertainty Blurred discrimination Confusion Conflictedness	Discrimination paralysis Sabotage of one or another option
Undeservingness	Discomfort with change Disbelief of praise Fear of being "found out" Resistance to or ignorance of advancement possibilities	Self-sabotage Apathy

The FEELING Is (cont.)	The ATTITUDE Is (cont.)	The BEHAVIOR Is (cont.)
	Guilt over rewards Reluctance to delegate or give up outgrown responsibilities Self-deprecation Insecurity	
Vacant hope	Tolerance of waiting False optimism masking defeatism Lack of initiative Rationalization, gullibility to alibis Inappropriate patience	Passive action Lack of movement toward goal
Guilt/grief/ loss	Fear that loved ones will become powerful or independent Fear of own independence Overcompensation Overattentiveness Possessiveness Refusal to delegate or relegate outgrown or no longer appropriate responsibilities Obsessiveness	Relinquishment of goal Retreat from independence Self-submersion in others

CHAPTER 2

Ambivalence

"What Do I Really Want?"

I have never met a woman who wasn't willing to sacrifice at least a little of her career for a relationship.

I have never met a man who thought he had to.

And this disparity is what makes for female ambivalence.

Ambivalence, the dictionary tells us, is "contradictory emotional or psychological attitudes . . . simultaneous attraction toward and repulsion from an object, person, or action." It is also "continual oscillation (as between one thing and its opposite)" and "uncertainty as to which approach, attitude, or treatment to follow." Now, how does this relate to men and women?

Men consider their work the fixed pillar around which the people in their lives must bend. Women see the act of having and keeping gratifying personal relationships as a pillar—an end, a goal—in itself. Today, with career added to their lives as a priority, women find themselves doing shuttle diplomacy between two very different goals: love and work. And such constant, uncertainty-breeding oscillation constitutes one dictionary meaning of "ambivalence."

Also, since men take their work to be an unimpeachable duty and right, they assume that love is a constant attendant: something that someone will continue to give them even if that someone is taxed or inconvenienced by the demands of their work. But most women view work as an option or even a privilege—as part of their identity, not that identity's cornerstone. So they don't assume they are owed unwavering love and accommodation by those who may be inconvenienced by their work. (Such inconve-

nience, the woman assumes, is her fault.) For this reason, women
don't pursue careers in the clear-minded, wholehearted, hungry
way that most men do. Some nagging fear of the price such pursuit
will exact from their valued personal lives keeps them ambivalent.

"I want a stimulating career, money and success," the women I
counsel all say. They believe they mean this. And intellectually
they do. But scratch the surface of that commitment and you find,
80 percent of the time, that they'll trade off some of that bounty
for love.

The trade-off is subtle—so subtle that usually a woman doesn't
even know she is making it. Gone are the days when college girls
cheerfully admitted to majoring in marriage and doing graduate
work in putting hubby through. We're much too sophisticated for
any of that now. And very rarely does a woman with an interesting
career tender her resignation to be a full-time wife. She probably
won't even reduce her working hours at all.

Yet how far she's gotten (or, more often, not gotten) in that
career—and what kind of ambition propelled her that distance—is
another matter. For often the presence or imminence of a lasting
love relationship (and sometimes even more so a tenuous one) can
chip some of the edge off a woman's raw need to accomplish, can
dilute the urgency of work as a primary goal. With relationship as
something to fall back on, work doesn't count as much.

Surprisingly, even some women in their twenties—women who
came to maturity during the height of feminism in the seventies—
use the sheer anticipation of love and marriage to hold a part of
their identity—and their future—in abeyance. Many such women
have come to me for therapy, ambushed by a subconscious reasoning that goes: Why should I go out of my way to look deeply inside
myself to ferret out what I might want to do with my life—and
then go through the pains of pursuing it when something else
(usually a relationship) will come along soon enough to cover that
lack and fill that need?

Because these women have not yet given themselves a chance
to go for a career—to feel truly in charge of their lives—I will refer
to them here as the *Comers.*

On the opposite end of the spectrum are those women I will call
the *Havers.* They have high-flying careers, status and power. Yet
for all the mastery they wield over their workaday lives, their
relationships are often in shambles. They find it easy to win points

at the boardroom negotiating table and on the stock market floor, yet they are exasperated and vulnerable in their dealings with the dazzling go-getter men to whom they're invariably attracted. These men want love affairs run their way—and having that sometimes involves the women's giving up more than a little of their work time (and the peace of mind needed to do that work well) for love.

Both of these women have opposite forms of the same problem. The Comer is stuck in ambivalence-leading-to-confusion-leading-to-apathy because, though she says she wants work, she has never known the terms and rewards of work, so she unconsciously looks for the process of love to fill the "work" space in her. The Haver is stuck in ambivalence-leading-to-conflict-leading-to-self-sabotage because, though she says she wants a relationship, she has never known the terms and rewards of true intimacy, so she unconsciously looks for the style and values of her work world to fill her "love" void. Each woman is trying to fit a square peg into a round hole. Neither is filled. Both know what they don't have, and so they are ambivalent about that which they do.

"I'm not sure what I'm going to do on my own, but I sure won't live in the shadow of another charismatic, authoritarian boyfriend," vows Gail, a Comer client of mine who has yet to find sustenance in work.

"Sometimes I think I'd give all this up for one good man," sighs Haver Audrey, referring, with a sweep of her hand, to her expensively furnished office in a television network's executive wing.

Part of each one's ambivalence is healthy. For aggressively questioning the unfulfilling life choices you have made (indeed, merely discovering that something you'd thought was immutable *is* a choice) is a good first step toward change.

But what steps come after that first one?

BREAKING THROUGH "COMER" AMBIVALENCE

"What do you love?"

Whenever a woman (or a man) comes into my office steeped in the fatiguing ambivalence that leads her to say, "I don't know what I really want to do with my life," I begin by posing that simple question.

"What do you love?" I repeat.

. . . And the silence that usually follows my question is deafening.

It's amazing how many people have no passion in their lives—and are puzzled by the expectation that they should.

When I asked this question recently of Gail, the young Comer I mentioned, she was one of the many who fell perplexedly silent. She was making a comfortable salary as a private secretary at a brokerage firm, but she had no interest in finance as a career. I judged her to have the style, intelligence and education (four years of college) to be making five times as much.

While she was living with Martin, a dynamic but dominating young lawyer, Gail's underachievement was comfortably obscured by the social and personal demands of their relationship. Between attending to Martin's ego, arranging the household and participating in a social life composed largely of his friends; between learning the skiing that Martin loved and perfecting her stroke on the tennis court that served as his weekend office, Gail had mercifully little time to confront her own career malaise. Her passion had always been reserved for a person, not a proficiency or a goal. The question "What do you love?" had stumped her because she was so used to concentrating on the who.

But now that Martin's narcissism and insistence on having things his way had convinced her that life with him would not make her happy, the question "What do I want to do with my life?" loomed in front of her like the stack of unpaid bills one returns to after a very long vacation. She'd made a trial split from Martin. She felt good about her decision—but raw and vulnerable, too. Having dispensed with her safety net, she wanted to build a solid base for herself from within. I wanted to help her find the materials with which to do so.

"I want you to come back here Monday with a written description of your idealized life—and what that life feels like to you," I told her after our first session.

She returned that next week with a tentative picture of herself as an interior designer. She enjoyed design, she explained. She had helped Martin shop for office furniture, had rearranged his house and, years before, had spent a summer stripping old furniture down to its natural wood in an apartment she shared with two college roommates.

Furthermore, I noted, she had a distinctly aesthetic touch in the way she accessorized her clothes. And her work as private secretary to a busy executive had honed her skills as a negotiator for hard-to-get services. (How different, after all, was the knack for finagling her boss onto a fully booked flight to Denver from persuading a temperamental craftsman to alter his mural design to conform to a customer's taste?)

But the more we talked about the details of this possible career, the more uncomfortable Gail became. She protested that she would have to tie up her evenings with design courses and that even if she succeeded in those courses (and she wasn't sure she would) she'd have to quit a secure job to apprentice, for a lower salary, in her new field.

The sacrifice and risk of it all became frightening to Gail, and the hard work and mundane details involved in getting to her idealized life forced her to call her own bluff. Deep down, she was thinking of career as she'd thought of love: as something that rides in on a white charger to rescue and transform you. If it wasn't easy or automatic—something she could receive rather than go after—she wasn't interested.

"I guess I just don't want to be a designer badly enough," she said dispiritedly. To which I thought of Jean-Paul Sartre's remark "To be free is not to do what you know; it is to want what you can do." Gail wanted that wonderful, empowering freedom to be able to feel enthusiastic enough about her talents to put them to use. She wanted to break through her deadening ambivalence—to change from someone who had never acted aggressively on a career possibility in her life to someone who could.

The first step was to show her that she was much more capable of change than she thought.

I gave Gail a simple assignment: I asked her to do one new thing each week for eight weeks: alter a pattern, drop a habit, add a ritual to her day. "For example, go to a Greek restaurant for lunch instead of your favorite Japanese one," I said. "Don't watch TV before you turn in at night; read a book instead. Get up a half hour earlier in the morning."

Though petty and arbitrary by themselves, these changes, cumulatively, served to shift her picture of herself in the same minute way that turning the tube of a kaleidoscope inch by inch alters the mosaic within. She was experimenting with change and breaking down apathy on the smallest, most elemental level: that of idiosyncrasy. Those small actions began to rev up her internal motor—to prepare her to make crucial large actions.

"I feel habits frozen in me are being defrosted," Gail said one day.

She was shifting from a waiting mode to a mode of action.

To take best advantage of this new readiness, I gave Gail a second exercise: I asked her to sit down with a pad and pencil for an hour each night between two of our weekly sessions and to make five lists. (See Table 2, p. 15). Under FANTASIES, she was to free-associate all her yearnings and dreams, from the prosaic ("to marry a man I love and have children") to the fantastic ("to be a spy in the Kremlin"). Under FEELINGS, she would write down her reaction to each fantasy: laughter, enthusiasm, anxiety, etc. She was to spot-check her reaction on several separate nights and finally cross out those fantasies she deemed were not rooted in some authentic, if remote, desire or need—leaving those that *did* tell her something about herself. (For example, though far-fetched in itself, did the spy fantasy strike her as an expression of her real desire for risk-taking, for travel and for making a dramatic change of identity?)

Under column three, SKILLS, she was to brainstorm, over time, all her talents, competencies, and assets. Here I ask all my clients to go beyond standard résumé items (fluency in French, managerial experience, horseback riding proficiency, etc.) and to look deeply into themselves and pull out all the temperamental qualities, attitudes, intellectual capacities—even things they might otherwise dismiss as idiosyncrasies and quirks—that could possibly be considered assets. (Do you have a capacity to do several things at once, to deflect criticism with humor while objectively evaluating the truth in it? Are you good at analyzing the problems of your friends? Are you a master of timing? All of these count.)

Under column four, CONTACTS I, she was to free-associate all present and past colleagues, bosses, boyfriends, roommates, neighbors, mentors, teachers, advisors, relatives, friends and friends of friends whom you like and trust and who are even vaguely and indirectly in positions to help you better your working life or extend your professional horizons.

The next step is analysis. Look over the first column and see the pattern that emerges from the strong clues yielded by your fanta-

Table 2

FANTASIES, SKILLS AND CONTACTS

FANTASIES	FEELINGS	SKILLS	CONTACTS I	CONTACTS II

sies. You might find that you're not really a technical person but a people person after all; that you really crave, and would do well in, an independent, entrepreneurial role instead of the umbrella environment of the corporate world you've *been* in; that you'd flourish best as an idea person—in a rural setting, not as a follow-through person in a city one.

You may begin to see that you do have the skills to shape the clues found in your fantasies into a direction for yourself. Or you might find that you don't have those skills, that training is indicated (and, you see now, very possible).

Whichever you conclude, you are shaping up a picture of a truer, more focused self—a self full of prospect and potential. Not surprisingly, as you turn to the fourth column, you begin to see that you have many contacts to help you put that self into action. In fact you even see that there are people you've left off the list. The closer you get to defining a job, a field or an environment that you really want to go for, the more people suddenly "emerge" in your life (they've been there all along of course) to help you.

So now move on to column five and add the new contacts to the ones you've already listed in column four. You might want to break them down according to function:

1. *Sponsors* are people who will write letters of recommenda-

tion for jobs and schools in any of the fields that strike you as possible.

2. *Mentors* are people who can guide you through the "ropes" of that career.

3. *Teachers* are those who can impart in you specific needed new skills.

4. *Networkers* are people you know who are good at connecting and introducing people to each other and who enjoy doing so. They can do so for you now.

5. *Brain trusts* are learned, wise, experienced people—often much older than you—whose broad and knowing overview of a career, or simply of life in general, will be of value to you now.

6. *Clients* are those who can hire you, buy from you, commission you, use your services.

7. *Indirect facilitators* can ready you for your new career launching: the hairstylist and makeup artist who'll revamp your personal image, the graphics designer friend who'll print up your business cards and resume; the child-care person who'll take care of your kids while you go back to school, get a job.

8. *Horn blowers* are people who can informally promote you or talk you up in the circles where you want to start moving.

9. *Fans,* whom we'll learn more about in Chapter 8, are those wonderfully—uncritically—supportive people in your life who believe you can do no wrong. When you're making a big life change, they're great to have around.

10. *Truthtellers,* about whom we'll also learn in Chapter 8, offset the fans. They're the very valuable people who can give you constructive criticism and can save you from self-delusion and ill-advised moves—all without making you feel bad about yourself.

When my client has gotten to this point, I plan a five-point strategy with her that involves:

1. Make a decision (to make a change, take a leap, change fields, actively investigate the new indicated career).

2. Gather information (about how to do all of this most effectively).

3. Write letters and make phone calls to your contacts (to get the assistance you need at each step).

4. Plan interviews (with the contacts, with career counsellors, schools, employment agencies, prospective employers, etc.).

5. Get ready to disengage from what you're doing and use your waiting time to plan your move.

After completing this exercise and working with me on the strategy, Gail actually *felt* (rather than intellectualized) the desire for a design-related career in which she would work laterally and collaboratively with people (rather than "beneath" one person, as she had done as a secretary and as Martin's lover). She saw for the first time the possibility of having that kind of career—one in which her domestic leanings and talents, far from being at odds with her career (as she always assumed they'd have to be), were actually nurtured, highlighted and would serve as a springboard to valuable creativity.

She has enrolled in a program of courses on the acquisition, preservation, display and curating of folk crafts and antiques; has arranged for an apprenticeship setting up model eighteenth-century rooms for a new New England preservation society; and is looking into historical societies, museums, nonprofit foundations, and the like for future jobs. She is on her way.

Now, once, like Gail, you're equipped with your blueprint for action, you're ready to remove false supports and reliances—to zero in on yourself as the sole agent of your life. You're ready to look in the real or metaphorical mirror and say, "That's all there is: me."

Nothing cuts through Comer ambivalence faster than those words—and the jolt of belief that accompanies them.

Naomi is a good example. A film-industry story editor, she had recently—and amicably—separated from her fairly well off husband, Phil. Since he'd helped support her financially for the twelve years of their marriage, she expected his largesse to extend to her new life as a free-lance producer if she got in trouble and needed it.

Naomi rented an office, printed up stationery, shifted funds from savings and stock accounts to a checking account—all the while taking her new work at a leisurely, though conscientious, pace, assuring herself, "Most indie prods take two years to make their first deal."

When her rent check was returned stamped UNAVAILABLE FUNDS, she blithely phoned her landlord to have him put it through a second time. But when he appeared at her door a week later with the check that had bounced again, Naomi realized—in a flush of humiliation: there was no longer any backup from Phil. She was all there was.

Seven months later, she had her first production deal.

BREAKING THROUGH "HAVER" AMBIVALENCE

At a weekend seminar in which I recently participated, I met Peggy, a sharp, highly motivated woman. She was the public relations agent in charge of the event and I was very impressed with the deft, confident, creative way she juggled speakers, guests, press and the executives of the sponsoring corporation. She had that extra touch of savvy and wit that separates the exceptional members of her profession from the pedestrian. It didn't take long to realize that she had everything it took to soar.

Everything, that is, except a proper appreciation of her need to be nurtured.

I found this out when she took me aside after my first afternoon's lecture and confided her ambivalence about Ted, the man she was engaged to marry. "I think I love him," she said, "but everybody tells me he's not aggressive enough for me. There's a lot that I want out of life. My own business is just the beginning. And yet as much as I care for him, I wonder if over the long haul we'll really be compatible. I'm having a hard time deciding if I should marry him."

The next day she introduced me to Ted. He owned a small graphics business but he was patently uninterested in working the twenty hours a day it would take to expand. "Look," he said, "I have plenty: a house in the mountains as well as one in town; a boat; a car. I like to ski in the winter and hunt in the summer. I've got a balanced life. Everybody tells me, 'Go for more. Expand.' But I don't want the headaches that go with all that. I don't want life in the fast lane."

I found Ted to be charming, frank, at peace with himself and delightfully noncompetitive. He seemed to love Peggy and to respect her values and goals, even when some were different from his own.

By Sunday night, after two long days in which she'd played producer, hand holder, troubleshooter, camp counselor and press agent from morning to night, Peggy and I had a drink. As she talked briskly and brightly about the success of the seminar and her plan to sponsor more such events independently, I glanced from her wide, fatigue-fighting eyes to her right hand, its fingernails drumming the tabletop in giveaway tension.

"You know," I said, "if a man were in the exact same position you're in, and a woman as centered and supportive as Ted came into his life, he'd marry her in a minute."

She was startled for a moment—and then she agreed. Why, after all, was she looking for a male clone when what she really needed was a complement: someone to soothe her after a hectic day, to balance her earnest ambition with a dose of good-natured skepticism about the rat race; someone to take care of that part of her she was neglecting. Why was she, a "new woman," sticking to the old idea of what a husband should be?

I got a postcard from Peggy last week—from Bali. "So how many people do you know who got married in Paradise?" it read.

Peggy's story—minus her happy ending, unfortunately—is a typical one. Many of today's powerhouse women unconsciously arrange unhappy personal lives for themselves by being ambivalent about men who are anything less than gladiators. "Bor-ing," these women pronounce a whole range of men who fail to dazzle them with their achievements or their charm—but who may have the sensitivity and readiness to fill their intimacy needs.

These women have the tunnel vision that Peggy narrowly escaped. They train their sights exclusively on men with sizzling ambition, loads of charisma, and the showy, ruthless negotiating style that I've termed Jungle Fighter. Self-centered, exquisitely skilled at wielding power and getting their way, these Jungle Fighters leave their women exhausted, unfulfilled and hurt. And these women—dressed in the smartest designer suits, their hair and nails gleaming from steady professional care, their imported-leather datebooks filled with choice business appointments and their briefcases poised by their two-hundred-dollar pumps—lean toward each other across cocktail-lounge banquettes and ask, very wearily and rhetorically: "How come all you meet these days are bastards? Where are the *decent* men?"

The answer to that last question is, "Everywhere." In offices, at parties and receptions, on vacations, in discussion groups, in political action associations, at seminars and conferences, charity fund raisers, concerts, adult education classes, gyms, health clubs, company softball games, marathons, group therapy sessions, PTA meetings, theater groups and tennis matches. Finding them simply requires a new way of looking.

As I pointed out to Peggy, men have long known that a life of risking and battling in the work world can be sanely maintained only if one is regenerated at home. A go-getter woman is often disadvantaged in romance with a go-getter man, because he can still play the power game better than she—if, indeed, both find value in playing it at all. And, while she expects a relationship of equals, he has a need for—and expertise at—domination. This woman ends up carrying a double burden: she leaves her tough nine-to-five game at the end of a day to face a man who engages her in a similar showdown at night. Not only isn't she being filled, she's courting burnout.

What I try to get the female powerhouses who come into my office with this problem to do is see that the men about whom they're saying, "Oh, he can't give me anything," really *can* give a lot: sensitivity, supportiveness, a smoothly paved route through which the woman can fulfill her emotional needs. (For the fact is, only she, not a man, can ultimately fulfill those or any other of her needs.)

"But my emotional needs *are* met," such women often reply. "My work, my friends, my hour at the spa, my weekly shiatsu massage, my vacations . . ." They tick off their fingers. They are mistaking the symbols and privileges of success for a sense of internal nourishment that cannot be bartered or bought.

Make the effort to start measuring the worth of a man according to his interpersonal merits rather than by the external measures of success and the rewards, in genuine nurturance, will more than make up for the more directly material rewards you might not be getting through the reflection of another, more conventionally powerful or successful man.

We will explore these nurturance rewards in detail (and learn how all women, Comers and Havers can maximize them in their relationships with their mates) in Chapter 8. But for now, let's move on to the component of the Poverty Mentality that has to be confronted before a woman can honor her nurturance needs: undeservingness.

CHAPTER 3

Undeservingness

---

*"Once I know what I want,
am I really entitled to try to get it?"*

"When are they going to find out that my confidence, my expertise, is all a fake? That I'm a fraud?"

This is not the fearful lament of a struggling young career novice. It's a statement I hear all the time from most of the executive-level women who come to my negotiating seminars and into my office for counseling.

I hear other statements from these women, too:

"I was in the right place at the right time, that's all."

"My last promotion? I just got lucky."

"It's not that I'm so good; I just stay one chapter ahead of the competition."

"Anyone can be a winner if they're willing to work twenty hours a day like I do."

Why is it that women are so quick to hide behind modesty and qualification, to pull out a dozen little excuses for their achievement? Why are they so unwilling to give themselves credit for their phenomenal capacity and assets and talents?

Because women feel *undeserving*. Despite whatever bravado they may project on the job, they secretly fear that their success has been a fluke, a fortunate accident, an opportunity to be grateful for that they had better not mess up.

Consequently, these women act as if they haven't really made it at all. They have trouble asking for and expecting help. They're uncomfortable with their privileges—indeed, even with their most basic prerogatives. One of my clients, for example, looks, acts and dresses every inch the advertising account executive that she is—but she's still nervous when she isn't seated behind her office desk at 9 A.M. "But you're expected to make your own hours," I remind her. "You're not punching a time clock."

Yet in her mind she is.

When women feel undeserving, they operate in one of two basic ways. The Comers sabotage their chances of making it; the Havers punish themselves for having made it.

The closer a Comer gets to the goal that she's earned, the more she may use self-destructive behavior to push herself away from it. I know one real estate saleswoman who keeps teetering on the cusp of being asked to be a copartner in a small firm, and who uses her anxiety over those occasions to put on weight and act silly and sexy at parties. Another acquaintance could be one of the most successful caterers in northern California—if only she'd realize that the people she hires to handle her business affairs have never made a sensible decision. She seems to enjoy the friction between her culinary talent and her financial brinksmanship; she's always almost a star, and the next moment, almost bankrupt.

These women are too internally comfortable with not making it to do the very simple things it would take to alter the course of their lives. For them I use a strategy that proceeds in stages: First, I have them think briefly back to the roots of their self-value. Then we explore how the strictures and forbiddings of their childhoods have matured into the tools of their current style of self-sabotage. We find new tools to get them out of undeservingness. Finally, I show them how to ask for what they deserve in a way that increases their chances of getting it.

Then there are the Havers—women with enviable income, power and status who, like the advertising executive with the 9 A.M. jitters, feel secretly undeserving of their success. These women find all kinds of ways to punish themselves. They exhaust themselves doing their jobs and the jobs of their secretaries. Their refusal to delegate detail work siphons valuable time from the tasks that could propel them ahead. Their inability to forge advantageous relationships with both employees and bosses keeps them on a treadmill when they could be soaring. They're afraid to push new ideas—sometimes even to present them. Their high-profile façades harbor "What, little-old-me?s" inside.

My strategy for these women starts with our taking a tally of all the small punishments they inflict on themselves and the unnecessary work they cling to. I then work with them to recognize and enjoy their power and to let go of the peculiarly female desire to be both the delegat*or* and the delegat*ee*. We then work through the specifics of how to present their ideas and proposals in a confident, effective way that results not just in what they deserve but, sometimes, in what they hardly dared dream.

Let me show you how each of these strategies works.

ATTAINING DESERVINGNESS FOR COMERS

I was sick as a child, so the summer camp I went to was staffed with nurses. During one session, one nurse—hardly the nicest of ladies—responded to some minor mischief of mine by spanking me. A week or so later I mentioned the incident to my mother, who had come to see me on visitors' day. There she was, in the flush of enjoyment of her summer's reprieve from parenting. Yet no sooner did the word "spanked" slide off my tongue than she said, without a whit of ambivalence: "Go to your tent and pack your bag, honey. We're going home."

From that moment on, I knew I was deserving of good treatment, consideration, respect. Nothing—not my mother's month of freedom, not an unrefundable camp tuition, not even two more weeks of diving lessons and basket weaving—was more important than removing me promptly from an arena where something basic I deserved was being so flagrantly denied.

Today, when I negotiate with publishers, television producers, bankers, colleagues and seminar organizers, that childhood incident glows in my mind like a pilot light. How fortunate I was to have learned, so early in life, that I was worth it.

When I begin to work with women who don't feel worth it, I often ask them to briefly think back to some childhood incident or remark that fixed their self-value in their minds. People with a high sense of undeservingness report memories like:

"My mother always said, 'I'm on the phone; don't interrupt,' when I walked into her room." (Message: "You're not worth listening to.")

"My father teased me and put me down in front of others. He

was never affectionate toward me at home." (Message: "You're an appropriate subject of ridicule.")

"My parents made me take off my shoes before I could walk into their bedroom." (Message: "You're dirty—and we're not.")

It's not hard to guess that such remarks, when they accurately represent the described parent-child relationship, make an imprint on the child's self-image that doesn't wear off when she's an adult. (After all, if it had worn off she wouldn't have remembered the remark.) Still, I've always believed that it's not what happened during childhood that keeps a person down; rather, it's what that person learned to hang on to from childhood and adapt, all by herself, into an adult form of self-restriction. In other words, the responsibility goes not to your parents or lover or boss but to you.

And so goes the power to change.

But to be able to use that power to change, you first have to find out how deep your undeservingness runs and the specific way you are using it to keep yourself down. One measure of both is what you allow yourself to have, what you require yourself to do and what you forbid yourself from enjoying or indulging in. When you compare these accounts with a list of the same restrictions and privileges that your parents dealt you as a child, the result can be liberating.

It certainly was for Karla, who came into my office a year ago with the classic symptoms of Poverty Mentality high in undeservingness. At twenty-eight she had already turned herself into a has-been. A painter, just two years before she had been poised for the kind of success that others in her field only fantasize about: she had had a major gallery show, was part of a museum group show, and had an artist-in-residency at a prestigious Texas university.

Yet the defeated and confused young woman who sat across from me now was working at a loathed job as an office temp and coming home at night to a strong-willed, aggressive husband, a petroleum-industry junior executive, who didn't even "permit" (Karla's word) her to talk on the phone to friends, who kept her ignorant of his financial status, who had somehow caused her to dismantle her budding career without giving her anything in exchange.

"How did that happen?" I asked her.

"I'd say, 'Here's the *Art in America* article about the group show, Dave.' And he wouldn't even read it," she replied. "Or he'd start an argument just as I was going out the door to teach a class. Or he'd complain that my studio sessions were taking too much time."

Still, this couldn't have been the entire answer. Another woman would have fought such severe possessiveness and unsupportiveness or left the man who displayed it. Another woman wouldn't have given up so much, so easily, so soon. To find out why and how Karla did, I asked her to fill out two sets of lists.

In the first I asked her to fill out an exercise which I first learned from a colleague and which has proved so helpful with my clients.

In the exercise, she was to complete as many answers as applicable, the sentence AS A CHILD, I WAS ALLOWED TO _____, REQUIRED TO _____, FORBIDDEN TO _____. In the second I asked her to complete AS AN ADULT, I ALLOW MYSELF TO _____, REQUIRE MYSELF TO _____, FORBID MYSELF TO _____.

Karla's lists, exactly as she wrote them, comprise Table 3.

Several facts stood out to me as I looked over the lists. First, she was not encouraged to make her own decisions as a child (REQUIRED TO "go to bed at nine," "do as I was told," "come straight home after school"; FORBIDDEN TO "talk back") or even, it appears, as a young adult ("go to women's college—their choice"). That strictly enforced obedience, that tethering to a pole, has blossomed into her adult self-requirement to "keep peace in family," "keep husband happy," and her striking self-sanction against "having fun alone (without Dave)." In the case of the first two statements, what one normally thinks of as forms of pleasures ("peace" and "happiness") become duties; in the case of the third statement, a whole realm of pleasure is being denied.

That such denial was now adapted to her adult life is evident in her other comments. Diet and housecleaning are mentioned twice, the latter as something she makes herself do instead of "enjoying" something else (TV). She requires herself to "be on time" and views making money and "trying to be better" as musts, not as easy, natural expectations.

Looking over both lists, it was apparent to me that Karla hadn't really acquired any social skills, that obedience was a familiar (hence probably comfortable) mode to her and that she so mistook pleasure for duty that she could relinquish enjoyment without protesting at all.

Table 3

KARLA'S LISTS

AS A CHILD, I WAS

ALLOWED TO	REQUIRED TO	FORBIDDEN TO
paint	go to school	argue
go to school	go to bed at 9 P.M.	steal
have a pet	take naps	lie
create my own	do as I was told	cheat
world	come straight home	hurt other people
have a horse	after school	talk back
play dolls	study	
read books	keep my room clean	
watch TV after	do my weekly chores	
homework	love my brothers	
listen to radio	and sisters	
go to summer	get B average	
camp	go to private school	
	go to women's	
	college (their	
	choice)	

AS AN ADULT, I

ALLOW MYSELF TO	REQUIRE MYSELF TO	FORBID MYSELF TO
do my art	try to stay on diet	have fun alone
(sometimes)	be on time	(without Dave)
enjoy my car	make money	enjoy TV shows
buy books	keep house clean	when I should be
have an occasional	keep peace in family	cleaning house
milkshake	keep my husband	lie
	happy	cheat
	try to diet (think	steal
	weight)	
	keep trying to be	
	better	

Since she never learned to forge a relationship with another human being who would be fair to her, it was easier for her to deny and acquiesce than to relate to herself or to a loved one in any other way. She had training in those undeserving behaviors. And because she had played so solitarily as a child, the few social aspects of being a painter that put her in the thick of camaraderie (the university position, the gallery show), had been easy for her to abandon. She had handed her entire career—and her life—over to her husband, a man whose authoritarian streak was comfortably reminiscent of her parents'.

She did all of this; no one did it for her.

And when she realized this—when she saw her requirements and constraints spelled out in her own handwriting—she knew that she could also change.

Since her lists had pointed to her lack of any social networking as the main way she kept herself in undeservingness, we started by trying to reverse this trait. I encouraged Karla to go after and develop two independent friendships. She did. I worked with her on a strategy by which she successfully negotiated with her husband for more freedom with which to pursue the friendships and to go back to the performing arts.

Next, I worked on getting her to understand how useless were some of her constrictions. By starting a lot of sessions with sentences that started, "What's the worst that could happen if . . . ?" I got her to see that the house didn't get any dirtier if she cleaned it once instead of three times a week, that getting a little high on white wine in an outdoor café with a friend was no betrayal whatsoever of Dave. Taking a complimentary tack, I asked her to keep a list of things that gave her pleasure, with the stipulation that the list had to grow by a third every week.

She discovered something amazing: she had never really actively looked for satisfaction before.

Recently, Karla sought—and received—a commission to paint a mural on a new public building. The art critic whose job it was to choose the mural artist is hardly known for his effusiveness, yet when he saw her work, he exclaimed, "What were you doing, sitting on this gift for so long?"

Slowly, Karla is moving back into her career—this time with the attitude that she's entitled to have it. Her new sense of deservingness has had enough of an impression on her husband for him to change the deed on their home, putting it in her name as well as his for the first time in their six years of marriage.

When you adapt the ALLOW/REQUIRE/FORBID exercise to your own use, look for crucial links between the CHILD and ADULT statements. Ask yourself:

- Do both lists show obedience, assertiveness or stubbornness? Solitary work and play or high incidence of collaboration/group interaction?
- How has each of these tendencies made me comfortable with my state of undeservingness? Able to sabotage opportunities?
- Am I sitting on my talent with my requirements and constraints? And does this self-stricture derive from strictures imposed on me as a child?
- Is my list of self-allowances too limited to give me room to develop and flourish as I might?

The answers to all of these questions add up to your direction for productive change. Still, changing your level of deservingness usually involves another person—the person to whom you must say, "(Because I know I deserve it), I want more."

Often, this person is a current or prospective employer. (We'll get to husbands, lovers and children in Chapter 5, "Guilt as a Smoke Screen.") And it is in relation to him (and it's usually "him") that a lot of women trip themselves up.

The best example I know of deservingness going awry in negotiation is the case of two young women editorial workers who were interviewing, several years back, for senior editor status on a new national magazine. Both had been underpaid at their last jobs and when they sat before the new magazine's editor in two separate, private meetings, these women who had never met both made the same mistake.

"I have to tell you right here and now: I insist on twenty thousand!" each said, upping her previous salary by three thousand dollars, in a tone of impeccable assertion. "That's a requirement I will absolutely not come down from. I won't take a penny less!"

The magazine editor—who was not above exploitation—had spent the previous day rubbing his fingers raw on his pocket calculator, trying to find a way to build a sufficient secretrial staff while at the same time budgeting in the four senior editors whose salary range the parent company had set at $27,000 apiece. Here was his answer: he could have the two women cut-rate—and hire an extra secretary with the savings.

That's just what he did.

The two women's poignant adamance—and their ignorance of simple negotiating principles—gypped them out of what could have been a ten-thousand-dollar raise from their previous salaries. Hired at twenty-one-thousand apiece, they thought their assertiveness had earned them a thousand more than they'd asked for —until, two months later, they discovered it had gotten them six thousand less! Their two male counterparts, who knew enough to find out the budgeted salary before going into the negotiation, were hired at the full twenty-seven-thousand apiece.

The moral of that story is: You owe it to yourself to know what you can get, for your subjective idea of deservingness may in actuality be selling you short. If the salary of the job in question isn't offered before you meet to discuss it, simply say, at the time the interview is being set up: "I need to know what range we're talking about so I'll be able to negotiate with you fairly."

If the information's still withheld, find it on your own. Read the appropriate trade publications. Call a professional organization. Ask friends or friends of friends who've had similar jobs. Call a headhunter or an employment agency and say you're looking for that position. What kind of salary can you expect? The important thing is: Find out.

And if you're offered a salary you think is too low? Don't say yes or no on the spot. Graciously table your decision until you can get sound counseling from someone in the position to help you, for once you accept a low salary you cannot turn around and negotiate up.

ATTAINING DESERVINGNESS FOR HAVERS

"Grace," the deep male voice intones through the desk intercom, "could you come in here a moment. There's something I'd like to run by you."

Grace quickly turns off her electric typewriter in the middle of a letter.

There, astride the corner of his desk, sits young Mr. Applethorpe, in a pose of such intimacy and self-assurance that Grace is immediately, unaccountably flattered.

"Take a look at this report," he says, handing her a weighty sheaf of papers. "Let me know if I've got Allied's number with this assessment."

His secretary nods compliance. She will take the entire report home tonight after doing her own work; stay up till midnight reading it; return tomorrow with some valuable additions that Applethorpe (who will have spent that same evening relaxing with his wife at the theater) will then incorporate into the document.

He'll have gotten her time and expertise free. And, in the process, he will have made her feel not exploited but important.

Now, Applethorpe's female counterpart would do it all very differently.

She'd go home and spend one or two or three nights trying to fix it herself. It wouldn't occur to her to ask Grace for time-saving input. She wouldn't have thought she deserved it.

Men know how to ask for help from their employees. Women, unfortunately, do not. Most successful women do not know how to build a support system among subordinates so that these people will be loyal and helpful to them. Their wobbly sense of deservingness leads them to err in either of two extremes: by being too curt or by being too chummy. Since they don't feel entitled to get help, they're either defensively brusque (as if trying to prove to their doubting selves that they're boss) or apologetically solicitous (as if trying to extinguish any difference in status between their secretaries and themselves).

It is hard for these women to feel worthy and dignified when they say, "I need help." (I will deal in detail with how they can learn to do so in Chapter 13, "Interindependence: Negotiating for Help.") It is hard for them to relinquish, to delegate, to jettison the small tasks and detail work from which they have graduated.

Enough self-styled superwomen have come into my office groaning under the double weight of their new responsibilities and the old ones they're loathe to give up for me to see their dilemma as a genuine phenomenon. I call it The Two Faces of Deservingness. One face is the woman's self-punishment for having made it. Instead of letting herself be selective and choose only the most interesting and important projects, she wears herself out by designing the house and sweeping the sawdust out, too. The opposite face is that same woman's misguided self-rewarding. She wants today and yesterday. She doesn't realize you have to let go of in order to get. Even though it would be cost-effective to do so, she doesn't want to give up some of the simple pleasures she enjoyed when she made less money, wielded less power, had more time. So she not only cooks the standing rib roast for her dinner parties, she makes the fresh mayonnaise for the crudité dip as well. Instead of giving up one or two of her small tasks to nap, get a massage and then apply her fresh mind to the business proposal she's drafting before the dinner party, she tries to do it all, the little and the big.

As often as not, the big things lose out in the process.

How do you learn to let go, to delegate?*

First, you need to identify what you're wasting time holding on to—which is not quite as easy as it sounds.

Lynda, for example, is a highly placed woman in publishing who used to arrive at my office as if she were the mother of eight instead of boss to the same number of staff. "There are things at work that only *I* can do," she'd protest when I questioned her weariness. I felt that if she looked carefully, she'd prove herself wrong.

So I asked Lynda to keep a log of everything she did, minute by minute, during one typical day. She brought the log in to her next therapy session. The needlessly undelegated or time-wasting work included parking in a public parking structure instead of using the much closer executive lot; making her own Xerox copies, answering her own phone calls, making her own coffee, writing her own memos rather than dictating them; walking down the hall after someone instead of buzzing him on the intercom; hearing out people to whom she should have said, "Discuss that with so-and-so"; doing her own housecleaning when company was coming for dinner instead of hiring the help she could clearly afford; shopping for the flowers, liquor and groceries at three different stores instead of getting them all at the supermarket, picking up her dry cleaning instead of having it delivered.

I asked Lynda to go through the log and mark UNNECESSARY next to every task she considered so. She counted up the minutes spent on these and came up with eighty-three—an hour and a

* In Chapter 13, "Interindependence: Negotiating for Help," I will deal with delegating housework to husbands and children.

quarter lost. I looked over the list and found another two hours of make-work she'd not considered as such or had overlooked. I told her, "Here are almost three and a half hours you could have spent relaxing and being good to yourself—or making more money."

If you suspect you have Lynda's problem, put on a wristwatch and make your own log, recording every task, however small, that takes over a minute's time. After you add up your own UNNECESSARYS, give the log to a colleague or friend whose efficiency you've admired and have that person further edit your day. You'll be surprised at the freedom that opens up. And with that freedom comes power.

But one of the most empowering freedoms of all is the freedom to hope. By this I mean the freedom from self-deluded dreams, unrealistic expectations, plans that are actually traps: the freedom from that which appears to be hope but which is really an excuse to stay stuck and stay poor.

Let's move on to that freedom by turning to the next chapter.

CHAPTER 4

Vacant Hope

---

*"Do I really expect to be able
to get what I want?"*

Few of my concepts strike so many women so close to home as vacant hope. That's the term I've devised to describe a condition of futile, runaway yearning, or of unrealistic anticipation, or of false, self-bluffing preparation that ties up real options in activity that goes in fits and starts and circles—if it goes anywhere at all.

Vacant hope is a sort of waystation on the continuum of hope to hopelessness. With hope, people take action that leads to positive results. With hopelessness, there is no action, only despair. The main danger of staying in vacant hope is being swept along the continuum into hopelessness. When someone comes into my office with all the signs of vacant hope (which we'll get to in a minute), she's still motivated enough to work on herself. But when she's waited so long that she's slid into hopelessness, that motivation is much harder to come by.

Waiting—futile, draining, ultimately dangerous waiting—is the culprit here. Women are masterful at it. And at "understanding." We empathize with other people's excuses too well not to know how to do the same with our own. We're also excellent over-preparers. We always seem to feel we need to read just one more book, take just one more seminar, tie up just one more (often trivial) piece of old business before we take a stab at an opportunity the life-span of which (we often realize only too late) is mercurially short.

And while we're great at planning next week, next month, next year, our conscientiousness in the short term masks our innocence of the long. So rarely do we really stand back from the detail work of our existence to examine the big picture of our lives. So rarely do we make those present-for-future trade-offs that men make without thinking: trade-offs that would guarantee us what we really long for years down the line.

All of this means that we invest great amounts of energy earnestly wishing and longing and planning—but we somehow arrange our lives so we get very little return on that investment. We get so stuck in hope that we can't move on to having. We get so stuck in process we can't break through to goal. Fueled by feelings of ambivalence and undeservingness, we deeply and secretly do not expect to get what we say we want. Therefore, hoping becomes an art form we've polished, an end in itself, a substitute gratification for the action and outcome it was supposed to merely precede.

When Edna St. Vincent Millay said, "Hope is a subtle glutton," it was this kind of time- and energy-consuming hope she was talking about. I call it "vacant hope" because it can look to the outside world like real hope ("I expect . . . ," says the hoper, with often bright eyes; "I'm going to . . . /planning to . . . /waiting for . . .")—but when you knock on the door of its carefully crafted exterior, nobody's home.

Real hope is solid. It has content as well as form. When a person in real hope utters those same sentiments, the words are merely the tip of the iceberg of internal conviction and motivation, of self-perceived power to move and to do and to get. Vacant hope is hollow. Vacant hope is believing it's the thought that counts. Hope is knowing it's the action.

Vacant hope is having your energy scattered in five different places. Hope is being focused on one important spot.

Vacant hope is clearing your work desk, sponging your desk, rearranging the papers on your desk and finally deciding you need to go out and buy a *new* desk. Hope is blanking out the clutter, ignoring the desk, and diving right into your work.

Vacant hope is saying, "It'd be a pity to quit so soon. I've put so much into this." Hope is saying, "I've given this person/project/investment so many months for it to pan out and it hasn't. I'm going to pull out now while I'm still somewhat ahead of the game."

Vacant hope is beating a bushful of birds. Hope is working with the one in your hand. Vacant hope is the teenage girl's bulletin board, laden with pictures of rock stars. Hope is that girl's boy next door, the one who really thinks her crooked tooth is sexy, believes she'll be a surgeon someday, laughs at her jokes.

Vacant hope is asking, *"Why . . . ?"*—a word that keeps people spinning and wallowing in regret and rationalization. ("Why did this have to happen?" "Why didn't I . . . ?" *"Why* can't I just . . . ?") "Why . . . ?" is yesterday's canceled check. Hope is asking—unrhetorically—"How . . . ?" as in "How can I improve this situation?" "How can I make this happen?"—cutting past the hand wringing and going straight for the movement and remedy. *"How . . . ?"* is tomorrow's blank check.

Vacant hope is spending a lot of money on dinner with a friend at an expensive, trendy restaurant on the vague chance that you'll be noticed by somebody fascinating. Hope is living your life in such a fashion that you become fascinating yourself.

Vacant hope is dreaming of seeing your body on the stage and your name in lights. Hope is picturing the sweat on that body, the callouses on your toes, the compulsory rehearsal that coincides with your head cold—and yet feeling exhilarated about the whole image.

Vacant hope is ambushing your goals with a case of the yeah-buts—as in, "Yeah, but I'll be on vacation when that new account comes in next week"; "Yeah, but . . . remember? You promised . . ."; "Yeah, but a person like me has never gotten a job like that before." Hope is realizing you can use these yeah-buts to demur, wheedle, browbeat or overquestion yourself out of many grand possibilities in life. Hope is perceiving the opportunity quickly—then, while you're digesting it, being appropriately quiet.

Vacant hope is pining after. Hope is going after. Vacant hope is yearning for. Hope is strategizing for. Vacant hope is dreaming. Hope is wide awake.

When someone comes to me and I suspect that she's indulging in vacant hope, I ask her to listen very closely to her language. Does she speak in positive noun-verb progressions ("I'm doing . . . ," "I'm taking . . . ," "I want . . .")? Or does she saddle her sentences with hesitancies and qualifiers and other signs of tentativeness? ("I haven't made up my mind yet," "Hmm, that's a possibility; I'll think about it," "Maybe I'll do it tomorrow"). Or does she use the negative noun-verb progression? ("It won't work," "It won't do," "I can't"). Hope is indicated by the first use of language; vacant hope by the second, hopelessness by the third. Several clients have, at my suggestion, carried small tape recorders in their purses during the day and turned them on during key encounters. They've been shocked at what they didn't know they were feeling.

Havers and Comers have usually arrived at vacant hope in different ways. The Havers usually started out in hope—until a series of defeats or self-sabotages pushed them down a notch on the continuum. If they are open to change and willing to see things clearly, they can get back to hope before too long. After all, that's where they started; they still have the options and resources.

Comers have more to fight against—particularly if they don't have satisfying relationships and don't show signs of advancing in their careers. These women feel lonely, without power or options. Their vacant hope often teeters more on the brink of hopelessness. When I work with such women, I use great effort—lots of role playing, negotiating scripts, exercises, encouragement—to get them to push themselves into action.

But, however she got there and whether she's a Comer or a Haver, the woman in vacant hope usually plays out one of three distinct styles. These are:

VACANT HOPE AS QUICKSAND

When a person walks in quicksand, the more steps she takes the deeper she sinks. The sand exerts a physical lure, pulling her steadily downward.

Lures can be emotional as well as gravitational, and you can sink time and money and passion into projects and people just as you can sink bodies into sand. A sure sign of quicksand hope is the "logic" that posits the well-worked-for brighter day just around the next bend. The quicksand hoper, like the slot-machine player, desperately believes that her investment must be returned, simply because of all that she's put into the game. She cannot bring herself to cut her losses. She can only keep going a little bit further . . . then a little further yet . . . then a little bit further than that.

A classic example of quicksand hope is the woman who is involved in a long affair with a chronically nonmonogamous or once-burned, commitment-shy man. This woman believes her partner is going to change—and that such change is induced in the same way one housebreaks a puppy: with time, patience and stoic tolerance of things that smell bad. She considers the time she's sunk into the relationship (and "sunk" is the word she'll use later) as time invested in nursing her partner's emotional wounds, in promoting his slowly escalating trust of the female sex. Therefore, if she doesn't stay around to reap the harvest of all her hard work, why, then, some other woman will. Given this reasoning, the longer she stays with him the longer she must stay. But the longer she stays the more dependent, defeated and bitter she becomes.

Women going into business for themselves are sometimes stuck in quicksand hope as well. What they call "just getting our sea legs," "paying my dues," "learning the ropes" or "weathering" a bad first year before an "inevitable" payoff, someone else would more clearly assess as throwing good money after bad. The adverb "hopefully" a most overworked expression these days, is used again and again by these women. Naïveté about money matters, romanticism about striking out on one's own in the business world and the desire to be "good"—to not disappoint one's investors—can start a downward cycle whereby a great deal is risked, then more is risked to make back the original risk . . . and so on.

About two years ago, I visited what was hoped to be a unique speakers' booking agency for executive women: hoped for by the two women who came up with the idea and by others of us who wanted to see this good idea work. I saw flaws from the beginning: their overhead was high, they were concentrating on the wrong audiences, their brochure was expensive but dull. These were "kinks" they would soon work out, they assured me. But after those were unkinked, others emerged to take their place, including a national economic downturn that made their kind of business more vulnerable to recession and government budget cuts than most.

Instead of pausing to assess their mistakes and the bad omens, they went full force ahead, taking an even bigger loan to try to improve and prevail. They started their second year badly, and the more beholden to their investors they were for "rescue" money, the more there was to rescue. Instead of pulling out when they still had something to save, they went back in, this time liquidating—and losing—much of their personal assets. "But we hoped . . . ," they insisted as the roof fell in. They didn't hope; they vacantly hoped. If they'd been operating out of real hope, they would have been able to risk judging this one project as hopeless, enabling them to then rechannel the real hope into something that hope deserved.

VACANT HOPE AS CAMELOT

The future looks glorious—shimmeringly, mistily so. The hoper is continually conjuring up some fully hatched scenario—of success, love, fame, glamour, power—with not much thought, and less action, to her likelihood of and responsibility for getting there. The hope is like a mirage—impossible to grab hold of, but painful to assess as unreal.

When this kind of hoping persists over a very long period of time, the fantasy's warming quality wanes. The hoper becomes more deeply isolated—from friends (who want to point out the truth to her, and whose censure and pity she senses or imagines) and from other aspects of reality that must also be relinquished in order to keep her delicate delusion intact.

The married man's girlfriend who has been planning for the day Joe gets his divorce for three quarters of the length of their affair is a prime example of Camelot Hope. So is the "uncompromising" artist whose low-level temporary job is beginning to look pretty permanent to everyone but herself. And the unhappy wife who has remained in a barren marriage for all the years she's confessed her misery to her friends, while at the same time dreaming of being magically transformed into one of those glamorous, secure single women she keeps seeing in Jill Clayburgh movies.

The Camelot Hoper may also be the socialite whose idea of making plans to open a boutique or a gallery is having her chic designer friend design a logo, rather than taking herself down to a business school and learning about marketing, tax structuring and costs-benefits analysis. Or the single professional woman, now in her mid-thirties, who never saved up to invest in real estate, land, stocks or good furniture—even when it was a buyer's market— because "all that" was to come with the Married Good Life she somehow never imagined she wouldn't have.

VACANT HOPE AS THE LAZY LOVER

The bored, can't-be-bothered sexual partner lies on his or her back and says, "Do me." The message is: I won't resist, but I won't lift a finger, either. If pleasure comes my way, I'll be glad to receive it; if not, *c'est la vie.*

People take this attitude with their dreams and aspirations even more than they do with their erogenous zones.

With love itself, ironically, women are anything but lazy lovers. They usually work overtime to stoke the fires and make sure the enterprise thrives. But often the very same woman who is able to chart the daily ups and downs of her relationship on an invisible graph would feel remarkably unalert in front of a Dow-Jones board, even if she has a small portfolio. What stocks she has (and they've often been passively acquired—through inheritance, divorce settlement, employment at a shareheld company) she considers icing on the cake. (A man would consider these the first ingredient of a bigger, richer cake.) If she has a "good enough" job, she won't think of aggressively looking around for a better one (though she'll "keep her feelers out" and "stay open to the possibility") until something or someone makes it unpleasant for her to stay where she is. Yet most of these women will tell you very seriously that they "hope" to have much more than their lives hold now.

The lazy lover is also hooked on foreplay. As lovely as protracted foreplay is, it is still, when all is said and done, a segue to something more climactic and definitive. But the all-foreplay hoper likes getting there more than she likes arriving. For her, the pregnancy could go on forever, if only there weren't a birth.

So she will spend years in graduate school, switching fields to stay in a not-quite-finished state. Or she will spend more years in subprofessional dilettantism: trying on one, then another would-be career like so many clothes from a sale rack. Or she will always be "just about set" to spring from assistant to full-fledged, from junior to senior standing in her firm or profession—when something will keep her stuck where she is just three, then four, then ten months more. She'll be "on the brink" of putting her business in the black or opening up her own office—when a crisis, miscalculation or reconsideration will send her five squares back again, if not all the way back to go.

Life for her is an endless warm-up, but an oddly comfortable one, despite its surface frustration. For she gets to keep hoping for perfection, to imagine an idealized game instead of getting into the messy fray of a real one.

BREAKING OUT OF VACANT HOPE

Where Are You on the Hope-to-Hopelessness Scale?

Although vacant hope often sounds to the listener like real hope, it often feels more like hopelessness inside. And, as some of the examples I've presented make clear, the longer a person stays in that in-between state, the more hopeless, in fact, she becomes. That's why speed is critical in breaking out of vacant hope.

So when a new client enters my office in a state of longing that seems markedly unaccompanied by conviction or action, I often stir up the molecules right away by having her take a simple word-association test. I've duplicated it here. (See Table 4.) Quickly go down the list of twenty variables and circle the state—in the appropriate column—that is most descriptive of your feelings, attitudes or behavior now.

Table 4

WHERE ARE YOU ON THE
HOPE-TO-HOPELESSNESS SCALE?

HOPE	VACANT HOPE	HOPELESSNESS
Passion	Diminished passion	Lack of passion
Conclusiveness; ability to bring projects to completion, fruition, closure	Habit of flitting from one half-done project to the next; getting caught up in beginnings and middles	Inability to get much past very first stages of things
Drive	Diminished drive	No drive

HOPE	VACANT HOPE	HOPELESSNESS
Action when opportunity given or presented	Halting, half-hearted or erratic action when opportunity given or presented; opportunity often not clearly or immediately perceived	Sense of no opportunities at the present time
Assertiveness (One decides to act, then acts)	Mental/emotional assertiveness; behavioral passivity (One decides to act; then does not act)	Passivity
Clear, distinct, specific, concise communication	Mixed signals; beginning a thought and not following through	Scattered thoughts and sentences; minimal sense of abstraction; choice is made not to put any effort into communicating
Preparedness for exigencies, for unpredicted factors entering in	Sense of often being caught short, surprised, thrown for a loop	Overwhelmed by exigencies, unpredicted factors
Living in the present	Beginning to dwell on the past	Living in the past
Resilient but impatient in crisis; eager to get back on the track	Not necessarily effective in crisis but diverted, secretly excited by its element of novelty and relieved at the reprieve it offers	Innured to/powerless in crisis
Willingness to take appropriate risks	Sense of taking wilder than calculated risks; difficulty "making odds" on outcome	Sense that entire situation is a risk

HOPE	VACANT HOPE	HOPELESSNESS
Ability to separate constructive from destructive criticism—to absorb and make use of the former	Inability to separate criticisms; vascillation between feeling everyone else is wrong . . . and everyone else is right	Deep sensitivity to all criticism; projection of criticism where none exists
Consciousness of time; efficient use of time. Ability to separate and prioritize major from minor tasks, to work from big picture down to small	Comfortable with postponement; increased attention to trivia. Tendency to work from details up. Anxiety at prospect of having small nuisance or warm-up tasks totally dispensed with	Feeling of loss of control over time
Sense of proportion about money and people: neither overspending nor overbooking	Impetuous, excessive spending of money; frequent overbooking of schedule	Inability to control budget—or time spent with others/ time spent alone
Attentive listener	Distracted listener	Disinterested listener
Energetic	Diminished energy	Exhaustion
Willpower, moderation	Increasing use of one or more of the Great Saboteurs: drink, drugs, cigarettes, food, sleep	Intense use of one or more of the Great Saboteurs: drink, drugs, cigarettes, food, sleep
Sense of freedom, free choice	Need for/dream of something/someone to "come to the rescue" (though self-rescue is not ruled out)	Sense of entrapment; feeling that rescue is needed but is entirely out of own control
Ability to see through excuses and alibis of oneself, others	Clinging to excuses, alibis	Sense that excuses, alibis are now irrelevant, useless in kidding oneself

WHERE ARE YOU ON THE
HOPE-TO-HOPELESSNESS SCALE? (cont.)

HOPE	VACANT HOPE	HOPELESSNESS
Perception and appreciation of irony where appropriate	Sense that more and more of own life—and life in general —is ironic, that great (though possibly amusing) disparity exists between what is and what ought to be	Use of outright sarcasm—as a verbal defense and as a reflection of one's take on events in the world and in one's personal life
Trust	Increased suspicion	Paranoia

© Tessa Albert Warschaw, Ph.D. 1985. No reprint without permission.

If you have circled more answers in the middle column than in either of the other two, or if your answers are divided between the first and third columns, then vacant hope either literally describes your state of mind or (in the second case) serves as a functional "mean" or "average" condition for the two extremes—hope and hopelessness—between which you oscillate.

Moving from vacant hope to hope requires the courage to confront buried, unpleasant truths and the courage to risk making big changes. Most of us have this courage; it's just that we don't tap it until things get so bad we have almost no choice. Sarah is a case in point. By learning from her story, you can attain choice; you can get a head start on a process she waited until nearly zero hour to initiate.

SARAH'S LEAP OUT OF VACANT HOPE

When I first met Sarah several years ago, I liked her instantly. With her masses of curly hair, her bright hazel eyes, her jeans-and-espadrilles artiness, she projected a certain insouciance. Her warm serenity and direct gaze told you that the person you were talking to was deeply, thoughtfully there.

Then I began to detect puzzling discrepancies in the life lived beneath that winning facade. She claimed that she wanted to be a fashion designer, but she never got very far with that career. And though she was a devoted wife and expert seamstress, her husband of fifteen years hardly seemed to notice or care. She read voraciously and critically—everyone from Steinbeck to Colette to Virginia Woolf—and she was a skillful writer herself. Yet what writing she did was furtive, as if she were afraid to complete what she'd begun. Designing was her real work, her real identity. At least that's what she said.

Yet her career had never taken off—and she was now almost forty years old.

Her husband was a controlling father figure to her, adept at making the decisions that all her life she'd assumed she couldn't make for herself. What he wasn't particularly adept at was making a living. He stumbled in and out of businesses as a screenwriter (often losing his shirt). He was more than a social drinker. Her part-time jobs and his occasional profits were keeping both of them afloat.

It became clear to me what was happening: her fear of losing him—her subconscious decision to protect his ego (and with it, she assumed, her place in the marriage)—had led her to nip her writing talent in the bud. His entrepreneurial vacant hope kept her invested in her vacant hope designing career. Her effort at getting him to stop drinking was the vacantest hope of all. She began taking too many tranquilizers—all the more to blunt the realization that her life was a tightly sealed circle of fear, frustration and pretending.

That's why I was so moved by her courage the day she walked into my office and, taking me up on an offer that had been gently standing for quite some time, announced: "I'm ready to work." She and her husband had separated. She was clearly in great pain, yet there was calm resolve in her eyes. "I realize that what's been keeping me down for years is my sitting around and waiting for the day that things will be different," she said. She wanted to stop waiting and start doing.

And so we began.

Between sessions in which we worked on shoring up her resources to live alone* and to examine the marriage with enough distance to be able to know if she wanted a divorce, I worked on

---

* This process will be covered in Chapter 5.

getting Sarah to probe what I strongly believed—and she was just beginning to suspect—was a second area of vacant hope: her design career. Months of guided self-questioning went into a process I've now summarized as a blueprint for breaking out of vacant hope (see Table 5). It can be self-administered over whatever period of weeks—even months—it takes to address the questions honestly, thoughtfully and accurately. Here is how the exercise works:

After you've identified and described your suspected vacant hope (Column A), ask yourself (Column B, Action Taken) what you have done or are doing to make the hoped-for situation happen. What courses are you taking; skills are you acquiring, practicing, honing; contacts are you forging or maintaining; changes are you making in your physical or material self; strategies are you pursuing? List these. Then go through the list and find the actions you've taken two or more times before. People in vacant hope are often doing the same thing wrong again and again. Pause and relive the effect the action yielded in the past. Are you driving now down the same dead-end road you've driven down before?

And what about the action that you could be taking but are not? Why aren't you taking it? Is your integrity standing in the way? (You don't want to "fight dirty," "play games," "seduce my way to the top," do the compromised work that gets your foot in better doors.) Or is your temperament keeping you from certain means to your end? (You're just not a joiner. You avoid high-stress situations like the plague. It's not your style to paper the town with your résumé; you'll wait for that one personally arranged interview.) Is fear holding you back? Or is it your lack of resources—money, connections, time, child care, health?

Now that you know what you could be doing but are not, are you willing to make changes in order to take more effective action toward your goal? Or are you still unwilling? If so, might some of those reasons for Actions Not Taken be excuses for a deep and basic ambivalence?

George Bernard Shaw once said: "There are two tragedies in life. One is not to get your heart's desire. The other is to get it." For many people in vacant hope, the last part of that aphorism is particularly true, though often hidden from the conscious self. This might be the right time for you to bring it to light and explore it.

Table 5

BREAKING OUT OF VACANT HOPE

A	B	C	D	E
SUSPECTED VACANT HOPE SITUATION	**ACTION TAKEN/ NOT TAKEN**	**TIME**	**AM I KIDDING MYSELF?**	**ACTION TO BE TAKEN**
Select one vacant hope situation that you are ready to change now	Actions previously taken or avoided that led to vacant hope or hopeless situation (i.e., how did you get there in the first place?)	1. Time (and money) invested in hoping	Do I really want—and am I effectively going after— what I say I'm hoping for?	1. List action
		2. With whom am I spending my waiting time? a. Productive friends supportive of my goals and of my means b. People who encourage my postponement, passivity, excuses	If not, what am I willing to hope for?	2. This is the time I will allow myself to make the changes for the new hope

Lastly, assess your true state of readiness. "Readiness" is a tricky and much misused term. You can run around getting ready, getting ready, getting ready, only to have that flurry of activity obscure the real opportunity when (as often as not on little cat feet) it arrives. You are left like a car in a ditch, spinning your wheels in the mud. Or you can think you are poised for ascent, all buttons polished, all systems go, when, in truth, you're not ready at all.

Are you in a state of readiness? If the job you say you hope for were offered tomorrow, would you not have to crash-diet off ten pounds, speed-read three books on the subject, borrow a briefcase? Would you not have to spend a week updating your files, looking for a babysitter for your children, assembling an office wardrobe from scratch?

If the love you yearn for were to come your way tomorrow, are you emotionally prepared for the sharing, the risk? Do you have a home comfortable enough to welcome a partner? A schedule flexible enough to enjoy his company? Relationships with the others in your life—children, friends, parents, ex-husband—sound and resilient enough that you can accommodate the new intimacy without any painful consequences?

And if none—or few—of these things are true, then what is this telling you about your true expectations? If, indeed, you're "hoping" for something, then why are you living your life around the probability that it will not materialize?

Next, turn your attention to Column C, Time. Time, to the vacant hoper, is like debt to the chronic gambler or pounds to the binge eater: something that piles up as if uncontrollably. The net accumulation is very hard to face.

Brave it. Sit down and tabulate the weeks, months or years you've invested in the hoped-for situation. Where applicable, figure out the money you've lost in the process, for example, by sticking with a low-paying "temporary" job while waiting for your dream career to take off; by insisting that a fruitless business venture be on the verge of turning around; by so subtly but thoroughly expecting to be taken care of one day (by a man, an inheritance, or "things finally coming together") that you let a lot of career or investment opportunities fly by unnoticed.

Then ask yourself: *"Can I afford my life?"* When I suggest my clients put this question to themselves, they initially reply "Of course I can. I'm *living* it, aren't I?" But then they actually *think* about the question—and it's an eye-opener. For, almost invariably, the life they are currently living is in some way not the one they consider their Real—aspired-to, ultimate—life. Rather, they're in a kind of limbo, full of financially or circumstantially determined for-the-time-beings: one child instead of two, rental apartment instead of condominium or home, hack work instead of creative work, a week at the seashore instead of a month in Europe, first-apartment furniture instead of those really good pieces that express their own taste. Of course, there should always be room for improvement and further striving in life, but if the gap between the real and the Real has been glaring for a long time, it is best to pause and assess things. How much more time are you willing to let pass while you nurse that chasm? And how much more time are you willing to throw away on a platonic ideal of a life when you could instead be improving a situation that is real right now. Think hard about both of these things.

Finally, look at the people you're investing time in as you wait for what you hope to happen. Are you nourishing your own sense of fatalism by hanging around with "empathetic" fellow "aspirers" who lament about "the rotten economy" or "the lousy market-place" that is holding you all down? Is your friends' idea of supportiveness the willingness to let you get away with your delusions? Or are you spending that time with realistic people who can see through excuses—yours and their own—and who care for you enough to be, when they must be, constructively critical? Waiting time is usually not spent alone. It can be squandered, or it can be utilized. Which are you doing—and whom are you doing it with?

What all of this self-questioning leads to is the blunt master question that heads Column D: Am I Kidding Myself? Answering that question in the affirmative, as Sarah finally did, takes great strength. It is painful to let go of a dream, even when that dream is full of holes and has been keeping you down for years. But sometimes you have to let go of to get. This is just what I helped Sarah to do.

The Action to Be Taken (Column E) we decided on for her was (1) that she give up her dream of a career in designing—and all the motions connected to it. Instead, (2) she would decisively and wholeheartedly commit to her writing. A loan from her family would support her for a while. I helped her negotiate for it from a feeling of strength rather than one of dependence. We both felt that borrowing money was preferable to her going back to work in the time-sapping "secondary careers" she had dabbled in while waiting for her designing career to take off. We wanted a clean break from all the diversions and detours that had fed her vacant hope in the past.

We also wanted to build in supports for Sarah's new work. So, first, she enrolled in a good writing workshop. Second, she committed to a definite project: a novel. Third, to get her past her anxiety about isolation, self-discipline and the sheer newness of writing, I offered her the use of the typewriter in my office's reception area for a block of hours several times a week. The deal was, I would read whatever pages she wanted me to, if she wanted me to, but I would not judge them. And she was under no obligation to write a certain number of pages—even sentences—a day. I was simply providing a supportive workplace outside of her home with set hours and people around for intermittent conversations. She began typing away.

We also strategized her working habits at home. She would fix up a work space but not waste time fussing over its decor. She would designate specific hours of the day for her work, after certain anxiety-releasing chores were done and before a scheduled meeting with a friend or other "reward"—a movie, a run on the beach with her Sony Walkman, a chance to try out a new recipe.

She phased out and severed those one-way and destructive friendships in her life and told her genuine friends to please not call her during working hours. (She was amazed at how quickly they understood and agreed.) When other calls came through, they were met by an unplugged phone. Finally, when she was well on her way with her book, she did what she had never dared do before: she set a deadline for herself—a workable deadline, but a deadline nonetheless.

Today, not quite two years later, Sarah is well on her way to completing her novel. Her divorce is final. She feels more responsible for herself than ever before in her life. And she is living with a man she met in the writing class. He's demonstrative, charming, funny, a talented fellow writer—and so supportive he makes her lunch on the day her writing is "hot" and his is not.

Yet Sarah occasionally fights to tell herself that solitary work behind a closed office door should not make her guilty, does not threaten loss, is not somehow Less.

Which brings us to the nut that's left in the bowl after all of the others have been cracked: the final, most complex and pervasive women's Poverty Mentality component, Guilt as a Smoke Screen.

CHAPTER 5

Guilt as a Smoke Screen

"I'm going to fall back on easy self-blame and the facade of selflessness to avoid the question, If I do risk and try for it, what love and comfort will I lose?"

The woman would like the man she is involved with to be more responsive to her emotional needs. When she's provoked enough to mention this to him, he replies with angry variations on "What do you want from a guy?" In the pure, silent second between her delivery and his rebuttal, she is sure that her needs are legitimate, that he is almost purposely not hearing them, that this time she will have the clarity to hold her ground. No matter how aggravated he may seem, she will let him know that she has rights and that it is *he* who must change.

But then he replies—and a familiar jolt of anxiety shoots through her system: Keep this up and you'll make him leave. In another minute, she has felt it and, in one way or another, said it: "You're right. I'm nagging. I'm demanding too much. It's my fault." It's amazing how that assumption of guilt instantly dissolves her anxiety. Even if the feeling of guilt doesn't hold up in her mind for more than an hour, it is functional. It short-circuits her anger just at the point that it could really erupt and—she is sure—do harm. It keeps her from rocking the boat. (And who wants to be tossed into those rough, murky waters of aloneness?) It keeps the relationship if not very good at least very safe and intact.

The woman is single, sophisticated, successful: a three-star Haver, it appears. But as you get to know her, you realize she would feel naked without her professional title, that she would be mute without her constant shoptalk, deal-making, industry gossip. She does not know what it is to have a lunch, a tennis game or a conversation that is not somehow tied in to her work.

Somewhere, underneath her polished facade, she is starving for intimacy and connection. But she has so thoroughly bought the male model of success and she is so terrified of the enormity of her "contrary" needs that she cannot admit her feelings—not even to herself.

What does she think she is feeling?

You have a drink with her and, once loosened up, she leans back and pats the thickly stuffed briefcase that's perched at her side like a presence. "I feel guilty as hell when I don't take this home," she says.

The woman is a wife, mother and professional. Sometimes when she has had her office door closed for hours and often when she goes on short business trips to another city, a sense of unease and sorrow clouds her mind. "Why am I here, alone—and not with them?" some tiny inner voice wails.

She is ashamed of this "regressive," "irrational" feeling. (If the man she beat out for that recent promotion could only hear her thoughts now!) So she "corrects" the feeling by inverting it from "I miss and need and want my husband and kids" to "They miss and need and want me"—adding, automatically, "And right at this moment, I am letting them down."

How easy it is to make that inversion and to add the kicker at the end. After all, society expects her to feel remiss for not shuffling the deck of her commitments in such a way that her family is always the first card upturned. So she denies herself examination of the challenging full spectrum of her needs (needs that could be negotiated if she'd only respect them) and settles instead for the catchall response that, for women, is as American and endless and monochrome as a wheat field in Kansas: guilt . . . guilt . . . guilt . . . guilt . . . guilt.

Most of us, in one way or another, have a little of one or more of these women inside of us. We have deep needs for human attachment. What we fear losing more than anything else *is* that attachment. (What men fear losing is control.) We value our relationships —with husbands and lovers, children and parents, colleagues and bosses and friends and peers—to such an extent that keeping those relationships satisfying feels to us as important a goal as the kind of end- and result-oriented goals that men have always valued.

Yet we live in a society that has always honored those latter values, while characterizing our "emotionality" as a quaint poor cousin to men's "rationality." To make matters worse, the early gospel of the women's movement—Love Thy Work; Beware All Attachments As Diversionary—(now, thankfully, revised) and the me-first edicts of the seventies only increased the pressure on women to bury and be ashamed of their desire for connection. "Symbiotic" and "dependency" have become the new dirty words in intelligent women's vocabularies. (Unfortunately, the subtle shadings in these complex terms have been glossed over, if not downright misunderstood, by many of those who have used them most frequently.)

We have boxed ourselves into a place where, in effect, we're not allowing ourselves to be women. We've discredited and thrown away the Female Principle at the very point in time when it could be doing us so much good.*

And since we have denigrated this Female Principle for so long, many of us enter the various emotional negotiations in our lives severely handicapped. We simply do not trust ourselves. When, for example, an intimacy need is not being fulfilled, we cave in to the assumption that there is something wrong with us for having that need. We don't test the waters of commitment early enough in a new relationship. We don't confront the man soon enough. We are certain he will argue better than we do. We do not expect him to be able, much less willing, to give us what we want. (Half of the time, we don't even think he'll understand what we're talking about.) Yet, as my colleague Dr. Dee Barlow notes, we practice a sort of selective denial. We know that the relationship isn't working, that our needs aren't being met. We just won't admit it.

But even when we do admit it, and even when we feel we could get results, we're terrified of the risks involved in holding out for

---

* I'm reminded here of the remark made to me recently by the thirty-eight-year-old male partner in a major Los Angeles law firm: "Women have so many more arrows in their quivers than they know. In so many cases in my business, I've seen how they could use certain distinctly female qualities—their empathy, their nuancing of situations, their concern for feelings and process—to defuse a situation that men approach like two ramming bulls. In a pure business sense, they could win a lot that way."

them. Losing our "niceness," creating a chasm so he'll know we mean business—all this seems intolerably threatening for even a short period of time. So we nag and we fear and we stay where we are: needy, angry, confused. And we cover it all up and defuse it by taking the blame.

Along with this, we've bought the myth that it's a Noah's ark world, that an uncoupled woman is as useless as a leftover sock. A thousand books and articles have told us in a thousand different ways that alone doesn't have to mean lonely, but we don't seem to be getting the message. Many of us still feel that even a very bad relationship is better than being alone.

(The truth is that our society exists on multiple systems of groupings. "The couple" is only one among many—not the biggest, not the best, and certainly not the only one capable of rewarding a person with a rich private life.)

Add this all up and one thing is clear: we're stuck. Because we feel our relational needs and values are illegitimate and immature, we cannot take them out of the closets we've recently crammed them into and examine them with the dignity and precision they deserve. We cannot therefore demystify them. And without demystifying them, we cannot possibly strike the necessary balance between our need to be close and our need to be separate. We can only hide our needs and deny them until, untended, they grow out of control. And the more they grow in this wild and unexamined way, the more enslaved by them we feel.

Then along comes one adaptation—one response—that sucks up all the resultant emotional detritus like a high-powered vacuum zipping across a littered floor: guilt. It serves as a smoke screen for our fear of separation (not just from loved ones but also from bosses, colleagues and others) and our grief over loss (of fusion, niceness, approval). But, as every woman knows, guilt is not just a smoke screen. It's a vividly alive emotion in its own right, feeding the very dilemmas and ambivalences it is covering up.

The woman then becomes an exhausted "broker" of an imagined, ever-accumulating cross fire of IOUs. For in order to justify the endless obligations to others that she has taken on, she has set up a system of others' compensatory obligations to her. If she owes a cooked-from-scratch meal to her husband every night, then *he* owes *her* attention and flattery. If she buys her son a "Dukes of Hazzard" lunchbox, he then owes her good behavior. Soon, life loses its spontaneous flow of give and take. Everything becomes an obligation.

There is also great anger involved. For underneath the fear of loss (which is underneath the guilt) is a woman's fury at whomever she's afraid to lose (husband, child) *and* at herself for getting herself into this bind to begin with. Peel away one negative layer, and you get to yet another one.

If we are to break this complex, exhausting and seemingly endless syndrome of self-sabotage, we need to do three things:

We need to find—and to act on—a whole new, positive view of our need for attachment, so that we can negotiate for the fulfillment of that need in a proud, aboveboard, result-producing way.

We need to find a whole new, positive way of regarding and experiencing the uncoupled female state so we don't stay in miserable relationships for "security" or cripple our chances of improving flawed but otherwise promising ones.

And we need to understand the seductive power of guilt: to find out what it is that makes us so much more susceptible to guilt than men are: to see how our society creates guilt rabbit holes for us to fall down, and to discover what's in it for us to keep falling into them.

After years of addressing these subjects, I believe I've come up with some useful, effective answers. Let's take the third issue first.

DOWN THE RABBIT HOLE OF GUILT: THE TYRANNY OF INTERROGATION AND THE TRAP OF VALUELESS, BOTTOMLESS COMPASSION

One of these days, I am going to give a lecture or a seminar to a group of women, and a member of the audience is *not* going to stand up and proudly announce: "I was able to come here today because my husband is home watching our child." And no ten, forty or two hundred women in the audience will smile delightedly at the "lucky" speaker or applaud her noble, absent husband.

When all that happens—or, more accurately, doesn't happen—I am going to go out and break open the best bottle of champagne I can find.

What I will be celebrating is the end of a double standard that makes us regard nurturing activities expected and unremarkable when assumed by women but sacrificial and praiseworthy when assumed by men. What I will be celebrating is the fact that no more will those tasks that elicit a "So what? That's the least she can do" when the performer is female elicit an "Isn't that marvellous?" when the performer is male. What I will be celebrating is the end of what I call the Tyranny of Interrogation, which women live with every day of their lives.

If I've titled the concept a bit hoarily—in the manner befitting a stentorian voice booming through an echo chamber—it's because the dozens of big and little, voiced and implied, questions that comprise that tyranny *do* resound on a woman's conscience that way.

What are some of these questions?

"You mean you're letting them eat convenience food—with all that sugar and those additives—when it's so easy to just run fresh fruits and vegetables through a blender and . . ."

"How much longer are you going to be on the phone, dear?"

"How do you handle it when your work is going well and his isn't?"

"Working on Saturday again? But, gee, I thought today we could sort of sleep late, then do a little planting in the backyard, then maybe make a barbecue."

"What happens when his clients come to town just as your job gets the busiest?"

"Are you the lady of the house? I'm taking a survey on behalf of the butter and margarine association and I'd just like to ask you a few brief questions about your family's preferences and what you think about certain brands in regard to taste, freshness, price, spreadability, nutritional value and availability at your local supermarket."

"You've really got time for a movie/massage/long novel in that busy life of yours?"

"Honey, where's my olive-green tie?"

"And exactly when did you purchase this appliance, Mrs. Hansen?"

"You told him you wanted two nights a week just to be by yourself? Didn't he get upset?"

"And your phone number at work, Mrs. Barnes, so our PTA and fund-raising committees can call you when events of special importance come up?"

"*Wow*, hon, did you catch what Dan Rather just said? Oh, I forgot you can't hear the TV over Billy's bath water."

"C'monnnn, can't you sneak out of that boring sales conference for just half an hour? I want to show you the new car I'm thinking of buying."

"Oh, that yucky stuff for dinner again?"

You get the idea. We are assumed to be accountable for all of it: husband's needs, lover's needs, children's needs and, if there's any time left over, our own needs. The administrivia, as I call it, of daily life falls squarely on our shoulders, as does the emotional shopkeeping. And if we're ever brazen enough to forget that fact, there are plenty of needling questions to remind us.

Often, the questions are there even if no one else is raising them. We've become our own chief interrogator—and, not surprisingly, she's the toughest interrogator of all.

For example, I know a woman named Meg who's an excellent, accomplished photographer. So is her husband Josh. They have two children, six and eight. They often work together on projects, and those projects they work alone on are equal in value, quality and prestige. They respect each other's talent with a rare mutuality.

But their attitudes toward work and family are notably different. He can cleanly prioritize and negotiate and make trade-offs between the two. She cannot. Like many Haver women with families, her life sometimes feels as if it were being lived inside the spin cycle of a washing machine. Needs and demands twirl and jumble and mesh and tangle. Choice is difficult, conflict painful to resolve.

Last year, during the course of a photography workshop she was giving, Meg became friendly with the top aide of a highly placed Asian diplomat. Through this contact, she and Josh were invited to spend a month photographing life in a village in the People's Republic of China. The only hitch was, it was during their children's school months, so the kids could not come. And one parent would have to stay home with them.

Josh felt that, since it was Meg who had gotten them the assignment, it was only fair that he be the stay-at-home parent. But she couldn't see it that way. She knew she'd feel too guilty being away from the children to enjoy the adventure or take good pictures. So she stayed home, he went on the exciting assignment and, in place of guilt, she suffered regret, ambivalence and resentment, the latter made all the more frustrating because it could not be fairly directed at anyone.

"But what," I asked Meg, "if you'd spent the entire month before the trip and the entire month after doing little else but being with the kids: putting aside and turning down work to double up on mothering?" She shook her head and, in a voice at once helpless and adamant, protested: "I couldn't do that! You just can't put a fixed value on certain things."

Why on earth can't we?

My friend and colleague, anthropologist Dr. Susanna Hoffman (author of *The Classified Man*), tells me that among all world cultures there are three bartering currencies. There are words (including titles and positions); there are items (including all money); and there are bodies, the recognized value of which is not just sex and labor but caring and nurturance as well.

Men understand and respect the value of caring in this original, anthropological sense. They know how to cross-barter: bodies for items; words for bodies; items for words, and so forth. They see companionship and nurturance and compassion as things that are of value—assigned, estimable, negotiable value. The rich man marries and supports his doting, caring wife or showers presents on the young mistress who makes him feel as if he were the center of the world. The father, only half teasingly, orders his son, who is playing Pac-Man in their resort hotel suite: "Go out and enjoy that sun. I'm spending a lot of money on this vacation." The husband retorts to the wife who's just complained about his emotional withdrawal: "What do you mean, I don't 'give' you anything? Didn't I buy you this house? this car? Don't I praise you in front of our friends?"

Whether or not we always agree with their tactics and tone, we go along with men's cross-bartering. Yet we cannot cross-barter ourselves, even in a more humane and loving way. When it comes to what we consider our ultimate commodity, nurturance, we feel it is sacrilege to even attempt to quantify it and use it as a medium of exchange. We place caring so "above" conventional measures of value that, in effect, it becomes valueless: worthless in negotiation. We assume our compassion to be bottomless, unending. And, as such, we are its constant, unappreciated slaves.

The further hitch is that, unlike men, who know that knocking yourself out to earn money to support a child is a real demonstration of love for that child, we don't make that connection for ourselves. We may exalt our "caring" beyond all value, but it suddenly does take on value, for negative purposes, when it's placed in apposition to other forms of love.

Just let her child whine, "But Mo-om, all you do these days is work!"—and a woman will shrivel with guilt, thinking, "My God, I'm not caring enough!" So that atmospheric, "unquantifiable" nurturance—that is what counts, after all—not this rising-at-6-A.M.-slaving-till-8-P.M. routine, which counts so mightily as Daddy's love to the same child.

Women simply have to learn to say, with conviction, "But my working has everything to do with my caring for you. I'm working to make money to keep you clothed and fed and schooled and happy. I'm working because I wholeheartedly embrace my responsibility for your welfare. And I'm working to learn things about the world that I can bring home and share with you. So you must understand that there is an exchange of love going on in my absence as well as in my presence, that my work is a form of love for you."

BREAKING OUT OF GUILT: "WHAT'S IN IT FOR ME?" AND DISASTER FANTASIES

As self-punishing as guilt is, it is also chock full of hidden advantages to the self-punisher. The next time you are feeling guilty, take pen to paper and ask yourself, "What's in it for me?" Table 6 is one woman's list:

Table 6

WHAT'S IN IT FOR ME?

Feeling and acting on guilt enables me to . . .

1. *Maintain* my nobility ("What a much better wife/mother/ worker I am than she is because . . .") ("What a martyr I am!") and *elicit* sympathy, admiration and self-satisfaction for that nobility.

2. *Protect* the status quo by not changing routines—other people's, my own.

3. *Ensure* my popularity ("What a good kid/good sport/generous, giving person she is!").

4. *Remain* in control of other people's habits, mutual territory and shared projects. (e.g., if, out of guilty good-mothering, I drive the kids home from the ball game instead of making them take the bus, I can make sure they don't stop at McDonald's. If, because other people in the office are too busy and I'd feel bad putting them out, I do most of the work in organizing the firm's Christmas party, then the party bears my stamp and reflects my taste.)

5. *Deflect* complicated issues (such as "How *can* housework and emotional support be fairly shared within this family?" and "What does 'being a good wife/parent/lover/employee/ company coprincipal really consist of?"); *spare myself* the hard work of thinking and working through creative, individualized solutions.

6. *Handily fixate* on one overwhelming subject (my responsibility to others) so I always get to feel emotionally occupied, so I don't have to feel vulnerable to new feelings—or to boredom.

7. *Bind* people to me now by making them dependent on my goodness and my service to them and guarantee favors from these people months and years to come; have something to throw up to those who are ungrateful or unreciprocating.

8. *Avoid* all the anxiety that comes with the possibility that someone will be mad at me, will move away from me, will take my assertion or demand or movement in a negative fashion and will respond to my action with one of their own.

9. *Bolster* the myth that everything is okay.

10. *Corner* the market on virtue. Reduce other people's efforts and caring to second best next to mine.

11. *Sidestep* all responsibility for going into action.

12. *Hide* what flaws and shortcomings I might have that are not related to caring and giving by looking only at those, real or imagined, that are.

13. *Comfortably see* myself and others in a safe, superficial, one-

dimensional light, rather than as creatures of often baffling complexity, contradiction and nuance requiring more careful insight and response.

That's quite a list.

Thus, far from being benign and other-directed, acting out of guilt and from the caring-is-bottomless philosophy is highly self-serving. Trading in that mind-set for some degree of cross-bartering is not a step in the direction of selfishness but is a step in the direction of sharing with others the credit, the truth, the risk, the control.

The longer we stay on guilt's straight and narrow path, the more we blow out of proportion the consequences we imagine that any deviance from that path might bring. We cut off our freedom to a terrifying extent and in a tragically (sometimes pathetically) unnecessary way. Several years ago, for example, a woman came to me locked into the years-long practice of fixing her artist husband three hot meals a day. This time-consuming routine was, she felt sure, part of her job of being a supportive wife. The longer she suffered silently, the higher seemed the risk posed by "rebelling." I finally got her to muster her courage and suggest that her husband either take his lunches at a nearby coffee shop or fix them himself. He agreed without resistance. And for years she had expected their marriage to be threatened if she dared make that demand!

Though this woman's case is unusual, her wildly exaggerated worry is not. It is shared by a great many women every day, whenever they contemplate making a demand, a complaint or a move (temporary or permanent, physical or emotional) away from those they are tied to by business or love. "The kids will turn to dope if I leave them to take this job!" "My lover will feel I'm withdrawing if I go off skiing with friends this weekend instead of staying in town with him. He'll drop me for someone more safe and predictable!" "I could get fired if I make any more demands on the job!"

These are Disaster Fantasies. And the only way to defuse them is to start playing them out.

This is what I worked with Jocelyn to do.

A talented and accomplished illustrator, Jocelyn had been badly managed for a long time by her business manager, Noel, with whom she'd been romantically involved years before. Every time I'd suggest that she sever their relationship and find a new person (male or female) who could do much more for her career and her finances than he, she'd hoist up a familiar flag: "I can't possibly leave Noel! I'd feel too guilty!" Then she'd start in on the litany of deals and lawsuits he'd represented her in that were really, she insisted, her doing, her fault.

She seemed to cleave to their tangled history of mishaps in order to justify her entrenchment in a relationship that had never quite lost its personal meaning for her. Even though Noel made it very clear that he only wanted a business relationship with her now, Jocelyn continued to make of him a sort of fantasy lover. He occupied the "man" slot in her mind. (That way, of course, no real, possible, available man could find any room there.) His presence in her life on an emotionally tinged professional level made her feel she wasn't alone.

And being alone was what she dreaded more than anything.

So guilt wasn't the real issue; fear of separation was. And, like many women who find themselves drumming up all kinds of reasons why they "couldn't possibly" leave their dead-end jobs or love affairs, Jocelyn chose to stay in a disadvantageous business and delusory personal relationship just to avoid the consequences of that separation.

But what would really happen if they parted ways? Upon what was that deep and terrible fear based?

Working with the Disaster Fantasy exercise (Table 7)—the same exercise, in fact, that helped move Sarah of the previous chapter out of her fears of leaving her unsatisfying relationship—Jocelyn and I set about finding out.

Jocelyn described her problem (item No. 1) as "feeling that, objectively, I should find better representation than Noel seems to be giving me—but being afraid to act, afraid to let go."

Under No. 2, she listed the consequences with predictable negativity: "upsetting and hurting Noel; feeling disoriented; having to start from scratch finding a business manager and explaining my whole career—and life—to them and learning to trust them, etc." But that list, as is often the case, was a mere warm-up for her

Table 7

DISASTER FANTASY

1. Describe the problem.
2. Describe the consequences of the problem (what could happen to you).
3. Select the most severe consequence (the "worst" thing) that could affect your life.
4. If No. 3 did occur, what could you do?
5. Who is there to help you?
6. Who is there to hurt you?
7. How might you sabotage yourself?
8. What are you willing to do *now?*

© 1984 Tessa Albert Warschaw, Ph.D. No reprint without permission.

bottom-line fear, which she blurted out under No. 3: "I'll never find work as a commercial artist again!"

"Just what do you mean by that?" I asked her, trying to pinpoint the specifics within that calamity scenario. "No other business manager will want to handle me," she began, "either because they'll figure I'm temperamental for leaving Noel, or because the truth is I'm really not good, and Noel was getting me more work than I deserved all those years.

"Then I'll have to try to get accounts for myself, and I'll screw up the negotiations. And I'll get a bad reputation and I'll be afraid to knock on doors and I'll get rejections and the phone won't ring and I'll be too discouraged to even try anymore. And I'll stop looking and people will stop wanting me and there'll be too many other talented newcomers to take my place for anyone to miss me —and that'll be it!"

Jocelyn recited that speech in a tone that told me that she knew she was being melodramatic, if not irrational, but that knowing that didn't alter the grip that the fantasy held on her mind. And "grip" is the right word. For disaster fantasies are hammerlocks, neatly foreclosing all possibility, designed to stop the internal dialogue dead in its tracks. (That, after all, is their value in keeping a woman stuck in inaction.)

I pushed for an opening in that inner dialogue by taking the fantasy seriously. "All right," I said, moving us on to No. 4. "Let's suppose all of that did happen. You *are* finished in commercial art in this town. What then?"

"What then?" She seemed puzzled that I'd even ask. Wasn't The Worst a huge brick wall behind which nothing, good or bad, could exist?

Well, we chipped at that wall, brick by brick.

If The Worst really did come to pass, she decided, she could always:

1. Take her retailer cousin in San Diego up on a standing offer to go in with her on a children's store; move to San Diego;

2. Sell her car, her coop apartment and her stocks in order to finance labor-of-love projects she'd dreamed of for years: starting a girl-detective comic strip; doing silk-screen; starting a very small printing press for quality-papered and -bound illustrated books;

3. Utilize her extensive use of foreign languages (she speaks five fluently) to go into an entirely different, non-art-oriented line of work: interpreting, translating, offering her services to embassies and consulates, teaching;

4. Relocate abroad—in one of the countries whose language she speaks, with money gained from the investments detailed in option No. 2;

5. Pursue a long ago, still appealingly idealistic plan to join the Peace Corps or a Peace Corps–like group.

So there was a road beyond that brick wall. Not only did post-Disaster options exist; they were feasible, interesting and glamorous. Knowing this, a great deal of the bite (and the bluff) was removed from the Disaster. Leaving Noel was reduced to a life-sized choice. Now, in fresh (and still uneasy) contemplation of that choice, she had to wrestle with the very real steps she would have to take to replace him. So, moving on to No. 5, we pondered the question, "Who would be there to help her?"

"You're there to help yourself," I began. Then, brainstorming and telephoning, we came up with a list of six local women's groups, graphic artists associations, and commercial art networks, all of which had formal or informal free-lancer grapevines that could put her onto agents and to jobs, and some of which had advisers who helped people act as their own agents and managers on deals.

We went on to list Jocelyn's individual friends, colleagues, ex-workmates and miscellaneous contacts. This list grew to twenty, though advancing it was like pulling teeth. ("Oh, I couldn't ask him for help," she'd demur.)

Given that attitude, "Myself" was at the top of the list of possibilities under No. 6, "Who is there to hurt you?" Second on the list was Noel. Third was "Anybody who corroborates my idea of myself as a victim."

How (No. 7) could she sabotage herself? There were many ways. One, by ignoring the possibilities outlined in No. 4 and the people in No. 5. Or by staying with Noel and reinvesting in the delusions that (a) he'd come through for her romantically and professionally; (b) she would be "lost" without him; and (c) their failures had been all her fault.

Finally, using No. 8 as a lever, we took a step away from the hypothetical and into real action. "What are you willing to do," I asked her, "now that you know you have resources and that you could survive the severance of your business relationship with Noel?"

When she drew a blank, I suggested that she write Noel a civil—even gracious—letter, severing their business relationship and detailing the reasons. She laughed briefly, uneasily. "I've already written that letter—dozens of times," she admitted. "In my head."

"Good," I said. "Then the next step won't seem so daunting. Write it on paper this time. Reread it to make sure it expresses you accurately, that it's neither angry nor apologetic. Then type up a clean copy, address it and mail it—to me. That way, the act will seem realer than it ever did before—but not so real that it will frighten you."

By offering myself as a transitional step between her fantasy of and her action in letting go of Noel I was enabling her to "rehearse" her emotions for the real break which, four weeks later, she made. In addition to defusing her fears of the worst, Jocelyn needs to open herself to a whole new attitude. For her and for other women in this situation the next step is:

OWNING YOUR POSITIVE NEEDS FOR CONNECTION AND ACHIEVING MONAHIMU

I remember, about half a dozen years ago, watching a documentary film about the great highwire family, the Flying Wallendas. In one sequence the wife stood on the husband's shoulders as, balancing a pole, he walked the length of the wire.

I marveled at the profound degree of trust, teamwork and the intimate connectedness of this pair. Then my marveling was abruptly interrupted by a wisecrack emanating from the back of the screening room. "When one falls, the other comes all the way down with a thud: typical of a marriage!"

The voice was a woman's—and much of the supportive, sardonic laughter came from other women, too.

That incident spoke volumes for the way most educated women had come to view the act of depending. The Wallendas' feat was not viewed as a symbol of exacting and eloquent trust, and their reliance on each other was not seen as the artistry of interplay toward a shared goal. Rather, the intricate balance of dependence between husband and wife was interpreted as a rigged system by which people lost rather than gained.

For years, fueled by pop psychology books and self-liberation rhetorics of various, interlocking stripe, we let ourselves malign dependence across the board. Properly "self-realized" or "evolved" people weren't supposed to need each other, only want each other—in a way that sounded suspiciously dispassionate, if not downright sterile. In furiously rewriting the psychology of our gender, we women wanted to pave over every urge to attach, to connect, to rely like so many potholes in a pocked city street. We became very wary and ashamed of the fact that the people in our lives mattered as much as the goals. "This is no way to conduct life!" we remonstrated to ourselves. The desire (not to mention the urge) to nurture and, yes, even sometimes to please seemed to throw up constant roadblocks, barring us from the clean, straight-ahead route that men cut to their goals.

I think we overreacted. I think we threw the baby out with the bath water.

As a therapist all through these years of social and personal change, I have been seeing and hearing hundreds of men dying inside of the Poverty Mentality because of their lack of attachment, of commitment to relationship, of the ability to take primary joy in the interpersonal—of, in short, those very things that women have been so eager to overturn and deny. I think it is time we started proudly, happily, owning the good side of our female need and proclivity for connection, instead of dwelling on and blowing out of proportion the bad.

The time is right for this owning up. After years of recognizing only one emotional and moral developmental standard (the male one), academic psychologists are now seeing that women do think and feel differently from men and that different is not only equal but, in some ways, may even be better. Harvard University's Carol Gilligan speaks for many theorists and practitioners, for example, when she points out (in her book *In a Different Voice*) that women do live their adult lives embedded in relationships to a greater emotional degree than do men, that the highest moral value for women is not some system of abstract justice based on principles but a system of situational, personal, concrete justice based on needs and circumstance and care. Women, she confirms, see choices not one-dimensionally but multidimensionally: from the nuanced points of view of all the people involved. Furthermore, she says, all of these differences comprise a strong, important, positive and mature alternative to the male mind-set. I couldn't agree more.

For, in addition to the negative symbiosis that has been given much attention in recent years, there is also something known as healthy symbiosis, which is not at all the contradiction in terms it may strike one as being. Negative symbiosis is one person using the other as his or her virtual oxygen tank—and both people fearing separation and individuation from one another. Healthy symbiosis is an intense attachment that is functional, mutually beneficial and finite in length of time. Here, the two partners do not fear separation. They break away from their nourishing connection to individuate, to grow. The Wallendas were involved in healthy symbiosis. So are a breast-feeding mother and child. In both cases, the attachments are life-giving—yet when the attachment runs its course and is severed, no one suffers.

Less extreme than healthy symbiosis are other forms of positive needingness that are part and parcel of the human state. We must learn to stop denigrating this positive needingness, to trust and respect it again. Perhaps we need a new name for it—and I'd like to propose one. The word is *interindependence,* and it describes the fact that people need each other to further their own independence; that we can develop our best, most particular, even most stubbornly idiosyncratic selves by linking to one another in certain deep, steady and mutually beneficial ways. Just as a young child learns independence best by doing things alone while her mother is within earshot in the house, adults of either sex can get their best work done—and their best lives lived—when their separate, autonomous acts are performed in bold relief against a background of connection—of answerability to and support by others.

If Jocelyn had been able to own her positive needs for connection, she might have cultivated a satisfying relationship with a man that left her free to see Noel's professional service (or disservice) to her in an objective light. She then would have been able to disentangle herself from him.

And if Meg, the photographer I mentioned earlier, had been able to come to terms with her need for connection with her children—if, early on, she'd based her entire family philosophy on the notion of interindependence—she would have been able to go to China with no one suffering.

How would this have been possible?

When a family is based on interindependence, any member's separation is seen as an act made possible by—and made in collaboration with—the others. The children's going off to camp, for example, would be presented and experienced as the act of two members going away from the rest in order to have adventures that they could then take home and share with the others. In this same way but even more so, the trip to China could be presented and experienced as something the entire family, even those left at home, could participate in.

Meg would cast herself as the family's emissary to the commune. For a month or two before the trip, she would get the children busy on a project—a book of pictures and text explaining their city and family and customs to the Chinese children, for example— that she would then implement in the village, in their behalf. She would charge herself with coming home with an album of photographs, taken by her, of responses from the children of the village to her own children's project. Meg's children, in short, would be actively and legitimately included in her assignment. She would be going to China as much for them as for herself. The trip would seem less a separation and a loss than an interindependent family venture, based as it would be on the attitude (voiced, in this case, by Meg but shared by all of them): "I can reach and stretch and risk and sometimes even go off by myself for a while because—not in spite of but because—you are there. And I'm glad this is so. And I'm grateful this is so. And because this is so, there are real, concrete ways that all of us can benefit."

But interindependence doesn't apply only to families and to lovers. It applies just as well to women who live alone.

I live alone. I have been divorced for several years. Yet, far from being the quietly desperate "odd sock" that the term "single woman" flashes on the public's mind screen, I am in the thick of so many matrices—of emotional support, intellectual stimulation, professional networking and just plain play—that I can scarcely enumerate them all.

For example: I have joyously close relationships with the members of my family.

I have a rich array of friendships, some going all the way back to my high school years, others as new as six months old. Over the years, as well, clients have become friends and friends have become clients. Contacts are shared, as well as life support. My busy schedule of professional meetings, lectures, workshops and seminars brings me in constant touch with some of the most vibrant professional women and men not only in the cities I live in, New York and Los Angeles, but in the dozen others that I visit as well. My ventures in the worlds of publishing and cable television have expanded those circles and friendships even further than that.

I live alone, but I can honestly say that I am almost never lonely.

And I use myself as an example here not because I'm exemplary or unusual but, on the contrary, because I think there are many, many women whose lives are like mine—and even more women whose lives could be. This kind of rich interindependence outside of the strict nuclear family context—this alone-but-not-lonely state —is more and more common now, for women and men, especially in the big cities. Yet our society still does not honor it with a name. The Greek word *monahimu* (roughly meaning "by myself, in pleasure, by choice") comes the closest.

Monahimu. I like the sonorous, rolling sound of that word. It conjures, to me, a state of affairs in which you are keeping your own self full and excellent company.

The toddler talking busily to himself as he raptly puzzles out a new toy . . . the elderly Parisienne doyenne eating her full-course restaurant meal with appreciative languor and gusto, being not the slightest bit self-conscious (as we would be in this country) that she is seated at her table alone . . . the young teenage girl dreamily writing in her diary and listening to records in her room at night, or zooming down the street on a skateboard, hair flying behind her, wind smack in her face—these are common pictures of *monahimu*. But there can be so many more of them. Whether coupled or single, parent or nonparent, worker in office or at home, we can all learn to live our lives in such a way that solitary pleasures and interludes—whether there are many or few of them —are spent with delicious self-engagement.

Only when a woman is capable of this *monahimu* can she make decisions about her relationships on the basis of healthy, not neurotic, need. And only when she has owned her positive need for connection can she help show the man in her life—whether he's a new man or a husband or lover of many years' standing—how to honor that need.

LOGICAL CONSEQUENCES: NEGOTIATING FOR INTIMACY IN AN EFFECTIVE, NONTHREATENING WAY

All of us know of cases in which a man and a woman have been involved for years in a romance characterized by lots of wearying "hard work." The woman is not getting what she wants from the man. He is commitment-shy, closed to communication, emotionally irresponsible—"impossible," in a word. They finally go their separate ways, this woman who always sighed about her mate's misbehavior and this chronically misbehaving mate.

In time, the mate finds another woman. Does history repeat itself? No. Years of fighting commitment and communication have melted into an apparently smooth-as-silk new union in which, by all accounts, he is giving his new lady what she wants—the very same behavior that her predecessor tried so hard and so vainly to wrest from him.

The moral of the story? Men do know how to have relationships.

Men do know how to give women what we want. It's just that for years women have been giving men permission not to be responsible for their relationships.

The second woman knew all of this. The first woman did not.

The second woman also, most likely, had enough of a sense of internal integrity to know that she had a right to have a relationship that was, at the very least, mutual, harmless and trusting. Owning her need for positive connection and intimacy, she did not approach the man wondering if what she wanted from him might be too much to ask.

Thirdly, she probably operated out of logical consequences, showing the man that certain behavior elicits certain responses; that if he wants B from her, he must therefore take it upon himself to come through with A.

To understand what logical consequences is, we first must understand what it is not. And what it is not is the two other tactics that women often use to try to get the same results. One: They plead and cajole for "good behavior" or intimacy from men—or they try to "earn" or "bribe" it by inappropriate tenderness, flattery, favors and nurturing. The message such a woman is sending a man is: "You will be rewarded for not giving me what I want."

Or, *two,* they punish their men—with scoldings, tears, withdrawal, fury, airs of great aggrieved disappointment or long self-righteous speeches about what they are doing right and the men are doing wrong. Often, these same women threaten to leave "unless. . . ." But they do not make good on their threats. The threats become empty, meaningless: an ever expanding bottom line, the predictable harangue of the Girl Who Cried Wolf. The message this woman is sending is: "I'm going to bluster and stomp and blame, but, beneath all that noise, I continue to give you permission to repeat the very transgressions to which I object."

Logical consequences, on the other hand, is neither a bribe nor a bluff—not inappropriate coddling or an empty attack. It is simply a method of showing a man (or a child, an employer, a friend—anyone with whom you are negotiating) that he is responsible for holding up his end of the relationship with you; that his actions toward you have clear outcomes for him, and that those outcomes are most pleasant when those actions are most fair.

Here are some examples of how logical consequences works, as opposed to the other two tactics.

1. A woman goes to the hospital to visit her teenage daughter, recently laid up with a broken hip after a skiing accident. The girl is snippy and sullen, both attitudes she has been adopting toward her mother of late. She barely mumbles a thank you as she takes the mail, books, portable tape casette and memorabilia that her mother has brought at her request. She spends most of their visit talking on the phone to her girlfriends and ignoring her mother, who spent an hour in heavy traffic just to get there.

The mother has a choice. She can try to "win" her daughter by being even more solicitous the next time. Or she can rebuke her daughter for her rudeness before coming to visit again. Or she can deal logical consequences: decide to cancel her next visit since, quite apparently, neither one of them is enjoying it. (And canceling the visit means no more items brought from home to make the hospital stay more comfortable.) Thus, only by doing this last will the mother make the daughter see that her rudeness is affecting their relationship in a way that is disadvantageous to them both.

2. A woman has noticed that the man she has been seeing has taken to insulting or ignoring her when they are in the company of others. She has a choice. She can assume that he is just "naturally" trying to fight off his deepening feelings for her and prove to her that he's not the nice guy she thinks he is. "Understanding" all this, she can patiently put up with his behavior until it "just naturally" passes. Or she can take the defensive: ignore and insult him in front of people just as he does her, or rebuke him for his behavior after every occurrence. Then there is a third alternative: She can simply take along taxi money and calmly but immediately excuse herself from the party or gathering every time he exhibits this behavior. When later, baffled, he asks, "Why did you leave?" she will say, without anger: "I was made to feel uncomfortable. I did the only logical thing I could do." Only in this way does he know he has a price to pay for his behavior toward her.

3. The couple—both busy professionals—have a long-distance commuter romance. When they're together on weekends in Los Angeles (her turf), he's relaxed and caring and delightful. But when he flies back home to Chicago, he becomes demanding and possessive on the phone, calling her as many as a dozen times during the day at her office, becoming miffed and argumentative when she is too busy to talk.

The woman can react in one of three ways. She can empathize

with the vulnerability and fear beneath his bullying and so indulge his phone calls. Or she can call him a self-centered chauvinist for assuming she is able and willing to drop her work whenever he has the time and desire to call. Or she can take a third tack. She can say: "Look, I'd like to talk to you, but I can't have a good conversation when I'm preoccupied with work or if you're raising your voice at me. So I'm going to hang up now. If you want to have a different kind of conversation, I'll be free to talk at three-thirty."

Only when she takes this last tack does he see that altering his behavior will get him what he wants: wholehearted contact with her.

All of these cases are real. The woman in each scenario was a client of mine. And, in each case, she effected change in the behavior of the person—the daughter in the first instance, the lovers in the second two—by simply dealing logical consequences.

Dealing logical consequences takes forbearance and courage. You must hold out for results. You must stick to the systematic cause and effect implicit in the arrangement, and not give in to either of the two other superficially easier (but ineffective) tactics. You must be willing to take on a bit of short-term discomfort and anxiety in order to come away with long-term gains.

But you *will* get those gains. And as you get them and make them, you will wonder why it was so hard for you to see how easy it was to have them in the first place!

Breaking out of the basic feelings, attitudes and behaviors that comprise the Poverty Mentality is, as we have seen through these past five chapters, a process of taking a roundabout route to finally arrive at a principle, a point or a tactic that, once finally mastered and internalized, seems so simple and clear, after all.

Breaking out of those feelings, attitudes and behaviors requires, in short, a new way of seeing.

Now that you're armed with that sight, let us train it, in depth, on an area of life in which the Poverty Mentality flourishes: the male-female relationship.

II

MEN AND WOMEN AND THE POVERTY MENTALITY

CHAPTER 6

Brand-New Poverty Games Couples Play

I once had as a client a very successful man who was stricken with the fear that women were out to "get" him through his bankbook, whenever his guard was down. This man's boyhood was spent watching his parents play out a classic weekly living room scene. The mother, a timid housewife, was still and obeisant as the father, wearing his Breadwinning Head of Household badge on his sleeve, gruffly doled out her week's allowance.

When my client was eleven, his father suffered a stroke. The mother wept, endured, dutifully nursed her now partially paralyzed mate. The boy empathized with his mother's despair and was moved by her selfless demeanor—until his father whispered to him one day from his wheelchair: "Don't be fooled by all your mother's crap. She's loving every bit of her new power."

For the most part, thank God, those terrible days—of wildly imbalanced power, of lying and emotional bribery and raging distrust between men and women—are over. In income, financial savvy, prerogatives within the relationship and society, we're more equal now than ever before (though there's a lot of room left for improvement).

But as old wrongs are righted and traditional gaps are closed, fresh problems arise—"better" problems, to be sure, since they're not based on the old men-have/women-have-not chasm, but thornier problems as well, because they're unprecedented and, being unprecedented, they have no proved—sometimes no known—solutions.

So if my client's fear had no literal base, it did have something of a figurative one. For the sorry truth is, men and women do "get" each other through their bank books in myriad subtle ways, every day of the year. Even couples who sincerely love each other play the Poverty Games with each other, games often as hidden from their own eyes as from the eyes of the outside world.

What is a Poverty Game?

It's a style of relating between men and women in which money is used as a lever to keep both parties down. It's two people mistaking quid pro quo for trust, and confusing cold, rote, fifty-fifty splits for genuine, nuanced partnership. It's two people thinking that the avoidance of issues is the granting of freedom. It's one member of a couple expecting the new rights and privileges to apply when it's convenient and advantageous, and falling back on the old rules whenever it isn't. It's the other member of the couple putting his or her ego in the way of their mutual success.

A Poverty Game may reflect a veiled or unconscious hurt, anger or aggression. (Many more people brutalize each other with ledger books and paychecks than with explosive or sharp-edged weapons.) Then again, it may simply be the result of one Poverty Mentality meeting another, and the two of them careening to mayhem down a road paved with the best of intentions.

A Poverty Game is most often played by people who are mated, domestically if not legally. But it can also be played between a single woman and a professional financial adviser of the opposite sex. Here are four common ones, all new twists on the old Poverty Games they aim to replace.

POVERTY GAME I:
DOUBLE MONOPOLY/DOUBLE SOLITAIRE

The most classic Poverty Game men and women have played through the ages is Decision Monopoly. We all know what that is: one member of the couple—almost always the man—makes all major decisions regarding money. The woman may be indulged with the illusion of holding the family purse strings, but the purse she is holding is a puny, innocuous one next to the whopper of a satchel *he's* controlling.

In traditional upper-middle-class households, for example, the woman may oversee a ten- or even twenty-thousand-dollar house-remodeling project—she may even initiate it—but the man put up the two hundred and fifty thousand that purchased the house, and with that outlay came the privilege of making basic decisions about the house. In working-class households, the woman may decide which supermarket to patronize for family shopping, but the man decides which of his union's health and life insurance plans he'll tether his entire family's security to.

Decision Monopoly is symptomatic of the entire old order of male and female power and privilege. And though it's still unfortunately prevalent, many modern couples—especially Haver women and their mates—are consciously reacting against it. But by correcting Decision Monopoly's injustices these couples often fall into a new poverty game. Based on (1) women's achievement of professional and financial parity over the last twenty years and (2) the enlightened couple's aversion to subjecting each other to unfair demands, this new game might be called Double Monopoly/Double Solitaire.

Here, both partners make their own, independent decisions about their concertedly separate financial bailiwicks. They rarely talk to each other about how and where they are spending their money. "Space" and equality within the relationship is somehow used to justify a vague and reckless kind of laissez-faire with the bankbook.

Those who have plumbed depths of sexual and emotional intimacy unknown to past generations of couples now find they're timorous of and embarrassed by the one intimacy that those past generations always embroiled themselves in: the tremendous intimacy of money. To face one's mate and ask: "Where did you spend the five hundred dollars you got from that commission last week? Mightn't we have put it to better use together?" seems as much a gauche violation of that mate's right of privacy and freedom as demanding: "Where did you spend your lunch hour? What restaurant? What street? Were you with another woman?"

These couples are silent because they eschew the old oppressive/repressive rules for making money decisions together. And there are no new rules to take the old rules' place.

So what you end up with is two people coming together with two separate—and sometimes polar opposite—styles of handling and accounting for money, two separate—and often very different

—sets of priorities for what money should be saved for and spent on, two separate, hidden statements they want to make about themselves with their money.

What you end up with is two ships passing each other in the night, their lights respectfully dimmed.

One night, they accidentally collide.

And then, of course, there is panic.

Nora and Todd are such a couple. Both in their late thirties, with divorces behind them, they clearly love each other deeply. They also seem to love the contrast of their personal styles. He's a flamboyantly creative restaurant chef-part owner, always dazzling friends with his witty takeoffs of gourmet pieties. His idea of handling money is to brandish his credit cards until they're over the limit and to write checks impulsively, without tallying them in the checkbook.

Nora, who's a market research executive, smiles with fond aggravation at those blank spots in their checkbook. The levelheaded yin to her husband's feverish yang, she's the bookkeeper of the pair. She provides the common sense; he provides the flash. He's the absentminded creative force and enfant terrible, she's the classy earth mother. "I have no right to make him change such a fundamental part of himself," she says, of his approach to money. "Anyway, how can he change? He is who he is."

And who she is is a person whose money style is, in a different way, just as inviolate as she claims his to be. Her meticulous ledgers are written in a code Todd couldn't crack even if he wanted to. And aside from the kitchen and his small office, their home is furnished to reflect her deep concern for serene and serious good taste.

All of this describes them a half year ago: a delightedly dissimilar married couple with lots of goodwill, as well as lots of avoidance and denial of potential problems.

Potential became actual six months ago. The second trust deed on their home was due. There was no money to pay it. The bank threatened unpleasant consequences. Nora and Todd "had no idea" how any of this could have happened. Resentment was aired and blame was spewed where none existed before.

This was not, they finally admitted to me, the first time that they'd backed into this kind of financial panic. This time, though, they wanted it to be the last.

I worked with Nora and Todd to come up with this five-step program to break their pattern of Double Monopoly/Double Solitaire, and to forge, instead, a system of financial accountability that would enhance, rather than jeopardize, their freedom and their closeness.

Step 1: *Explore how the hidden statements that each of you separately makes through money is costing you money and causing you stress.*

Where, how and on what you habitually spend money—all of these choices give impressions to the world as distinct and telling as your fingerprint, and as clear and visible as your style of dress. These impressions are the result of hidden statements you're asking your spending style to make for you.

If you spend a lot of money on services—housekeepers, service people, personal secretaries, masseurs or masseuses—to make your life easier and more convenient, you are saying "I'm important." If you're spending it on clothes, cars, furnishings, you are saying "I'm fashionable." If you shower presents on your mate and children, entertain frequently and expensively, are the first to pull out your wallet at the end of a restaurant meal with a friend, you're saying "I'm generous."

Todd was clearly saying "I'm playful" with his footloose spending style. Nora was saying "I'm in control" with her private ledger keeping, her tight rein over their house's interior and exterior design.

It didn't take them both long to see how they were causing tension within the relationship, cramping each other's styles and losing money by making these hidden statements in an unacknowledged and therefore unnegotiated fashion.

For example, Todd liked to think of himself as an amateur electrician. But knowing Nora's penchant for order and respecting her prerogative as household administrator, he never thought of saying to her: "Hey, to save money, why don't we let go of the maintenance man you hired and let me put in a new lighting system and tinker with repairs for a while?"

Similarly Nora felt it was unreasonable to demand that Todd obtain and hold on to receipts for small purchases made during the course of his day (stationery, magazines, lunches eaten at coffee shops, etc.) that might be deductable on their joint return. So Todd silently resented Nora for his lack of permission to experiment with the lighting system. And Nora silently resented Todd's irresponsibility in losing them tax-deduction money. And neither of them had ever admitted these feelings to the other before.

Thus, we moved to:

Step 2: *Give your partner permission to give his or her statement "right-of-way" in one situation. Exact a trade-off from your partner in return.*

Nora agreed to let go of the maintenance man and turn the lighting and home repairs over to Todd. In exchange, Todd promised to try to remember to bring home receipts for his personal expenses and give them to Nora for her accounting. They figured that one month of this bargain would save them a full $350 ($250 for the maintenance man, $100 in tax deductions). If both of them could live with the negotiation over a year's time, that meant an annual savings of $4,200!

They posted the monthly and yearly figures on their refrigerator door as an incentive to continue the deal, despite their initial adjustment qualms. (Todd's at first scattershot repair work drove Nora a little crazy. And having to get a receipt for a three-dollar snack was a pain in the neck to Todd.) In time, however, both of them got used to it. Todd's electrical and repair work and his accounting improved; Nora became more tolerant and relaxed, less invested in being the overseer. And they *loved* saving the money.

Step 3: *Let the one who is better at it do a little research to find out where all the money (yours, mine, ours) is going.*

Because talking about money was so unfamiliar to Nora and Todd, it was decided that one evening per month would be officially designated as a time of financial reckoning and accountability. They marked that night on their calendar, one month from our meeting.

In the month that elapsed, Nora went over their books—her books and what she could discern of his books—to try to find out just where their money had been going. She kept a diary of expenditures as well.

Then came their first month's meeting, which I helped them negotiate through. I had Nora and Todd make the first of their monthly two-column lists of issues and risks. Issues are possible new expenditures (vacations, housekeepers, renovation, clothes, office equipment); risks are all obligations and complications on the budgetary horizon (the second trust deed, a tuition payment coming up for Todd's child from his previous marriage, a projected rough few months for Nora's firm).

Through this list they saw—for the first time—their separate incomes and separate circumstances as part of a larger, truly mutual design.

When it came to drawing up the budget, they opted for maximum breathing space, so they operated on the unlikely but prudent assumption that all the risks would materialize. That meant they had to veto twenty-five hundred dollars' worth of issues.

The quandary became: Which ones?

In the looks that played on their silent, thoughtful faces, I saw Nora decide not to come down on Todd for the new stove he was dying to order and Todd decide not to insist that Nora's Louis XIV settee for their library be reconsidered. They were left, then, with the hard work of finding $2,500 worth of neutral or mutual expenses to void. After some discussion, they decided to forgo some work on their garage and a planned week's trip to Taos and Santa Fe, New Mexico—with the option of rescheduling both projects in three months if one of their big risks didn't materialize or was comfortably met.

Step 4: Make a plan to be as intimate with your pockets as you are with your bodies and minds.

To crack the money avoidance that kept Nora and Todd locked in their Double Solitaire mode, we decided:

a. that all of their bankbooks—his, hers, ours, checking, savings and money market accounts—be kept together in one special drawer, opened flat to the current page;

b. that all purchases over seventy-five dollars that each of them was thinking of making be run past the other. (That way, you get a prior and aboveboard opinion from your mate—honest, solicited, with no ax to grind—rather than "See, if you'd asked me, I'd have told you it was totally irresponsible to buy that new sports jacket when you didn't know if you were getting that new ad account."

c. that the money administrator—in their case, Nora—keep the other partner apprised of all major moves with the insurance policies, taxes, interest rates on their holdings, etc.—even if that other partner says, "I trust you; you don't have to tell me the details." Even the most impatient, distracted or "creative" person can learn to accommodate details. It's much better to slightly "inconvenience" yourself that way than to stay in the dark and leave the "responsible" partner with all that lonely privilege.

Step 5: *Make a plan for the enforcement of the monthly meeting —and for the entire process outlined in steps 1 through 4.*

New habits take a little doing to keep. Nora and Todd felt they needed to use a form of Logical Consequences to make sure they'd stick to their monthly appointments with each other. So they changed their IRS payment plan from annual to quarterly, and scheduled four of their monthly appointments with one another on the day before the last day they could file without penalty. That way, keeping their appointment would be clearly cost-effective.

That took care of four of the twelve appointments. For the other eight, they told their secretaries to record the appointment in their respective business calendars and to remind them of the appointment, as they would of any other business engagement, on the morning of.

After six months, the system is working well. The tension is gone from the relationship. They're saving $350 a month. They each know where all their money is going. They're breaking out of their roles as indulged child and prim controller—and seeing fresh areas of one another, and of themselves.

POVERTY GAME II:
WHAT'S MINE IS MINE; WHAT'S YOURS IS MINE, TOO.

"What's his is ours," went the edict of the classic old Breadwinner/Homemaker game. Of course, with that old one-makes-the-money/one-makes-the-beds split went all sorts of privilege and power disparity, and modern, two-paycheck couples are right to eschew the whole package.

But is it really the whole package they're eschewing?

I don't think so.

Over and over again, I see Comer and Haver women playing a whole new Poverty Game, one that their partners tacitly corroborate. This Poverty Game rejects what's disadvantageous to them in the old game (the male decision monopoly) but doesn't quite get rid of what isn't: the assumption of one-sided, his-to-her sharing.

In What's Mine Is Mine, the woman in a couple claims full control of her salary. "I worked for it!" her attitude goes. "[Just like a man] I deserve to be able to do anything I want to do with it!"

This attitude romanticizes male privilege while ignoring male responsibility—or, rather, conveniently leaving that responsibility just where it was. For it's her mate's salary that is subtly but firmly held accountable for holding down the fort—for providing the household maintenance (rent or mortgage, food, kids' school, etc.) and financial leveraging (moving from one income level to the next through promotion, job switching, creative investment).

Even if she's involved in a serious career, the woman who plays What's Mine Is Mine often treats her income as a form of sophisticated pin money. She sees it as the icing on the cake, the overflow, the gravy—the putty that may occasionally fill in the cracks of the family nest rather than the mortar that holds that nest together. I call these women *nouveau* breadwinners because in the same way that the *nouveau riche* rush to acquire the flashy externals of wealth without giving thought to wealth's sober obligations, they rush to acquire the externals of careerism (status cars, clothes, vacations, imprudently expensive offices, staff and equipment where smaller, shared or more modest versions of the same would do) while leaving the internal sense of necessity—for maintaining and maximizing money—to their mates.

And with that sense of necessity comes hunger. And with that hunger comes motivation. And with that motivation, ultimately, comes power.

And that precisely is what the men get out of this Poverty Game: continued power—the assurance that, despite outward signs of change, their wives are still safely dilettantish, still dependent on them. "Jill's career may be taking off now," such a man might unconsciously console himself, "but she still can't read a financial report. Her new Mercedes is cute, but she's leaving the school tuitions to me. I'm still the bottom-line provider."

To the outside world, these couples seem enviably coachieving, their goals smoothly in sync. Outwardly, the woman feels in clear control of her income, down to the last dollar, the man in control of his ego and the family's financial reins. They're the picture of "supportiveness." They appear to share.

But what is going on inside the relationship, usually unbeknown to them both, is the opposite. The woman, having robbed herself of the urgency of breadwinning, is almost certain to be under-achieving in some way. The man is comfortable with her under-achievement; he does not think to protest. He is letting his male ego get in the way of their joint financial success. The family coffers are being reduced by as much as 30 to 50 percent from their potential. Instead of marshaling their resources to soar to-gether, they've arranged a kind of emotional/financial détente: what they're each so "supportive" of is not the other's best self but the other's frightened and compromised self. They're sacrificing long-term benefits and growth for short-term, day-to-day survival of the relationship. And since they're frittering away their real and potential money and leaving themselves vulnerable if a crisis should strike, they're not in but out of control.

Harriet knows about all of this intimately. Ten years ago she was a perfect example of someone who played What's Mine Is Mine. . . .

She had just received her Ph.D. in education. Her husband, Lloyd, had his own small import-export business. Her leap from Comer to Haver, not just in the outside world but within her marriage, could have been liberating and beneficial to both of them.

Instead, secretly afraid of it, they cushioned its blow. She was appointed to a nonpaying yet prestigious seat on the State Curric-ulum Commission. They leaped at the honor. They could afford for Harriet to take the appointment since Lloyd was making a lot of money. With the new professional's enthusiasm and her skewed sense of priorities, Harriet rented an office in a smart part of town for her yet unproved speech therapy practice and immediately got all the proper accoutrements: phone, answering service, printed stationery.

Instead of burning with urgency to make good on her daunting investment in her educational consultant career, Harriet felt com-fortable enough to take things easy, accepting what clients were referred to her way while spending the bulk of her time on the Commission work, which was high in social and professional status but irrelevant in practical terms to her new career. What she should have been doing was not renting her own office but subleasing someone else's three days a week; not "accepting" what clients came her way, but actively seeking them out; not wasting her time on unpaid work but building up a steady, lucrative professional practice. In that first year, what little money she earned was instantly eaten up by her high overhead. What she could have been doing instead was establishing a practice that by year's end might have been worth $25,000—which is equivalent to $40,000 today.

But she didn't think of doing that. And Lloyd, who knew better, never told her she ought to or had to. If they'd taken her seriously as a professional and if they'd taken seriously their financial partnership, they would have seen the idiocy of that first year right off the bat. Instead, moored in their respective Poverty Mentalities (Harriet's naïveté and dilettantism and Lloyd's need to keep taking care of her), they merged to play "What's Mine Is Mine; What's Yours Is Mine, Too."

What happened to Harriet and Lloyd is what often happens: The "yours" that was "mine, too" collapsed. Lloyd's business fell on hard times. So Harriet quit her post on the Commission and got a job. Like so many Poverty Mentality couples, instead of intelligently and profitably planning ahead, they waited for crisis to snap them to their senses, then started on a dime in a one-down position.

Harriet finally started her consultant practice a full year and a half later than she could have.

Hers was a classic case: woman in transition from Comer to Haver plays What's Mine Is Mine with her husband as an unspoken pact to keep their marriage in status quo. But this isn't the only— or the most frequent—form of this Poverty Game. Often it's played by women who were Havers well before they met the current men in their lives, women whose unions seem marked by a high degree of generosity, sophistication and lack of sexism— until a closer look reveals one of these subversions of What's Mine Is Mine:

1. "I'd be letting him get away with something if I let him benefit from my higher earnings" or "Since the man's income sets the tone for the couple's financial outlook on the world, I'm scot-free to play with my 'extra' goodies."

Joan is a television reporter who makes about thirty thousand a year more than Mark, her painter-craftsman husband of three years. Together, their incomes approach a hundred thousand—an amount that, for a childless couple, would allow for the making of smart, solid investments: coop apartment or home, stocks or additional real estate.

Yet Joan and Mark live like a couple of chic, forget-about-tomorrow sybarites. Their apartment is tiny and cluttered. Aside from her fancy car (and his not so fancy one), they own nothing. Joan's entire investment portfolio consists of her IRA. But meet her at a party and she'll knock you out with her designer clothes and expensive jewelry.

Clearly, leveraging their money as a couple is a prerogative that falls to Joan. As a free-lancer, Mark can't get the kind of credit Joan can get for real estate mortgage loans. And it's her higher salary that would provide most of the financing. Joan could view their marriage as a partnership, could exercise her leveraging prerogative, could find a good investment that would pad their joint coffers over the next twenty years.

But she isn't doing so. Why? On some deep, inarticulated level, she sees their marriage as short-term, not long-term. On that same level—and despite her external pride and supportiveness for Mark's work—she sees his lower income and less stable circumstances as a kind of latent character flaw, one that might suddenly bloom and thrive if she made things too easy for him, if she "capitulated" to the breadwinner role. Despite an unimpeachable public record for feminist remarks, Joan is really uncomfortable with and resentful of being in the position to steer her family's financial ship. It seems an imposition, not an opportunity, to have the responsibility to put her money to work for her, to make more. All those decisions, all that research, all the initiative that leveraging and investing implies—that's something the man is supposed to do. So she hides behind this very unstated "logic" and frees herself from "hassling" with long-term money plans at all. And by partaking of that false freedom, she's enslaving the financial future of her marriage—and herself.

2.   "I perform like a man with my money all day, so don't I deserve to be indulged as the most feminine woman alive by night?"

Katherine, unlike Joan, has been very smart and aggressive with her money. At forty, she's amassed a real estate portfolio that, along with her income as a service-industry executive, gives her a comfortable six-figure income, enviable security and options.

Yet she still expects her lover to take her out to dinner, take her on vacations, to share theirs while she holds on to hers, to foot the whole bill, as if in symbolic recompense for her laudable leap from an indulged childhood and first marriage to financial self-suffi-ciency.

Katherine's attitude—"Look what I've done! I deserve being taken care of on my off hours"—is an important illustration of the fact that, at this point in time, most women still think that maxi-mizing their own money is a sacrifice, an act of "going out of one's way," a hard, rare good deed meriting a reward. (Men regard this same thing as a sensible, natural act that is its own reward.)

Having long ago graduated from the need for the nouveau breadwinner's kind of reward (fancy clothes, cars, trinkets), shrewd investors like Katherine look for this other kind of reward —traditional courtliness from men—without realizing that it's a reward with a dangerous boomerang. For the man who most readily agrees to one form of nonmutuality is also the man most likely to subscribe to a second. I've known Katherine to leave a venture capitalists' meeting in order to go home and iron a stack of Brooks Bros. shirts.

How do you break out of What's Mine Is Mine?

1. See yourself in genuine partnership with your mate.

Ideally, a couple trusts each other deeply enough for each of them to throw almost everything they have into a common pot. The mine-yours distinctions—and the nitpicking and scorekeep-ing—dissolves in a genuinely felt and experienced context of mu-tuality, of teamwork.

It's useful to see your relationship at least as a financial partner-ship. In other words, the two of you are combining your talents, assets, resources, moneymaking potential. The one holding back or stinting harms the partnership and denies the partner his/her rightful benefit. To put it simply: You're in it together. The more each of you is able to make, the better it is for the other.

As noted New York divorce lawyer Julia Perlez told me: "The biggest mistake a woman can make—whether she's married or single or on her way in or out of either state—is to not maximize her potential as a money earner."

2. Look at where your money is going every day of the month, and compare your list with a man's.

If you suspect you may have nouveau breadwinner habits, that you may be treating your income as sophisticated pin money, keep an exact record of all purchases made and checks written for one month. Compute the percentages that go to (1.) savings and investments, (2.) household and family maintenance (including food, housing, schools) and (3.) personal luxuries.

Ask a male friend or colleague with a similar income and in similar life circumstances (same number or absence of children, property holdings, etc.) to make the same accounting.

Compare notes.

If the man is spending 15 or more percent than you are on 1 and 2 and 15 or less percent than you are on 3, then you are in some way playing What's Mine Is Mine. Consider trimming your personal luxury sails and funneling that same money into savings and investments instead.

3. When faced with the opportunity for personal indulgence, try "borrowing urgency."

You are starting your own business, but your husband or mate or father has enough money to cushion you for a while. You are walking down the street, and a Norma Kamali cocktail dress in a shopwindow catches your eye. You don't feel too guilty contemplating buying it; there's a business function next week that you could wear it to. On the other hand, you don't really need a new dress and you could be putting that same $250 toward a used dictaphone, a special promotional mailing, a paint job for your office's reception area.

What to do?

Quickly imagine yourself without your cushioning. You are the sole support of yourself, your business, your kids. There is no help coming in from the sidelines, no margin for splurging. What do you do? Buy the dress or put the money into the business?

Do what your "urgency-borrowing" self dictates about three out of every four times, but not all the time. Too much concerted and artificial denial makes for resentment and lack of a realistic perspective.

POVERTY GAME III:
THE NEW "GREAT SACRIFICER"—
AND HER NOT-SO-SILENT PARTNER

Faye is a client of mine who is a free-lance political consultant to various officials in national and international public life and in industry. She is looking ahead two weeks to the state primary election day because she's been working on the campaign of a senatorial candidate. She yearns to spend a whole week playing with her two-year-old daughter, Maura. "I feel filled up when I'm with Maura," she says. "I missed that total connection—when I, not some hired young woman, am feeding her and rocking her to sleep—all those months I was getting up at six and getting home at ten p.m. Maura misses it too."

But an important economists' convention is opening the day after Faye's client's primary. There she could make valuable contacts that might lead to a lucrative next assignment. She wants that too.

"It'd be career idiocy for you not to strike while your iron's hot," says her husband, Bill, also a political consultant. "We'll all go to the convention—as a family. We'll take the au pair girl along for Maura."

What Bill has proposed, Faye feels, is a technically sensible solution with a gaping flaw that, alas, the male mind doesn't understand. "We'll go without the fallback of the au pair," Faye amends. "Maura needs full-time parenting right now. You and I will take turns going to the convention activities and spending full quality time alone with her."

Bill balks. He's going to the convention for work contacts, not to sit in a sandbox half of each day! If Faye insists—rather pointlessly, he thinks—on stranding them without childcare, well, then, he'll take Maura for an hour or so each day—say, to breakfast, but—

Faye feels she has no choice but to say no to the convention. Bill tells her she's throwing a big career opportunity down the drain. Faye gets angry at Bill for what she considers his uncooperative hypocrisy: he benefits from the fact that she owns her need for intimacy and values relationship in a way that he does not (she's so often the first to bend to keep harmony in their home). And now he's using this advantage to him against her all the more, by causing her to have to give up the convention—and the work opportunities it would confer—entirely!

"Damn it," Faye says, entering my office. "Are we career women doomed to be always sacrificing one thing for another, simply because we're conscious of the value of caring and love as well as work, while men are impervious to the value of anything but work?" She pauses. "And is my not going to the convention in order to be home with Maura really a sacrifice?"

Faye is the new Great Sacrificer.

The old, classic Great Sacrificer sighed. The new Great Sacrificer gets angry. And then she gets confused.

The old Great Sacrificer was a woman who was expected to give up everything—identity, desires, ambition—for the good of her family. When she did so, it was with a sort of blessed ignorance: since her "potential income" was never acknowledged as existing at all, neither she nor her husband ever counted the actual thousands of dollars they lost by the arrangement in which she was stuck. When she suffered, it was silently, invisibly, "illegitimately."

The new Great Sacrificer is a woman who, having lobbied for and lived by the changes of the last twenty years, expects not to have to give anything up, at least not without a fight. When she indeed gives something up, it's with an acute consciousness of the cost of her action in real or potential income (a consciousness shared by her mate). When she suffers, it's visibly, vocally, legitimately—but not very effectively and with no small irony: for she's subtly directed to view the trade-offs and choices she makes as "sacrifices," even by those very people for whom or instead of whom she is making them—and especially when those people would not make those same trade-offs and choices themselves!

The old Great Sacrificer lived in a society and a relationship in which little that she did was interpreted as sacrifice but much, in fact, was.

The new Great Sacrificer lives in a society and a relationship in which much of what she does can easily be interpreted as sacrifice —but how much actually is is something about which she is honestly baffled. She is often left trying to fit the round peg of her owned-up-to intimacy needs and relationship-valuing into the square hole of male definitions. (Just because a man would not freely choose act A over act B, does that then make that decision a sacrifice when a woman—a woman who does not want to be denied the work and money options of the male world—makes it?

Or: The New Great Sacrificer is the woman who has gotten so wary of yielding that, counterphobically, she holds her ground, refuses to give an inch—to the extent that she actually pushes away what she wanted to be strong enough to have on her own terms: love.

The man in the New Great Sacrificer's life is a silent but very active partner in this Poverty Game. He can indulge, exploit and refuse to help her resolve her confusion, leaving their relationship and their bankbook diminished. (Result of this round of events between Faye and Bill: she's angry at his hypocrisy and his refusal to help; he's angry that her obstinate refusal to have the au pair girl at the convention is making her unable to go. They're both angry at the loss of potential money for their partnership, and they each blame the other for that loss.) Or, construing her "no-sacrifice" policy as a sort of Berlin Wall against his attempts at intimacy, he can leave.

To break out of this Poverty Game, you must do the following:

1. Distinguish choice from sacrifice.

I was making notes on this chapter while sitting one morning in the New York apartment of a friend. Right outside my window, a young couple in night-before discotheque clothes were standing on the stoop, arguing wildly. The girl was screaming at the boy in a tone of pain, rage and accusation that fairly vibrated entrapment.

At that instant I realized: This is a blown-up picture of what sacrifice feels like. That bullied, choiceless, cornered, do-or-die feeling that it's this person or no one, this activity or nothing; that someone or something has put you up against the wall: that's sacrifice. A sacrifice is turning down something you want to do for something you do not want to do.

A choice, on the other hand, is turning down something you want to do for something else you want to do. Choice involves doing a quick costs-benefits analysis of several conflicting possibilities at hand, then selecting one while rejecting or postponing others. Choice involves preference, freedom and some sense of pleasure or benefit, though it may also involve regret. You can't always have everything—the steak, the salad, the potatoes and the plate. The complexities of life in a value-transitional time, the adding of responsibilities that come with privileges, with options, with fulfillment—all of this makes for the need to winnow out, to select.

2. Don't confuse sacrifice with sharing.

Being with another person just naturally involves making trade-offs. But many Haver women, I've noticed, are so afraid of slipping back into the Old Great Sacrificer mold of their mothers (or, perhaps, of their first marriages) and are so defensive about preserving, unalloyed, all the options they've worked so hard to attain, that they refuse to make these little compromises. Even tiny concessions—going out instead of staying in; having seafood instead of steak—spell danger to them, seem the first pebblefalls in some inevitable rockslide to total surrender.

These women are making the mistake of confusing sacrifice with sharing.

Often, these women have lived alone so long they've become set in their ways. They've gotten used to not having to change one habit to accommodate another person, and this simple by-product of circumstance gets dressed up in all kinds of political and emotional trappings that it really doesn't merit. If a woman likes to listen only to classical music, to sleep with a light on and on the diagonal of the bed, to have the kitchen counter cleared of scraps before not after, the meal is served, and if meeting another person threatens these precious prerogatives, well, is compromising one or two of them really such a loss, a sign of being dominated or bamboozled? A woman in this situation should ask herself: Am I really being asked to sacrifice, or am I simply being inflexible?

3. Ask yourself: "What do I really want to do?"

Related to the two steps above, you have to steady yourself amid a sea of constantly changing values and imperatives. You have to listen to yourself alone. If arranging a five-course dinner from scratch is your guilty pleasure (even if it takes an entire day), forget the fact that many "experts" on women's liberation, time efficiency and leisure would call it unnecessary drudgery to do so. No one else—not your mate, your neighbor, your best friend, the writers of magazine articles and books, not even your therapist—can tell you what is or is not a sacrifice for you.

So the first three things you must do involve determining

whether or not you are indeed making a sacrifice. Let's say you've determined that you are. Say, for example, you'd like to read the newspaper and watch television at night, just as your husband does. But the kitchen is a mess and the dishes are piled in the sink. You get no pleasure at all from washing and straightening, but you do it anyway, because you have to use the same dishes and area for breakfast tomorrow. What do you do now?

4. State your complaint to your partner now.

Don't wait till your resentment mushrooms into conversationally unmanageable proportions. Say: "I feel this isn't fair: neither of us likes cleaning the kitchen, but I'm forced to do it every night, because you simply will not move."

5. Have an appealing trade-off ready.

"If it's missing your favorite TV show that's bothering you, why don't we move the TV set into the kitchen for an hour or two, and eventually consider buying a small kitchen set, so you can watch it while you clean?"

6. If this fails, deal logical consequences.

Bite the bullet and ignore the mess. Let the unwashed dishes pile up until they interfere with your ability to get out a meal. When the chaos and unpleasantness of the kitchen really hits home, he will begin to do his share of the dishes.

7. Recast a sacrifice as the choice it's able to be by creating a strategy for recouping your losses.

At a decision-making seminar I once took, I learned a handy trick. You write each different choice you have for pursuing an activity on a separate strip of masking tape. You tape the strips directly over one another on your cupboard door. Whenever you're feeling deadlocked, stuck, resourceless, you just tear one piece of tape off . . . and then the next . . . and then the next. . . .

You are reminding yourself of the important fact that most of us have multiple options, even when we believe we have none.

In situations such as Faye's—situations in which what is technically a choice appears to be a sacrifice—this masking tape trick translates into a strategy: list, as specifically as you can, all the things you are giving up in Option 1 (in this case, the economists' convention) for Option 2 (being a full-time parent for a week). Then devise a contingency plan for recouping as many of those losses as you can.

Faye kept saying she'd be losing "work contacts" by not attending the convention. "You can't really pin down or measure the loss," she insisted, rather helplessly, "because you have no idea who will be there, who you'll click with and talk to."

"You can find out some of those things," I told her. "It just takes work."

Faye hired a researcher and, within a week, got a fairly complete list of projected convention attendees. Within another week, she found out what projects half of these people had in the works.

She then zeroed in on fifteen people or groups—financiers, institutes, international development corporations—who she felt, for various reasons, were good prospects for giving her work that she wanted to do. She had a private meeting with her business partner, then a second meeting with the partner and Bill together. The aim of both of these meetings was to come up with the best ways to introduce her work to these people and groups by proxy.

Two groups she met through informal, social connections that were brainstormed. With four groups her partner tried to set up formal meetings. The other nine were foreigners. In three cases, European contacts she had worked with could and would act as liaisons at the convention. The rest, it was decided, would get a letter and proposal from her. If responses were good, a European business trip would follow. This time, Bill, Maura *and* the au pair girl would all come along.

With this strategy, Faye felt she was coming close to having the best of both worlds: time alone with her daughter, unadulterated by work politics, and the convention "preshrunk," as she put it, "preedited to meet my needs."

Women can have their version of "it all"—with a little work, ingenuity, planning and the mind-set that recasts a "rejected" option into a merely "deferred" one.

CHAPTER 7

Breaking the No-Win Bind

It happens with depressing frequency.

I am giving a speech, or a seminar, and among the people waiting to speak to me afterward is a woman with a disturbed, distracted air undercutting her aplomb. She is dressed for success, but something is clearly eating away at that image from the inside out.

"Dr. Warschaw," she says, "I now make twenty thousand dollars a year more than my husband. I love my work, but it makes me feel awful to know my success is 'showing him up,' is hurting him. It's not that he doesn't act proud of me—and, really, he is proud of me—but . . . well, you know men's egos. I know what it's doing to him inside."

Isn't it time all of us stopped taking this self-defeating attitude? Stopped automatically assuming that just because a woman makes more money than, or is otherwise more "prestigious" than her mate, that mate's self-esteem will be blown to dust?

For the more a woman buys into this assumption, that making more money or being more prestigious than her partner is somehow dealing him a blow, the more deeply she will plunge into downward mobility. She gets so hooked in to the anxiety that her partner will suffer that she starts flicking off the switches of her ambition, one by one—and, one by one, flicking on the four components of Poverty Mentality.

Here's how it happens.

The belief that we spoke of in Chapter 2, "Ambivalence," that love and work are opposite ends of a seesaw, the one plunging down in direct proportion to the other's ascent, will underscore everything she does. "Thanks for thinking of me, but my hands are full at the moment," she'll say—in words or demeanor—to anyone who holds out an offer for her to further her success. Using this "benign neglect" of her own best interests, she will freeze herself at her current level, then justify that freeze with guilt as a smoke screen for fear of separation from her husband or lover and grief over her feared loss of him entirely. She may even go so far as outright self-sabotage: losing her job, destroying her chance for promotion, using undeservingness ("Who am I to merit a promotion, after all?") to keep the lid on her recognition that she's doing this—and on her accumulating rage.

Or, if she doesn't choose to go that far, she will verbally undercut her success, minimize each new triumph, vacantly hoping (for she really knows better) that playing dumb about her competence will save her partner's ego. She'll "forget" how much money she makes—or become helpless in managing and leveraging it. She'll ascribe all she's accomplished to sheer wild luck. I call this the *Flake/Fluke Syndrome,* because the message a woman is sending out here is: "I'm really a flake, not a powerful woman; my hundred-thousand-a-year job is an incredible fluke. (It could all crash tomorrow, darling. I still depend on you.)"*

The woman may not know she is patronizing her man with all this, but the man does. Men are not coy about success, are not ambivalent about their achievements. So what the woman intended as a kindness will be perceived by her mate as the cruelest cut of all: condescension. His anger at her "outpacing" him is now fueled by the even greater anger that she dares to play him for a fool.

So he steps up his sarcastic remarks about her success in front of their friends. ("Where are we going for winter vacation this year? Ask Marge, the Breadwinner.") He becomes hostile, baiting and manipulative when they are home: purposely overspending to get her goat, acting truculent, petulant, insulting—or just plain withdrawing.

Finally, her buttons are pushed. ("Why, I've been sacrificing like mad!" she thinks. "And for what? He's only getting more resentful!") In words or attitudes, she lets fly with it: her rage at "having"

---

* An astonishing number of women are hooked in to this syndrome. In a recent issue of *Savvy* magazine, five out of the country's top ten executive women ascribed their success, at least in part, to "luck."

to apologize for her success, for "having" to make herself less so he can feel like more.

She tried to lose in order to win, but neither of them won. Bitter and blaming, they're stuck in what feels like a terrible no-win bind.

"But doesn't society make it a bind?" I hear some of you protesting. "After all, in today's world, a man is still suspect if the woman he's with makes considerably more money than he does. He's branded 'weak' or 'lazy'; 'kept,' 'opportunistic,' a 'mooch' or a 'gigolo.' At the very least, don't people tend to feel sorry for him?"

No. None of this need be true. A man is judged by others according to the attitude he projects about himself. If he is confident, secure, comfortable with himself—if he acts proud of his partner and generous-hearted toward her—he will be seen positively, as a success, no matter what kind of money he makes. The trouble is, far too many men still derive almost all their self-worth from their bankbooks, so their attitude about themselves is keyed more to that fact than to any other.

It is this narrow, stunting, "I am what I earn" thinking that must change. This male Poverty Mentality—not women's successes, not "the eyes of the outside world"—is responsible for the no-win bind that need not be.

Men must change. They must have the courage to broaden their identities, their perceptions of themselves and their worth. Women, after all, have already, courageously, carved out new roles for themselves. Now men must do the same. It takes two people to break the no-win bind. A woman can't do it alone. Neither can a man.

For breaking the bind is really all about partnership. It's two people refusing, flat out, to live by the impoverished old rule that says whoever brings more money into the marriage has more advantage, more power.

Ten or so years ago, I saw a lot of freshly minted Haver women sigh with exasperation and finally walk away from men who "just wouldn't grow up." Today, many of these women, feeling alone, look around and wonder "where all the good men are."

They're right back where they were left a decade ago: still in the bud, still groping with issues they only half-confronted then. These women got up and moved on rather than staying and forcing their men to grow with them.

It's time to go back and do that postponed work—for everyone's happiness and good.

WHAT IS THE PARTNERSHIP MODE?

My grandmother Tessie was a superwoman of her time. As a girl in Russia, she helped raise the eight other children in her own family. By age fourteen, she was in charge of a lumber yard, overseeing hundreds of workers. It's no wonder that she became one of America's first female insurance and real estate executives.

The man she married was her perfect complement. A rabbi and scholar, Grandpa Hyman was as soft-spoken and easy as Tessie was driven and dynamic. She hit the kids when they misbehaved; he soothed them afterward. She took care of the practical side of the family, he the emotional and the spiritual.

She made the money; he leveraged it. She'd come home from a day of collecting rents on the property they owned, sit down and hoist her big heavy leg up on the kitchen table. "Okay, Tessie, gimme the foot," Hyman would say. And out of her sock came the rumpled bills and clanking coins, which Grandpa would stack in meticulous piles and account for in his impeccable ledger books.

There was never any contest or power play between Tessie and Hyman. They each knew what the other did best—and let that person do it, social expectations about male and female roles be damned. They were true partners.

As much as I love their story and am proud to have been named after such an ahead-of-her-times woman, I hardly have to go back two generations to find examples of partnership. There's a Boston couple I know of. She's one of the youngest women ever appointed to a deanship at a major university; he's a sculptor. She makes about twice as much money as he does. She's also the one who puts on the business suit, picks up the briefcase and dashes out the door in the morning.

How does he feel about all of this? "Delighted," he says, with an easy laugh. "Her salary and schedule provide me with the freedom to get on with my work." What he provides her with is every bit as important: cultivated artistic style; the glamour, cachet and stimulation of the art world; a whole new visual perspective—"all of which," she says, "has tremendously expanded and classed up my life, which used to veer toward the dowdy."

Then there's the Chicago retailing executive I met during a seminar who recently married a playwright–theater director. When they first got together, she was struggling up the managerial ladder and he was knocking himself out trying to get his plays produced. One of her biggest drawbacks was lack of verbal confidence. She mumbled when she gave speeches; her hands went clammy. She preferred spending an hour drafting a memo to discharging the same information in a five-minute talk at a board meeting. One of his biggest drawbacks was commercial contacts. Financing and sponsorship were light-years away from the cloistered orbit of artists' colonies and small experimental theaters in which he lived.

They went to work on each other. Using his expertise and playhouse-borrowed equipment, he videotaped and role-played her through every speech she was to make, critiquing her here, rewriting her there, theatrically directing. In return, she showed him how to parlay his grant-application-writing skills into the commercial arena; she gave him contacts in and information about the business world. After a year and a half, she'd had two promotions, largely on the strength of her new communicative skills. And he had cofounded a small-town playhouse with sponsorship he solicited from a hosiery manufacturer who had a mill in the area.

Finally, there are my colleagues Dr. Dick Varnes and Dr. Dee Barlow. They share a profession; they share office space; they share a philosophy about their work and about the need to temper that work with play. They operate in the state of harmony I discussed as an ideal in the last chapter. And they throw all their money into one pot, with no need for "his" or "hers" distinctions.

Each of these four couples illustrates a different component of the partnership mode that they all share. To be partners, a man and woman (1.) must support each other's strengths, irrespective of social convention (as my grandparents did); (2.) must see their separate styles, talents and positions in the world as enhancing, rather than competing with, each other (as the dean and the sculptor do); (3.) must be able to mutually mentor each other (like the retailing executive and the playwright) and (4.), like Barlow and Varnes, must have evolved—or be evolving—to a point of such trust and goodwill that no scorekeeping is necessary.

Writ large over these four components is the tremendous pride these couples have in each other, the enthusiastic permission each grants the other to be his or her best self.

In all but one of these four couples, the woman made more money than the man, but that fact is irrelevant to their relationship.

Women who make more money than their mates have three choices. They can act just like men, equating money with power. Or they can capitulate, falling into the Flake/Fluke Syndrome, playing dumb, making themselves less. Or they can opt for the partnership mode.

Men who are with women who make more money can either resent and retreat or grow, change and enjoy—again, opting for the partnership mode.

Here is how you can do it:

SEVENTEEN STEPS TO BREAKING THE NO-WIN BIND AND WORKING TOWARD PARTNERSHIP

She's gotten a significant promotion or raise; he has not. Or: They meet, become infatuated; the infatuation turns into something more solid; but here's that income gap, suddenly rearing its head. The processes described in the first pages of this chapter threaten to emerge. How do you stop them and replace them with positive alternatives?

1. Separately attend to your feelings.

Listen closely to what is going on inside you. Be particularly conscious of tiny blips of anxiety, resentment, distrust, jealousy, ambivalence, guilt and anger that pierce through the otherwise smooth surface of your emotional screen. When are you experiencing these feelings? What remark or incident triggered them?

Attend just as closely to the giveaway clues to those feelings. Are you suddenly smoking more, coughing nervously, laughing inappropriately, raising the pitch or changing the tone of your voice? Grinding your teeth, rubbing your fingers, toying with wristwatch or ring, playing with your hair? Doodling excessively, clasping and unclasping your fingers, constricting your neck muscles? Biting your nails, breathing heavily, sleeping badly, shuffling your feet?

Are you communicating with each other in a tense or stilted way? Women so often make the mistake of trying to rescue a man from the task of recognizing and articulating his own feelings. Don't fall into that now. Let the man recognize, find and articulate those feelings himself.

The man might ask himself: Do remarks like "Boy, you've sure got a wife who's moving up in the world" make me angry? Does her new dedication to her work, her new success, make me feel abandoned—or about to be? Am I often looking for the lucky—and reversible—break that accounted for this "sudden spurt" in her income ahead of mine? Convincing myself that I'll zoom past her again? Desperately counting the ways that she's still dependent on me, that I'm still in charge?

Am I more sensitive about wanting to pay for everybody at the table when we join another couple for dinner at a restaurant? Self-conscious—even maybe paranoid—about our friends and acquaintances finding out that our new car was mostly paid for by her?

The woman might ask herself: Do remarks made at work or by friends about my success make me edgy, guilty, confused? Do I have the urge to retreat from the course I'm on? When I have the choice of sharing with my mate some praise or raise I just received, do I opt not to? Or think very hard before I do? Am I trying to keep my work and intimacy more and more separate these days? Do I find myself looking more closely and critically than before at his imperfections as a breadwinner, his lack of ambition, his lack of support for my success?

2. Address the issue effectively, forthrightly but with the proper gentleness.

First of all, find the right place and time to do so. The best place is at home, where you are certain to have privacy without distraction. Yes, there is something seductively atmospheric about starting such a conversation in a quiet, intimate restaurant or while you're taking a leisurely walk. But these two contexts invite intrusive elements, divided concentration. You owe it to yourself to be able to train all your energies on the task at hand.

Start the conversation with a *warm-up*, which is to the techniques of negotiation what a preface is to a book, an overture is to an opera. Say "I feel there's been something unsaid going on between us for the last few weeks and I'd like us to explore it" or

"I've been trying to figure out why we've been acting differently toward each other lately, and several things have occurred to me." Do not charge head on with the potentially threatening "You have a problem" or, worse, "I've been feeling you're resentful of my new salary."

Make use of the *probe.* A probe is a gentle inducement for your partner to unpeel another layer of his or her defenses, for you both to reach a deeper level of information and insight than the one on which you're currently operating. The tone of a probe is delicate, respectful, invitational, but not tentative, obsequious or apologetic. A probe might be: "You've been frowning while I've been talking. What are your feelings about what I've just said?" But avoid "Does this strike a chord with you? Has any of it crossed your mind?" or any other questions that can be answered with a yes or no, which shuts out any further dialogue. By using the probe, you're gently but firmly placing the ball not only in the other person's court but in his or her hands.

3. When talking about the issue, change SR behavior to SRR.

People communicate with each other in one of two ways: the *stimulus-response* mode *(SR),* which is reflexive, automatic—an action-reaction style; or what I call the *stop, reflect, respond* mode *(SRR),* which allows for a short but very important interval of reflection, analysis and decision-making before an answer or reaction is tendered to what the other person has just said.

Few techniques are as effective in changing negative communications into positive ones as the simple switch from the SR to the SRR mode.

Most couples have developed a kind of shorthand communication, and much of this shorthand bespeaks a very delightful intimacy. She cocks her head a certain way, he rubs her neck to loosen the kink. He starts a sentence, she finishes it. They operate in the SR mode so much of the time (and so pleasurably) that it is hard for them not to talk in the same way.

But when you're confronting something as sensitive as money and self-worth, the SR mode can be inflammatory, can shut off constructive dialogue before it has a chance to begin.

Allow a crucial "time out" period of as many seconds or minutes as you need to reflect on what your partner has just said instead of rushing in with your response.

4. Reach behind the smoke screen of money and pull out the real issue.

Is it really the income differential itself that is bothering you? Usually not. Usually the issue is something more personal—and therefore more malleable—than brute dollars and cents.

Delve deep and find out what that issue is. Men: Do you feel that her success has made her more critical of you, less understanding and nurturing? Or do you feel her new financial ascendancy has robbed you of your decision-making power about how the household money is spent and what your life-style is to be like?

Women: Do you feel he thinks you are really unworthy of your success? Or that he loved you as long as you were down and dependent and has no use for you now that you can stand on your own two feet?

Present the fear, the hurt. Be open to the other person's response. Be as empathetic as you can be. Aim for resolution: make a plan to go back to the conversation if you cannot resolve things now. Consider counseling or therapy as an option, if you need it, further on down the road.

Money is only the third living party in a relationship when two people allow it to be.

5. Close the time gap on "little" remarks that just "slip out."

It's silent history that kills relationships: the weeks, then months, finally years that go by between a "little" snide remark and its confrontation. One day, she blurts out, ". . . and that day, at that party four months ago, when you said, 'My wife's really become a little hustler; I'd hate to get in her way at the office!' What a nasty crack!" And he can't remember having made it.

The more time that is allowed to pass between making such a remark and acknowledging it, the more chance you give hurt and anger to fester in the dark. Finally, the two of you have evolved a relationship encrusted with bad will like stains on a neglected garment. And, as in the case of the garment, it's too late for cleaning, for repair.

Confront the remark as soon as possible after it's been said. (In the case above, that means right after the party, not at it.) These remarks are the presenting symptoms of a malady still in an early enough stage to reverse. Treat them that way—immediately.

6. Help your partner to unearth the many "hidden" ingredients of his self-esteem.

In the wonderful old fable "Stone Soup," an itinerant charlatan tricks a naïf into thinking a savory soup can be made from a stone. The charlatan drops the stone in the kettle of water and, while it brews, he casts about for one after another purportedly minor ingredient—butter, salt, vegetables—to add just a pinch of spice to the stock. Of course it's really all these "minor" ingredients that are making the soup; the stone is simply a decoy. But the charlatan's skill and the naïf's trust make it appear otherwise.

When it comes to money and self-esteem, men often play charlatan and naïf to themselves. They assume it's their financial clout that's making them hold their heads high in the world, but it's really a host of other "minor" ingredients that, taken together, account for their self-esteem.

Help your partner to see this fact. Consider his excellent parenting; his sharp decisiveness; his droll sense of humor; his prowess as an athlete; his sexual vigor, sensitivity and skill; his empathy with you; his loyalty to his friends; the judgment and clarity that make people come to him for advice—and the poker-faced cool and trustworthiness that make them know secrets are safe with him.

What about his handiness in the garden/woodshop/garage; his ability to keep cool and make good decisions under stress; his cleverness with split-second retorts and verbal rescues; his charm with new people; his ease-putting ability as a host; his talent as a raconteur; his deftness at the keyboard/at the barbecue pit/on the side of the fishing sloop; his good taste in clothes/food/wine/furnishings; his impressive knowledge of major league baseball records/eighteenth-century literature/Woody Allen films?

Make a list for your partner of all these things that give him pride in himself. Encourage him to allow himself that pride and the realization that these accomplishments of his have nothing to do with the money he makes.

Now have him remove the "stone" from his "soup."

7. *Help him to appreciate the nonmonetary assets he brings to your partnership.*

It can be enormously liberating for a man to discover how much he is valued and wanted by the woman in his life once the smoke screen of monetary support has been removed.

The woman in a partnership probably relies enormously on her partner's judgment, talents, humor, perspective, contacts and nurturance to help her achieve the success she has now. (Success almost never flourishes where supports are unavailable.) Almost surely, she relies on them still.

You might suggest to your partner the ways you complement and complete each other. If you're deliberate and meticulous, isn't his daring and spontaneity a whole new lens through which you can see—and tackle—the world? (Or if you're the hip shooter of the pair, doesn't your partner's thoughtful calculation temper your impulsiveness?) Does his nuts-and-bolts business mind extend the perspective of your whimsy and creativity? (Or perhaps things work the other way around.)

You may make more money, but mightn't he be the one who most skillfully leverages and manages it? Who parlays it into tasteful surroundings, establishes an atmosphere and agenda for play and meaningful leisure that makes the money worth having at all?

Women have long known how to count—and derive sustenance from—the many varied assets they bring to their relationships with men. But men's varied assets and contributions have been buried, unacknowledged, under the rock of their breadwinning skills.

Isn't it time now to lift up that rock? Indeed.

And hand in hand with encouraging your partner to expand the sources of his ego satisfaction, you might:

8. *Stand firm in your decision not to make yourself less.*

If you are undercutting of, apologetic for or uncomfortable with your gains, you are projecting the vague sense that your partner was right—that there is something to be feared in your making more money after all.

Your task now is to reinforce the positive, not the negative: to project an attitude that vibrates the truth (which you know and he is learning) that gains for one partner (be that partner male or female) means gains for both.

This means you do not hold back, at work, on those "optional" efforts and activities that might bring you even further money or distinction; you do not sit on opportunity, pretending not to see it; you do not tone down your aspirations.

This also means you do not fall into the Flake/Fluke Syndrome, exaggerating and celebrating and inventing ineptness in order to remain unthreatening and ever needful of the firm masculine hand.

The woman who makes these concessions out of the desire to save her relationship is really injuring it deeply by amassing the fodder for a martyrous anger she can—and probably will—level at the man, years down the line.

9. Don't underenjoy or overgift.

Women have a hard time striking the balance between a number of things—love and work, for one; elation and denial, for another. When a career triumph comes, we are torn between two extremes: (1.) wanting to paint the sky with delight, and (2.) feeling we should hold in that delight entirely. A lot of women think they are solving the problem by doing the former at work, the latter at home. But they only end up feeling confused, insincere and eventually angry.

There is a middle ground. And that is delight with your mate in your triumph, but with the same measure of tact that you would use with a female friend. To find that level, simply picture yourself as your best friend listening to you on the subject of the raise, promotion or award you just received. Now talk as you'd like yourself heard—with absolute pleasure but without flaunting, gloating, obsessing.

Also, some women, fresh from an income or professional triumph, suddenly lavish all kinds of out-of-the-blue praise on their mates. This torrent of "support" can set a man wondering, Does she really think I'm such a loser that she has to go into overdrive to shore me up?

A simple "You've been terrific; I couldn't have done it without you" will do. Continue to express your support and respect as you always have—appropriately, authentically—not falsely, nervously, guiltily.

Treating your triumph as a delicious but normal and natural event is crucial to breaking the no-win bind. The best "sales tactic," if you will, for any new arrangement is the demonstration that the people involved are just like what they were before, only happier.

10. Adopt the edict of "classy" generosity.

A friend of mine has an extremely proud father, a widower who lives on a modest pension. When the building this gentleman called home for twenty years was suddenly sold and remodeled, my friend knew what was about to come: a huge rent hike.

So he took the new owner aside and made a private deal to pay the difference between the new and the old rent every month, while his father was billed for the original amount, as always.

It's been four years and my friend's father hasn't the faintest idea he's being subsidized.

That is what I call *classy generosity.*

Classy generosity is quiet generosity. It's giving with the first priority being the recipient's pride and self-esteem—and with no importance placed on being acknowledged as the giver. Classy generosity is going to dinner with a man, and arranging in advance with the maître d' for the bill to be presented to you (or to be sent to the office) so there's no battle for it at the end of the meal. Classy generosity may even be occasionally passing such a gift—or meal —off as a company perk or an expense-account reimbursement when it really comes out of your pocket.

While most women would agree in principle to this kind of generosity, what happens in their real lives is another matter. The guilt and ambivalence of "surpassing" her mate in income leads many a woman to adopt a hidden agenda: she wants to be reaffirmed as "nice." And that means giving to him and being thanked for it. Listen very closely for signs of this hidden agenda. The need to give to be seen as generous is a relationship saboteur, especially now when your aim is to prove that who earns what is irrelevant to your intimacy.

11. Watch out for the "calloused hand."

Women who've been made to feel beholden to men who have equated money with power sometimes develop a very hard callous. They have a tendency to "remember when" the shoe was on the other foot, in a former relationship or in an earlier stage of their present one, and to rub that remembering in with the calloused hand.

"You made me ask permission every time I took money out of our account for a personal luxury," the woman might say, in word or in manner. "So why should I be any different with you?" Though that question is asked rhetorically, its answer is: "Because your aim is to break away from that old Poverty Mentality system of money equals power."

You must let the past go, and, with the past, the defenses, the callouses. Otherwise, you are dealing not in relationship but in retribution. And there is no way trust and intimacy can flourish in such soil.

12. Don't try to make him over.

So far, we've been assuming it is the *man* who is troubled by the woman's earning more. But in many cases, it is the woman. Here, the income gap exists not because of circumstance (i.e., an income-oriented man just happens to make less than the woman he's with) but because of a man's *choice* not to take on the gladiator role, to opt out of the competitive game in favor of other worthy values.

I see the following happening alot: An achieving woman finds it consonant to her own goals to be with a noncompetitive, nurturing man while she is on her way up. He has the time to listen to her work problems, perhaps even to take care of the house while she's out on the job. His own lack of personal investment in her career arena gives her a green light to soar, unimpeded by a competitive ego.

But when she gets where she's going, she suddenly turns around and plays What's Mine Is Mine. She wants him to transform himself into the earnest achiever who will coshoulder their higher lifestyle needs, who will be the conventionally "appropriate" mate for her at social functions—and to those ever imagined "eyes of the outside world."

She begins to want to restyle him: to get him to wear the "right" clothes, drive the "right" car, have the "right" ambition. She becomes resentful for being foisted into the very role that their complementary mesh had predicted all along: that of the higher earner.

Hurt, angry and put upon, the man retreats, exaggerating those very habits that annoy her in order to get back at her. (If he used to at least put on his one decent suit for her work-related parties, now he refuses to.) Their relationship descends into a tangle of power plays.

These cannot be untangled until the woman first realizes that she cannot expect to make him over and that, in many cases, and to a large extent, it is not fair for her to even want to.

Now that the emotional work is underway, move on to a negotiation of logistics of your arrangement.

13. Assess your minimal life-style needs, and make a fair plan for supporting them.

Figure out how much money you need to get through a typical month on a no-frills basis. Make a split that is fair and comfortable to you, proportional to your incomes.

14. Negotiate who pays for what specific luxuries and items over and above that budget.

This is where things can get sticky, so work them out in advance. Decide, for example, that she'll buy the dinners out, he the breakfasts; that the week-long vacation will be financed by her, the weekend jaunt by him. If there are items and entertainments that only the woman wants and she is the higher earner, then she should pay for them.

15. Understand that if you cannot stick to rules amicably something deeper may be wrong.

I recently counseled a couple who had an income disparity. The woman was a Haver intent on making over the noncompetitive man she'd been with, uneasily, for several years. He had been living rent-free with her; she charged him rent. She insisted on their going out more than he wanted to or could afford, so they struck a deal that she pay for two of their restaurant meals in a row, then he pay for the third. But on his night to pay, she invariably chose an extremely expensive restaurant. He protested; she got angry at his reluctance to conduct his life in a way that would allow him to treat her as she wanted to be treated—and so on, down the line. Their resentment of each other transcended negotiation. They are now living apart.

16. If it's preferable, arrange for an arbitrator.

I'm of two minds about using financial experts such as business managers and accountants. On the one hand, they can distance you from direct, hands-on involvement with your money, which isn't good. On the other, they can free you from having to focus on the income differential more than you'd like to.

Say, for example, a man enters a relationship with a woman and, some months later, moves in to live with her in the house she owns. Instead of writing a rent check every month to this woman with whom he is forging an intimacy, he can make the transaction through a hired third party. This may feel more comfortable and appropriate to both.

And should the relationship develop to the point where it feels right to consider the house a shared asset, remember that you can:

17. Renegotiate your finances at regular intervals on a state-of-the-partnership basis.

Partnerships are evolved over time. As time goes on, as trust and intimacy develop, as a sense of shared destiny evolves, couples chip away at the his/hers/ours rules they originally made. Once a year, you might sit down with one another and see if either the deepening partnership or special new circumstances don't call for a shift in allocations. And, if such a shift is called for, sit down and renegotiate, using the same guidelines as before.

Guidelines protect a couple on a technical level. But beyond that there's something that protects couples (and allows them to protect each other) on a far deeper level.

That something is nurturance. It is indispensable not just to partnerships but to the human spirit itself. Yet it has become a rare commodity today. I believe that the crisis in nurturance is the most affecting, the sharpest, the most painful underpinning of the Poverty Mentality. If we can face and defuse and cure that crisis, we've done a great deal.

I've made the next chapter the final chapter in this part because it is the most challenging, the most central.

And, ultimately, the most helpful.

CHAPTER 8

Making Peace with the Nurturance Gap

Not long ago, I assembled a group of women in my apartment to talk about what they were and were not getting from life. They ranged from Comers in their mid-twenties to Havers in their mid-forties. They were married and unmarried, parents and nonparents, and their conversation took off in as many directions as there were attitudes and experiences represented, which is to say a lot.

Then suddenly one question sucked all those scattered opinions together like metal dust to magnet. "Do you ever feel you nurture the man in your life more than he nurtures you?" I asked. The unanimous answer was yes.

Was this a one-sided grievance? A cut-and-dried case of one sex's wrongdoing to the other? As a therapist I very much doubted that.

To test my hunch a week later, I assembled ten men in my apartment. All of them were Havers. They were in their thirties to fifties, of diverse professions and eager enough to talk about man-woman issues to have left their offices early and be sitting inside around a tape recorder on a warm summer night. I worried that they would be a little too inclined to want to sound "correctly" liberated.

I needn't have worried.

For when I asked, "Can any of you think of an occasion in which the woman in your life gave you emotional support that was just what you needed before you asked for it?" there were a lot of shaking heads. Finally one man broke the thick silence to say: "I've got several great women friends. Why can't I get the same support from the woman I'm living with?"

Why indeed? has become the question of our age.

Those two evenings only served to underscore a conviction that had been growing in me, sadly, over the years of my therapy practice: We are facing a crisis of nurturance. Men and women are just not being fed emotionally.

(For many reasons which we'll explore in this chapter, women have the greater problem in getting the nurturance they need—and Haver women, the greatest problem. But to claim one-sided victimization is the worst kind of Poverty Mentality because victims are passive and self-righteous, and passive self-righteous people don't act. So when we talk about the crisis of nurturance, we have to take into account the situation of both sexes. It's too important to leave anyone out.)

When the feeding that is nurturance stops, nothing else can proceed very well. For lack of nurturance is the primary deprivation from which all others spring. Just as unnurtured children grow up to be adults incapable and distrustful of love, unnurtured adults are lonely, unproductive people. All their creative energy goes into the vain wanting of love. They become exhausted. They become cynical. They become scarred. The wellsprings of the self —ability to trust, self-esteem, enthusiasm for life—begin to dry out. They continue to do their work and to go about business as usual, yet they are dying inside. They are suffering from adult emotional merasmus.

What do I mean by this?

Merasmus is a Greek word that means "wasting away." We've always known this can happen from physical neglect—from lack of food, inattention during illness and injury, etc. But now we know it can also occur from not being held, not being loved, not—in a word—being nurtured.

Around the turn of the century, it was a puzzlement to doctors why certain healthy infants placed in foundling homes simply withered away and died during the first year of their lives. They were not starved, the doctors knew. They were not left untreated with colds or fevers. No, but they also were not touched.

Though they are not going to die from it, the people who come into my office with their tales of nonnurturance are suffering from merasmus as surely as those foundling infants were. Their merasmus is burnout due to lack of love—to a painful disparity between the nurturance they want, or think they want, and what they are getting, or perceive themselves to be not getting. (As we'll soon see, these distinctions are relevant.) They might be suffering from what I call false nurturance (attention and behavior that seems, or pretends, or attempts to be caring but is really not in their best interest). Worse, they might be suffering—and inflicting—mutual nonnurturance (whereby two partners act like mere roommates to each other, disregarding one another's emotional needs). Then again, they may just be suffering the less malevolent, but still problematic, confusion in packaging. (One party is attempting to nurture the other, but that nurturance is wrapped in such a way as to make it unrecognizable as care and support to the receiver.)

All of these states, which we'll explore, comprise the nurturance gap. The gap has always been with us, to some extent, because, psychologically and biologically, men and women are simply different. But it's been widened by the complexities of the transitional times we live in. Today, most of us are left to traverse (without a safety net) wide gulfs (1) between what women need from men and what men know how to give; (2) between what men have come to rely on from women and what women can no longer give without feeling false or diminished; and (3) between what women profess to want from men but secretly fear or are not ready to handle.

Mostly, though, the nurturance gap has been widened because women are not blind anymore. We cannot dismiss, ignore or make excuses for the emotional neglect we feel from the men in our lives. And we need nurturance as never before. Caught in the tough career fray every bit as deeply as men are, women now need—in order to thrive—the very balming and boosting and understanding—the "wifeliness," if you will—that men have been depending on for their sustenance for centuries.

And women are just not getting it. I've seen dozens of six-figure-salaried women being hollowed inside by merasmus. "Men just don't know how to be supportive," is their weary refrain. Some of these women try desperately—and fruitlessly—to nurture themselves through material overkill. I know one successful woman whose fabulous wardrobe could put her on any best-dressed list. Yet she goes home at night and she cries.

I probably care about this particular subject more than any

other in this book—and for good reason: when you see so many people who are "winners" on the outside—rich, successful, influential, talented, well dressed, well regarded, well heeled—suffering so inside, it becomes a challenge and a mission to try to reach, and help heal, that deepest, most elusive wound. I've spent a long time trying to get to the root of adult emotional merasmus; to ferret out the many causes and factors and signs of the nurturance gap; and to find out what can really be done—said and thought, reconsidered, communicated, practiced and written on pieces of paper—in order for the condition to be cured and the gap to be peaceably closed.

Nurture, the thesaurus says, means "to back, bolster, support, sustain." Support means "to be advocate of, to side with, applaud, approve, defend."

Who among us wants to live life without giving and getting this essential feeding? None of us do. And none of us have to. But before we learn how, let's learn why.

WHY THE GAP NOW? DIFFERENT DEFINITIONS, DIFFERENT DISTANCES, DIFFERENT NEEDS

Ask a man and a woman what it takes for each of them to nurture a loved one of the opposite sex, and you'll get two very different answers.

The woman will probably talk of "caring" and "listening," of "compassion" and "empathy." Trained since earliest childhood to tend to others' needs, to read facial expressions and body language, women know the argot of this deep and abstract nurturing as well as they know their own names.

Men have been the recipients of this first kind of nurturance, but most of them thought they never had to give it. What they were trained in—what they learned it was their duty to dispense—was a sort of pragmatic survival nurturance. Instead of the nuances of attention and expression and compassion, their medium of care has always been the wallet or checkbook and the strong assisting or avenging arm. Providing for and protecting, buying and shielding, flinging open their copious cloaks and drawing their women safely inside—that's what giving nurturance means to a man. In the old days, when the man took care of the outside of the house and the woman took care of the inside, that was enough.

It isn't enough now.

Today, of course, women are focused as much on the outside of the house as on its inside. We're facing all the stresses and exigencies of the working world and we're still doing our original nurturing. We've gone the double distance, while men are still traveling the single one. We don't need men to buy for us as we once did—or, except in emergencies, to physically protect us. But other things—a genuine, ongoing interest in our work; dinner made and cleaned up after every other night; the willingness to talk and listen deeply and wholly—this is the kind of bolstering and support that double-distance women need from men.

Why aren't the men providing it?

Some men just will not make the adjustment from the buying/ protecting form of nurturance to the more nuanced kind. Nurturance for them was okay as long as a woman was needy and weak. But it's not okay now that she can—and very impressively does—stand on her own two feet. A television producer in her thirties was recently the subject of an article in a national weekly magazine. The man she was involved with not only did not read the magazine that week; he made a point of telling her that he otherwise always did. "This man," she came to realize, "would bring me a cup of tea when I had a 102-degree fever, but not when I'd come home tired from a long and productive day at the studio." It was revelations like this that made her leave him.

But other men would make the adjustment in nurturance if only they knew how. They don't need, or even want, a weak woman. They simply never learned how to support a strong one. Just because a man hasn't yet gone the double distance doesn't mean he isn't able to. You just got there first.

What the woman involved with this man should keep in mind is that it does no good to get hooked into not-getting. By martyrishly thinking, "I keep giving and giving but he never gives back," you're foreclosing any growth and change on the man's part by refusing to see what he may well be trying to give you. The first step in closing the nurturance gap is to allow yourself to understand that it may be a gap in perception rather than in fact. Because, you see . . .

NURTURANCE COMES IN MANY PACKAGES

I have a close friend who always complains about her husband, a wry man of few words and an inability to be phony, because he doesn't effusively support those decisions of hers that he thinks are wrong. "He should stand by all my efforts," she says. You would think, to talk to her, that the man was critical and withholding.

Yet several years ago, when I was capitalizing a new project, this man anticipated my need for a short-term loan before I ever voiced it and had the check delivered to my office with a note that read, "Wishing you success." Like the words he wrote, the man got right to the point: He didn't wait for me to ask for the loan; he didn't require me to come to his office to get it; he didn't hem and haw (or say anything, in fact) about paying him back. He behaved with first-rank empathy and classy generosity.

This man is clearly capable of giving outstanding nurturance. But, sadly, his wife will never see it or receive it because she can't get past the package in which that nurturance is wrapped.

She is one of the many women who often lament, "If only the man in my life would support me the way my women friends do." Yet I have seen her women friends make the mistake, usually out of good intentions, of supporting her indiscriminately: urging her to undertake ventures for which she is unprepared or underqualified and to stand up to people when, in fact, a little standing back and reassessing might be the wiser, more appropriate move.

During the seventies, women scrambled to gain assertiveness. They felt they had underestimated themselves in so many ways for so long that the only way to correct the situation was a kind of mass mutual support not to be self-effacing or timid, not to "take crap." In a rush to heartily endorse each other's dreams and risks, they assumed it was better to err on the side of over- rather than undersupporting. I call this kind of nurturer the Fan.*

The wholly uncritical support the Fan gives feels good. It can be seductive. It's the sort of support we got from our mothers, who, if we were lucky enough to have a supportive mother, thought we were the brightest and the most beautiful, regardless of contra-

* The Fan, the Truthteller, the Shorthand Nurturer and the seven other most common nurturing stylists will be detailed in the next section.

dicting evidence. Sometimes, when we're down, we need the sharp hoisting up a Fan can give. Other times, though, nurturance that comes packaged by Fans can provide a dangerously skewed perspective and bad advice—and when this is the case, the Fan has unintentionally provided (or we have manipulated from her) false nurturance.

At these times, what a person most needs is the tougher-sounding but ultimately more helpful nurturance of the Truthteller, that friend or mate who may err on the side of bluntness but is never condescending or falsely flattering—or perhaps the understated support of the person I call the Shorthand Nurturer, who provides validation while also getting you to cool what may be overheated engines by giving the message: "You're doing great; so what else is new?"

My friend's husband packages his nurturance in a combination of these latter two styles. But since his wife was always busy looking for nurturance packaged by Fans alone, his potential supportiveness was lost on her long ago. She sent so many of his nurturance packages back unopened that after a while he stopped sending them altogether.

This happens a lot. And it's ironic because even though women claim they want the men in their lives to nurture them as their women friends do, this is usually not true. Women relish and depend on the more acerbic, pragmatic mien that men have—the male "edge," if you will, the male contrast. In fact, men who support women just the way other women do end up being described as "sycophantic," "wimpy," "overingratiating," "unctuous," "nerdy" and "insincere."

So we've set up a situation of thinking we desire something that, in fact, we do not. And we've set up a Catch-22 that says: "We want to be nurtured by men but (according to our narrow definition of nurturance) men are *incapable* of nurturing." Faced with this conundrum, it's no wonder so many men stop trying.

Women have to get used to delving beneath the wrapping and to accepting nurturance in different forms, different packages. Sometimes, in fact, the most effective male nurturance can come in the most offputting package. One of my favorite stories illustrates this.

Donna, a young photographer, was the only semiprofessional in a graduate seminar given by one of the country's foremost photojournalists. The man had covered three wars and his criticism, Donna was warned, could be as brutal as the action he'd seen. Yet during the first weeks of class, he was charming to Donna. He acknowledged her advanced status, asked her opinion often. She felt smugly delighted that she'd pierced his macho armor, that she'd become teacher's pet.

So it was with little surprise that, as she pulled her semester's-end photographs out of their manila submissions envelope, she saw, in his handwriting, the large letter A in the corner. Ah, she thought happily. The pictures she had taken were as good as she'd thought.

But as she pulled the pictures all the way out, she saw, with shock and dismay, that the A was not her term grade but the first word of a sentence that read: "A lazy, sentimental, irrelevant group of shots. . . ." The next four sentences were just as stinging.

Donna barely escaped the room before bursting into tears. Her first, not inappropriate, reaction was to call up her Fans. They all said the same thing: What a cruel, horrible man the teacher was! (And probably a much overrated photographer. And maybe impotent and unable to deal with her good looks.) She should quit his class and find a nurturing mentor.

She was on the verge of doing so when her brother, a third-year law student, called. He pleaded with Donna to stay in the class. "Don't you see," he said, "that man knows you've got promise. He's trying to provoke you, to get your adrenaline up so you'll really go out and make the most of your talent, if only to prove him wrong. That's what football coaches do. And Marine boot camp sergeants. And that's what I'm getting through the adversarial system of teaching here in law school. That's how men classically nurture men to achieve: by showing them how to be tough."

Donna stayed in the class, worked indefatigably on her second-semester shots and got them back in an envelope marked "How did you get so good so fast? Send these out to be published immediately."

This is not to say that boot camp nurturance—or creative aggression, as I call it—is appropriate in an intimate relationship. It most assuredly is not. (I can't even endorse it in professional or mentor-student relationships even though, as Donna's case illustrates, it often works. I think there are always ways to get to a given end without having to incorporate hostility into the process.)

What I am trying to point out, though, through the exaggerative qualities of this story, is that the man who says "You're capable of doing better than this" may well be providing a more valuable kind of nurturance than the woman or man who responds to you with bland, uncritical approval. This tougher, more discriminating kind of nurturance says: First of all, I take you seriously.

Patronization is what women got when they weren't taken seriously as intellectually discerning people, as high-caliber creators—when they weren't expected to achieve and excel. Just as blind adoration is what men got from their (unachieving, unexcelling) wives because those women secretly thought their husbands were too emotionally simple not to know the difference between that kind of "support" and real, discriminating opinions—and too weak-egoed not to have to rely on such patronization.

The challenge for today's new couples—people who respect one another, who refuse to patronize—is to know how to tell the truth to each other in a way that doesn't hurt—hurt the partner's ego or morale, hurt the relationship itself. We'll discuss this in more detail later in the chapter, but in the meantime, one couple's guideline (he's an illustrator, she's a sculptor): "We never critique each other's work—even if the work is lying around, in the other's sight —until we are asked to."

Sometimes a nurturing package isn't received because it's too overpoweringly big. (Your friend has just found out she's pregnant but is worried about having a miscarriage. In a well-meaning rush of exuberance, you start planning her shower and offering her all your own child's outgrown toys and clothes. The nurturance she really needs is your empathetic silence until her worrisome first trimester has passed.) Other times, the package is too small. (You need to talk and be heard and be held. He says, "Go ahead; I'm listening"—while he's emptying drawers and sorting his socks.) Still other times, the package has been sloppily wrapped; the sender hasn't taken the time and empathy to consider the pride and personality of the recipient. ("Hey, listen, if you ever get strapped, give a holler," you say to a friend who would sooner eat beans for a week than ask for a loan. But if she just happened to find the money deposited in her bank account, with the right kind of explanation from the bank or from you, the help would be gratefully felt.) Or the package may simply be the wrong shape. (He likes to do things collaboratively; you like to work independently. So his "C'mon, let's throw a great salad together!" strikes you less as the offer of help he intended than a cramp to your culinary style.)

Often, you don't receive a nurturance package because you have, so to speak, changed "address"—i.e., role, level of competence, priorities—and your partner doesn't yet see this. (For years, when you were a graduate student and junior staff worker, you relied on his advice. Now, out in the business world on your own, you can make your own decisions, and you want affirmation of that.) Just as commonly, neither of you receives the package because he has changed and you're still looking at him with old assumptions intact. A young woman I know spent so many years tolerating her boyfriend's irresponsibility that she continued to treat him like a charming, dope-smoking ne'er-do-well even after he (to use his former jargon) cleaned up his act. He stopped hiding behind marijuana; stopped coming to work late; started pitching in much more around her house and paying attention to her feelings and his own. But she didn't notice. Finally, one night, he almost shouted, in frustration: "See me for who I am *now*—not who I was yesterday!" Only then could she begin to see the nurturance packages he'd been piling up on her doorstep.

The lesson in that story, incorporated into what we've been discussing, comprises my Guideline No. 1 for closing the nurturance gap: *Respond to your partner's efforts at nurturance freshly, substantively, without prejudice or preconception. Forget about the past; see through the falseness of patronization and blind adoration; handle and ponder and* open *the package to get to what is being offered now.*

Guideline No. 2 is: *Go with a man's nurturing strength instead of trying to get him to improve on his "weakness."* If he's good at listening but can barely boil an egg, don't stress (to yourself or to him) your need of a home-cooked meal after a hard day's work. Enjoy, encourage and reinforce the way he is able to nurture you now. If he's an ivory-tower academic and you've written what you hope is a bestselling novel, it's unfair to expect him to turn into someone who'll delight in (and be good at) brainstorming publicity and promotion tactics with you. His literary support and his editing help is the nurturance that counts. A man is more likely to go the double distance if you don't turn around and suddenly triple it on him.

Guideline No. 3 is: *Stop assuming that your partner alone has to fill all your nurturance needs.*

Start realizing that even if he wanted to, he could not. Rather, understand that every person in your life nurtures you—or is capable of nurturing you—in a different style. It is the blend and alternation of these complementary styles that provides a richly textured matrix, a "patchwork" of supportiveness for your efforts and your ego and your decisions and your morale. This nurturance patchwork is every bit as available to unpartnered women as to partnered ones.

To understand what I mean by this, let's move on to an understanding of:

NURTURING STYLES—AND THE STITCHING OF A NURTURANCE PATCHWORK

Everyone nurtures in a certain style or combination of styles. Here are the ten most common ones:

1. *The Fan* is your uncritical booster—and God bless him or her for that. How dreary life would be without the doorman of your apartment building who thinks you look just like Ali MacGraw, or your hometown high school journalism teacher who, upon hearing you've joined a major wire service, writes: "I knew it would happen. Next step: the Pulitzer Prize!"

Sometimes a fan is an otherwise sophisticated person who suspends her critical judgment in order not to discourage you (a friend who is afraid you'll tear up your proposal if she tells you what she really thinks of it), or one whose savvy doesn't transfer from one field to another (your brother the physicist thinks your abstract paintings are gallery-worthy, but he hasn't been inside a gallery in fifteen years).

It's great to have fans as long as you know that they're fans and can take their boosting with the proper grain of salt. Otherwise, you're prying false nurturance out of people who usually didn't intend to provide you with anything but lovely, though limited, real nurturance.

2. *The Therapist* is that concerned, empathetic, emotionally oriented person—very often a woman—who draws you out and in-

duces you to share confidences and talk about your problems. When this person is proffering real nurturance, you are left feeling validated, unlonely, your problems at least partially clarified. When this person is proffering false nurturance, you have the uncomfortable impression that you've revealed too much of yourself to someone who has not done the same.

3. *The Pragmatist* is as uneffusive as the Fan is effusive, as uninterested in drawing out your feelings as the Therapist is interested in doing so. She (or, more frequently, he) specializes in solid information and distinctly unemotional advice and is very generous indeed with both.

If you've just come back from a two-week vacation to find out that your dog has grown ill in your absence, the Pragmatist won't sigh empathetically, shake his head and launch in on his own guilty-pet-owner stories. But he *will* immediately give you the name, address, telephone number and probable cost of a first-rate vet.

In a sea of roiling emotionalism, the Pragmatist's clearheaded problem-solving can be a welcome life raft. Yet when it's wholesale warmth you need, his style may leave you feeling hollow.

4. *The Diplomat* smoothly, deftly, sandwiches nurturance in between something he or she wants to get from you. She may phone you on business or for advice, or to ask a favor; yet her concern, praise and empathy seem so genuine you come away from the encounter feeling you've gotten as much as you've given. When the Diplomat is giving real nurturance, this is indeed true. But when the Diplomat is giving false nurturance, you are left feeling vaguely manipulated and distrustful.

5. *The Truthteller* is the opposite of the Fan and of the Diplomat. He or she is not out to win popularity awards (or, for that matter, to lose them). He or she pulls no punches and cuts through the cant, politesse and hesitations of these other nurturers to give you the difficult truth: "I think asking that of your boss would be inappropriate now." "Yes, you would look better if you lost those five pounds." "You're making excuses for why he's not calling. If you look at this clearly, I think you'll see he doesn't seem to want a relationship now." "That dress is pretty, but it doesn't show you to your best advantage."

A gentle Truthteller, whose judgment you deeply and justifiably respect, who waits to be asked before rendering an opinion, is one of life's most valuable assets.

6. *The Hangback Nurturer* waits a beat—or a day, or a month—before complementing you. He may feel uncomfortable telling you you look great in public, or even in person. He's not one to hurry an impression that may take a while to settle (and most of his impressions do).

The Hangback Nurturer is often male, never glib, and frequently from a region of the country and in a line of work that doesn't set great store on verbal pyrotechnics. Gary Cooper's screen characters were classic Hangback Nurturers.

The Hangback Nurturer's still water runs deep, and his few words about his feelings are worth two hundred of the Fan's, the Therapist's and the Diplomat's. But his inscrutability and his withholding may sometimes make you feel lonely or resentful—or both.

7. *The Shorthand Nurturer* may be seen as the Hangback's more stylized urban cousin. He's wry, cool, deliberately easygoing and even more deliberately understated. With exteriors as varied as the philosophical uncle and the low-key hipster, he deals in quips, nods, one-liners (sometimes one-worders), and writ large over all of them is the message: "Of course you did well/look great/will be terrific at the conference/I care about you. But then you already knew that, didn't you?"

The Shorthand Nurturer is the newspaper editor who reads the reporter's copy slowly, then looks up, hands the pages back and signals approval with a simple "Next?" Or the businessman who listens to an offer being spelled out in elaborate detail, then says, "You're on." The Shorthand Nurturer is the boss who watches you laboring earnestly—and sets your hectic pace at ease by inquiring, "Where's the fire?" Or the man who takes in his wife's new hairdo, new dress, new makeup—and condenses paragraphs of praise into a simple, proud "All right."

The Shorthand Nurturer can be just what the doctor ordered when you're getting too worked up over minutiae, taking a minor setback more seriously than is good for you, reading volumes into an incident or a slighting remark that would better be dismissed with a shrug. The Shorthand Nurturer cuts wounds down to size, offers tonic perspective. At other times, though, his refusal to acknowledge his own anxiety may leave you feeling lonely and uncomfortable with your own.

These seven are positive nurturers. Now for the stylists whose specialty is false nurturance:

8. *The Smotherer* appears to be eager to fill all your needs. He or she listens, soothes, helps you with your work, does your errands, promotes your projects, brings you that cup of tea just when you need it. But you never asked for all this—and much of it you'd prefer doing yourself.

You feel crowded by this nurturer and very often guilty for resenting his or her ministrations and presumptions. "What does he want from me?" you wonder, with increasing suspicion and discomfort. The answer, which you've partly known all along, is that you be totally dependent on and indebted to him.

Beneath his façade of helpfulness, the Smotherer is a master manipulator. He knows just when you're at your most vulnerable. That's when he leaves you to fend for yourself, all the better to make you feel more dependent the next time.

9. *The Punisher* is capable of great nurturance—if and when you do what he wants. When you're not "good," there's no nurturance. The Punisher is an emotionally lethal manipulator.

10. *The Foul Weather Friend* always seems to be there with advice and concern when things are going badly for you. But she disappears when things are good. Does she simply have an overactive Florence Nightingale complex? Can she only like you when you're down? Or does she actively enjoy witnessing your hardship? Whichever gradation of negativity is true, the Foul Weather Friend reinforces only the worst in your life. He or she should be avoided.

Not everyone, of course, is a pure nurturance stylist. Many are combinations of styles, or they change styles of nurturance according to the situation and the person. A woman may be a Fan with her invalid mother and young child, a Truthteller/Fan with her preadolescent, a Therapist with her younger sister, a Diplomat with her clients at work, a Pragmatist with her staff—and a Truthteller/Therapist with her husband. The point is, most of the people in your life respond to *you* in a predictable nurturance style. The constellation of those styles within a given day makes up what I call your nurturance patchwork, the uniquely patterned quilt of support upon which you rest and work and thrive.

I say "patchwork" because the units—the "pieces"—of nurturance, so to speak, are removable and interchangeable. You can learn enough about your nurturance needs (and their variations during a day) so that you solicit the right kind of nurturance from the appropriate stylist at the right time: you call a Fan when you need a quick jolt of confidence for a particular task; you post a question to a Truthteller friend when you suspect you may be operating under a delusion and feel ready to face that possibility. You relish going home and spilling out your day to your Shorthand Nurturer mate when you feel you're making an office mountain out of a molehill—but you'll reserve that same long conversation for a Therapist friend, instead, if you feel your anxiety is justified and that your husband won't easily honor or share it.

More often, though, and especially if you complain about being poorly nurtured, you may be sewing on the pieces of the patchwork in a way that's disadvantageous to you: going to a Truthteller when you're still too vulnerable for his hard assessment, letting a Fan influence a complex decision, appealing to a Pragmatist for demonstrative warmth—and, most commonly, expecting your mate to wear all nurturing hats instead of merely those of his style.

To find out if this is the case, and to find out where and how and from whom (and to what consequence) you get your daily nurturance: Turn to Table 8, make copies of the Nurturance Log and fill it out every day for a week. In the log, you will note down every situation that occurred during the day in which you solicited or received support, from whom, what result and so forth. From this log, you will get a picture of your nurturance patchwork.

Ask yourself now: (1) What pieces of my patchwork should be "restitched" to give me more of the nurturance I need, when I need it?; and (2) By drawing on his nurturance at certain times that I hadn't before, and by drawing on others at certain times when I used to go only to him, how can I make the best use of the kind of nurturance available to me from my partner?

Table 8

DAILY LOG OF NURTURANCE

DESCRIBE SITUATION WHERE NURTURANCE WAS SOLICITED BY YOU OR GIVEN TO YOU	TIME OF DAY	NAME OF NURTURER AND HIS/HER NURTURANCE STYLE	DID I CHOOSE THE NURTURER OR DID THE SITUATION PROVIDE ONE?
(I.e., preparing to make business presentation; wearing new hairstyle and it was remarked on; experienced anxiety over . . .)	(List in order, A.M. to P.M.)		

1.

2.

3.

4.

5.

6.

7.

8.

9.

10.

Table 8 (cont.)

AFTER THE NURTURANCE, I FELT	BECAUSE OF HOW I WAS NURTURED AND HOW I FELT AS A RESULT, THESE THINGS OCCURRED	EVALUATION
(a) Good: Describe, specifically, e.g., confident, worthy, validated, clear about options, right about decision, energized (b) Bad: i.e., confused, presumptuous, overly sensitive, depressed, unattractive	(e.g., I made a powerful presentation; I went out and ate a quart of chocolate ice cream; I skipped my tennis game and sulked)	(a) Did I really know what kind of nurturance I wanted/needed? (b) I got the nurturance I wanted/needed (c) I didn't; but might have had I instead called/consulted/gone to _____

NURTURING IMPASSES

All right, let's say you've made it to here. You recognize that it's unreasonable to expect your partner to provide all the nurturance you need in your day and your life. You've explored, and are continuing to explore, the alternatives.

You've also gone the double distance, and he seems willing to do so. You claim you want a man of tenderness and sensitivity; he claims he is proud of your competence and independence and will support all that you are. Your intentions, your exteriors, are good. But the insides of both of you have not quite caught up with the outside. And suddenly one night . . .

As you're unwinding before dinner, you replay a vexing scene that went on that day at your office. Perhaps you're rambling on a bit, but it's been a hectic day; you deserve to be able to vent.

Except he doesn't seem to think so. "Can't you be quiet?" your mate finally says. "I just got home; I need some peace and quiet." You put this together with an incident that occurred the other day: you gave him advice on a business matter (that pertained to your specialty), but you knew from his curt reply that the opinion of yours, contrary to his own, was not what he wanted to hear.

So, you are thinking now, he talks a good game of liberation, but he can't really play one. When the chips are down, he doesn't want to hear your problems, doesn't want the more meaningful nurturance of your educated advice but the ignorant yessing of a woman with no expertise.

You suddenly feel that the best, the most central part of you—your critical faculty, your judgment, even your cantankerousness—he cannot handle or appreciate, much less nurture. You are stung by this. Your resentment resumes. Your "I give; he doesn't give" litany continues.

And the nurturance gap remains.

Or:

He is talking to you about a problem, as you've told him again and again you want him to. When he's done this before, that problem (it only occurs to you now) reflected another person's insecurity, another person's flaw. Or it was a fear or worry so large and impersonal—death, war, illness—as to be heroic or cosmic or philosophical. He was being vulnerable in a way that you could respect: sensitive to feelings without betraying your old idea of how a strong, confident man should act.

Tonight is different. He's made a slipup at work, perhaps. Or he's been shown up by someone and he knows it. Whatever it is, he's fearful or abashed or angry in a way that is suddenly clumsy and banal. He's just crossed a secret fine line you never even knew you had drawn between vulnerability and weakness, between the manly and the insecure. Despite your better self, you are sharply disappointed. For an instant, you become the woman who wants that old buying/protecting indomitable-seeming man again.

He reads your disapproval, even if you pretend it isn't there. He feels that you've coaxed him into making the most difficult confession, only to strike him down now that it's been made. He is stung by this. His armor returns. His distrust resumes.

And the nurturance gap remains.

These are nurturing impasses and as painful as they are, they're a sign that at least you are trying, are risking. You're in a new social and emotional territory that doesn't yet have a language or map, yet, as frustrating as things can be, you aren't giving up. This is admirable because, the fact is, many couples do give up. They know they can't go back to the old form of blindness and rigidity—they're past the point of no return of the old buying/adoring kind of nurturance since they have two egos, two careers—so they've invented a new version. They live in states of mutual nonnurturance. Like children playing side by side in a sandbox with absolutely no interaction, they're indulging in emotional parallel play. While trying to get (and sometimes successfully getting) nurturance from other sources, they've made unspoken pacts of neglect with each other: "You don't support me; I won't support you. I'll expect nothing, and you don't, either." The challenge of responding to each other, of caring for each other, of taking pride and responsibility in one another's growth seems just too much trouble.

These mutually nonnurturing relationships usually contain so much fatigue and cynicism that nothing, short of a rush of new feeling and resolve from the hearts of both parties, can really save them in the qualitative sense. (Though they may remain intact, in name only, for years and years.) But other relationships—those with enough vitality to have reached the point of a nurturing impasse—are very savable indeed.

How to get past these big, final barriers?

CLOSING THE GAP FOR GOOD

True nurturance consists of several things. First of all, it must be natural: a flow of reciprocal care and support that is unconscious, untallied and without self-congratulation by either partner. When I asked men involved with women who felt well nurtured what specific things they did to nurture those women, I usually got pleasant bafflement. "Do I nurture her? I'm not even aware of it," they said. "Though I can tell you how she nurtures me."

Second, nurturance depends on the mutual decision to put the person you are with, and the quality of the relationship you have with that person, before any other considerations: work, luxury, the need for fame and success. Yet from this priority comes not denial or exclusion but expansion: the multiplication of possibility, of freedom. Nurturing couples enlarge rather than constrict each other—and they feel it. When I asked them what they sacrificed for each other, they invariably said they didn't sacrifice at all.

Three, nurturance depends on each partner's acting with the best interests of the other at heart—so forthrightly, naturally and consistently over time that a great web of trust is built up.

All of these things call on four essential elements, the foremost of which is empathy, which is the ability to emotionally put yourself in the cared-for person's place.

EMPATHY

Though we think of empathy as a talent, it is really a decision: the decision to attend to your partner, to imagine yourself in his or her skin. Once you make that decision, you can help develop your empathy. You can also "reality-test" it. Here are two simple exercises I often suggest to couples who come to me for counsel:

Empathy-Building Exercise No. 1:
What Is Our Nurturance Pattern?

Every couple gives and withholds nurturance in a different pattern. To find out how the two of you do, each of you take pen to pad and fill in:

I AM AWARE OF GIVING MY PARTNER NURTURANCE WHEN . . .
I AM AWARE OF WITHHOLDING NURTURANCE WHEN . . .
I AM AWARE OF RECEIVING NURTURANCE FROM MY PARTNER WHEN . . .
I AM AWARE OF MY PARTNER WITHHOLDING NURTURANCE FROM ME WHEN . . .
I MOST NEED NURTURANCE WHEN . . .
I MOST WANT NURTURANCE WHEN . . .
MY PARTNER'S USUAL RESPONSE IN BOTH SITUATIONS IS . . .

Exchange these assessments and talk over what you find. See the pattern of your manipulations, compensations, thrusts and parries —and congruences and efforts and care. What can be done to change your pattern so that the flow of nurturance answers real rather than imagined needs and is lovingly and purposefully rather than punitively or arbitrarily given? If both of you went so far as to fill out this exercise, you're strong enough to face the truth and care enough to change.

Empathy-Building Exercise No. 2:
How Do I Help My Partner Get What She/He Wants?

First of all, do you even know what your partner really wants? Each of you list the five things—success, peace of mind, to get a good finish time in the Boston Marathon, to see your daughter stop cutting classes at school, to open a wine bar (be as general or specific as you feel applies)—you think the other most wants. Then list the five things you most want, as they come off the top of your head.

Next, list the ways in which you think you help your partner toward those aims—brainstorming ideas, making specific phone calls and appointments, going, doing, listening, buying, humoring, critiquing, keeping your mouth shut, whatever.

Finally, list the ways in which you are helped by your partner.

Again, exchange lists. Discuss the differences in what you each perceive the other to be feeling and receiving and what is actually being felt and received. How can each of you use your own and the other's willingness to help to the better advantage of both of you? What signs were you misreading, and why do you think you were?

These exercises are particularly good demystifiers for couples who have the mistaken notion that empathy involves mind reading, and that, in order to be real, nurturance must come as a purely intuited gift. "If I have to ask for it, what good is it?" women now often complain, exerting the same rather arrogant demand on men that men have always exerted on women. Not true, this assumption. And not fair. Which brings us to:

DIALOGUE

Here, three simple rules apply.

1. Tell your partner what makes you feel good.

"What a pleasant surprise, your dropping by my office right before I went into that conference." "Can you give me ten minutes? I need your cool head right now." "Let's not talk. I'm too tired. But I would love a backrub." That's all it takes.

2. Take the trouble to learn to talk shop with each other.

Being deeply involved in a profession can do two things to people. First, it can make them solipsistic, make them feel that the world begins and ends with their particular industry. It can also leave them so mentally exhausted at day's end that having to spend any time translating that day in other than instant-shorthand terms seems too taxing to attempt.

The result? Many two-career couples in different fields are locked into two separate languages, two separate worlds. Their mates "don't understand" what's going on at work, they say with fatalistic sighs. They have to seek all their career nurturance elsewhere.

Reach out and bridge this gap. Make the effort to make the

dailiness and the broad strokes of your careers accessible to each other. Explain things nontechnically; keep up with events and issues in one another's arenas; and, above all, make it all interesting. Funny, how people who spend so much of their energy and consciousness on being successful and attractive in so many other ways don't think to put that same effort into the presentation of their work.

Just because you automatically assume the career world you inhabit is dazzling and relevant doesn't mean your partner does. Put a little time into letting him or her in on your zeal.

3. "Burn" your problems at the end of the day.

In certain American Indian tribes, it is custom to burn old, unneeded belongings at the end of each season. Households are cleansed and closets lightened. Old baggage is gone.

Old baggage, as we well know, can be emotional as well as actual. The woman in one nurturing couple I know is a Native American, and she and her husband have metaphorically adapted the burning custom to make sure they don't drag along unresolved tensions and unspoken problems from one busy day to the next. Every night, before they go to sleep, they spend a half hour talking about whatever is bothering them. They "burn" their problems at the end of each day.

But such deep, confidential talk is fraught with risk, so we now move on to:

SAFETY

"I will listen but will not judge."

"I know how difficult it is for you to say this; I'm on your side, no matter what."

"Your thoughts and feelings are safe with me."

These have to be the premises partners agree on if they are to feel free enough to let the other in deeply enough for him or her to nurture well.

Agree to safe zones: occasions when whatever truth one partner shares is guaranteed to be met nonjudgmentally by the other. Judgment and opinion can come later; advice after that. But reception must come first of all. Nurturance presumes intimacy, and intimacy is based on each partner's willingness to provide sanctuary for the other's most fragile feelings.

But confiding isn't always the answer. And there are times when intimacy needs the relief that only separation can bring. So let's conclude with:

SILENCE

Silence is tricky. For one thing, two people usually need it at two different times. For another, men and women use it—and eschew it—differently. For years, men have hidden behind silence, and, with the glorification of the Strong Silent Type, we've reinforced that hiding. Such silence has denied communication, cut off growth.

But just as men have erred in one direction, women have erred in another, tending to feel that the immediate discharging of words can fill all vacuums of anxiety, can heal all wounds. "Perhaps," says one woman, "it's because, as little girls, we always felt we needed to 'get permission' that now, as adults, we feel we have to come home from work to our mates and right away spill out our day." Whatever the reason, many couples are left with the frictional bind that the author C. D. B. Bryan summed up (in his novel *Beautiful Women, Ugly Scenes):* "Men come home to relax; women come home to relate."

Couples need to strike a balance between these two inclinations —a balance that both can feel comfortable with.

How can this be done?

Make it a policy to avoid the silence of manipulation and denial (those "What are you thinking?" "Nothing" exchanges), but make it a policy, too, to legitimize and honor what I call *restorative silence.*

Restorative silence is any period of contemplation, quiet, reflection or even withdrawal that one partner needs to emotionally regroup or replenish—in order, among other things, to be able to bring a refreshed, attentive self back to his or her mate.

Restorative silence might be the forty-five minutes of quiet a man needs to unwind, read his mail and shower before he feels ready to ask his wife about her day. Or it may mean two weeks of deep introspection and mourning a mate requires to absorb the death of a parent. (As my mother once said in explaining her own son's response to our father's death: "Everyone needs a little hole to curl up in and lick his wounds once in a while.") Whatever form it takes, it should be requested with goodwill by the mate who needs it and respected with trust by the partner.

Women need restorative silence, too—often even more than men do, and usually without understanding or acknowledging the fact. For the fuller a woman's life becomes, the more emotional output she feels is required of her. I'm not talking just about the mounting nurturance demands that come with being a wife and a mother; I'm talking about her family at home, and her friends, and her colleagues as well.

Women suffer from what I call the burden of depth, the presumed obligation to listen to and care for and be there for everyone in their orbit. Casual or limited or, worse yet, "staged-down" friendships (those that have moved from great to lesser intimacy) are looked on as signs of lapsed compassion and substance, of sloppy emotional housekeeping: the eighties woman's guilty equivalent of the fifties woman's less-than-snow-white sheets.

"I feel so bad," a woman who is juggling husband, toddler and stepped-up work demands anxiously told me. "I ran into someone I used to work with. We'd always gotten together for lunch every two or three months and talked about what was going on in our lives—before I had the baby, that is.

"When I saw her the other day, she told me she had just broken up with a man after three years. She was clearly so ready—so needy—for me to hear all the details and help her puzzle it through. But I was running to the bank—when *aren't* I running these days?—and couldn't stop, so I called over my shoulder: 'I'll call you—tomorrow. We'll have lunch. I want to hear all about it. God, it's been so long. We have to catch up!'"

Her sentence clattered, then derailed, like an overworked locomotive. "You know what?" she confessed, after a deep breath. "Even if I had time to have a long lunch with her, I don't want to. I can't handle any more deep caring. I can't pile one more person onto my list!"

This woman is suffering from nurturance burnout, an extremely common condition these days. How to prevent and cure it?

1. Carve out for yourself at least an hour a day of total Alone Time. Close out your partner, your children, your workmates, your friends. Read a book. Take a walk. Wash your hair. Do your nails. Do nothing. Do anything, as long as you do it without a concern in the world for anyone else but yourself.

2. Listen to your body for signs of stress and fatigue from escalating nurturance obligations. Before these can take their toll, tell your mate that you see the burnout coming, that you need relief. Reprioritize your day, your week. Delegate responsibility where you can. We will explore specific strategies in Chapter 13, "Inter-independence: Negotiating for Help."

3. Make yourself understand that you cannot be all nurturing things to all people. Explain your overload to those who expect more from you than you can now comfortably deliver. Make pacts with your close women friends to fight your burnouts together, to mutually lighten your burden of depth. Vary the format of these friendships: through long silent walks together, doing yoga or simply puttering quietly around in the same room, take your restorative silence in pairs. Start releasing emotional intensity together —through exercise classes, jogging, stripping an old oak chest, going to a mindless movie—instead of generating that intensity through your once-steady diet of long, deep talk.

TWO VIEWS ON THE MOUNTAIN, TWO PILLARS UNDER THE ROOF

It takes a lot of time and patience to make peace with the nurturance gap, to get things just right between two people. Life doesn't stay put. Babies; money; career, mood, house and income changes: everything shifts the balance of who needs more of what from whom and when. Just when you think you've got it all down pat, the sands start shifting again.

Then another upheaval comes, but this time something's different. The sands may shift, but—wonder of wonders—there's solid earth underneath. And no one but the two of you put it there.

During a stressful period after they had spent twelve years together—years in which the balance of nurturance sometimes resembled a seesaw—one couple I know went to visit friends who lived at the top of a Los Angeles canyon. They got out of the tension-filled car, stood by their respective car doors and almost simultaneously remarked on the beauty before their eyes. Except he was looking east at the mountain range and she, west to the ocean.

In that instant, they realized that they would probably always have different views—but that they would also always, somehow, where it mattered most, agree.

"We understood," says the man, "that we were going to go the distance with each other. We were two pillars holding up one roof. The pillars had to be of equal size and weight, or else the roof would be lopsided and eventually collapse."

So they took it as their obligation to conscientiously care for what they were building, to each be equally attuned to the wholeness and sturdiness of that other pillar: to protect it from stress and from harm. They were partners in strength, and by helping to keep the other built up, they knew, they were helping themselves as well.

Still there are times when the picture is not quite so hopeful—when it's not the nurturance gap that needs to be closed but the relationship itself.

Can such a seemingly bankrupt situation be rescued so that when the dissolution of a partnership occurs, destruction does not accompany it?

Yes. And in the next part and chapter of this book, I'll tell you exactly how.

III

LETTING GO

CHAPTER 9

Divorce As Positive As Possible

It may seem strange at first to be including a chapter on divorce, an essentially negative process, in a positive book.

But sixty-three out of every hundred American women are divorced. And of the four million of these women who are entitled to child-support payments from their ex-husbands, a full 47 percent are not getting the money that is legally theirs.

"Make something positive of *this?*" you ask.

Yes. It is possible to do so.

Preparedness is positive. To flinch from these stunning statistics is to court self-delusion—and self-delusion, of course, is the Poverty Mentality. A woman can say, "It can't possibly happen to me," and mean it, but she still owes it to her sheer sense of reality to look at those figures—and at their implications. It's positive and wise to have health insurance, even though you don't plan to be sick. In the very same way it's positive and wise to face the realities of divorce when you begin to sense something is askew in your marriage.

Preparedness means caring about your life enough to take responsibility for even those eventualities you regard as enormously unlikely. Preparedness means facing life with bravely open eyes. Preparedness means preventing or circumventing the worst, from a position of strength—rather than falling victim to the worst out of false optimism or sheer denial of reality or of options.

It is possible for a woman to end her marriage in a way that leaves her self-esteem, her finances, and the security of her children intact (and I'll show you how to do so in a moment), but most women fall into divorce (and the passivity implied by my choice of verb is intentional) in an entirely different way, with their Poverty Mentality in full furl. This is the case even when the woman wants the divorce.

We have seen how even when things are going well for a woman, the Poverty Mentality can afflict her, to one extent or another, in a number of ways. But when a woman is hit by the profound pain, dislocation, and blows to self-esteem that attend the breakup of a marriage, the Poverty Mentality can be truly overwhelming. It stops being part of her perspective—and starts being all of it. Ambivalence, vacant hope, undeservingness, guilt as a smoke screen are like open land mines on the emotional territory through which she walks. Even if there are no children and not much money involved, divorce is traumatic to women. But when there are children at stake and money or property to be divided, the trauma is greater—and the risk of loss, much higher.

She is more likely than ever to make dozens of large and small ill-advised, unthought-through, irrational, naïve or timid decisions. She waits far too long to make her moves—and misuses her waiting time. She fails to mobilize her resource people, sometimes fails even to know who they are. She settles for less—and she sets herself up to be taken advantage of. And all of this happens despite her most fervent hopes for equity and the best intentions in the world.

In divorce good intentions alone do not count. If they did, all those fair-minded, well-intentioned divorced women would be collecting the alimony and child support that they are owed. And —in almost epidemic proportions—they are not collecting it. A full 2.15 million men today (up 406,000 from five years ago) neglect or ignore their child-support obligations.

Why has there been such a tidal wave of support nonpayment by divorced men to their ex-wives? Why, between alimony and child-support defaulters, do almost a majority of divorced fathers and fully two thirds of the divorced men in this country feel their legal obligations to their ex-wives and children are a sham?

Why do otherwise law-abiding men who presumably love their children—or, at the very least, wish them no ill—systematically renege on this most basic of life's responsibilities?

Efforts to answer this question yield such weak and circuitous replies (these men are excising their responsibility to their children as a way of excising their pasts; or, in seeking to replay their lost youths with new and younger women, they "pretend" they don't have children by forgetting them financially) that even the authorities and men's group advocates who proffer them seem vaguely unconvinced and groping for a way to make sense of the baffling and disturbing phenomenon.

I believe the answer is much simpler than any of these half-hearted rationalizations. Men, I believe, do not pay because women let them get away with it.

And because those women let the men get away with not paying, the women are almost as responsible for that nonpayment as they would be if they were doing it themselves.

This is not farfetched. In fact there is a legal defense that is built around this very notion of the passive relinquishment of rights. It is called *laches,* and though it is not used in divorce law, it is a powerfully relevant concept that, I believe, should be introduced immediately into the vocabulary—and the mentality—of all divorcing women.

LACHES: A NEW TOOL FOR GETTING WHAT YOU DESERVE IN A SETTLEMENT AND FIGHTING THE NONPAYMENT EPIDEMIC

In equity (a form of law) laches is a defense based on a person's or business's obligation not to "sit on its hands." Here is how it works:

Party A has made a loose business agreement with Party B, one stipulation of which is that Party B not distribute Party A's merchandise. Party B does distribute the merchandise, and the fact is not kept secret from Party A. After three years Party A accuses Party B of violating their deal. Party B then uses laches as its defense. "You knew," Party B's lawyers say to those of Party A, "that we were distributing your merchandise. And you had that knowledge for a long enough time for us to be entitled to assume that your lack of protest or intervention constituted your tacit relinquishment of the nondistribution clause of our agreement."

When the case is heard, it is Party A, not Party B, who is judged remiss—and Party B, not Party A, who was operating within rights. Party A did not act on its laches.

Not legally but in everyday life, the same thing happens in

divorce. The divorced man takes the role of Party B to his ex-wife's role of Party A in situations ranging from negotiating custody settlements to honoring those settlements to honoring visitation rights with the child. The ex-wife may lament, wring her hands, even threaten—but nothing counts except doing what is legally and/or interpersonally effective. In order not to lose and lose again, she has to go out of her way to find out what's effective—and then to consistently practice it.

Divorcing women, particularly those with children, have the obligation—not the opportunity, not the option, but the obligation —to negotiate smartly, toughly and upfront to get the settlements they deserve; to reinforce, deal logical consequences and take fast action to ensure the enforcement of their settlements. By saying this I am in no way condoning or excusing the shameful record of the men involved; I am simply saying that we finally have to frame divorce in such a way that women are denied the profoundly self-dangering postures of passivity and victimization. Simply put:

In every phase of divorce—from the earliest consideration of separation to the filing of the papers and the negotiation of a settlement, to divorce's continuing aftermath of support payments and custody visits—a woman must act on her laches.

In a moment I will show you how to do so. But first let's take a brief tour of the pre- to post-divorce process and see just where in that time continuum each of the four components of the Poverty Mentality is most likely to strike.

THE DIVORCE TIME LINE AND THE
FOUR COMPONENTS OF THE POVERTY MENTALITY

First, there's the pre-divorce stage, when it's becoming apparent to a woman that the tremors in her marriage are no longer isolated, occasional and due to passing circumstance but are built into the marriage and are growing, in size and in frequency, to near earthquake proportions.

Most women know, years before they finally divorce, that their marriages are dead. But ambivalence keeps them from acting on that knowledge.

That ambivalence is three-staged. First, the woman oscillates between recognizing and denying her feelings: "Do I think that something is wrong with my marriage—or am I just having a bad day and thinking ill of everything?" Once she realizes that the former is the answer to that question, her ambivalence moves on to the question of whether her feelings are justified. ("Is there something wrong with my marriage—or is there something wrong with me?") When that question has been resolved, the ambivalence comes to settle in the only place left: "Should I get a divorce or not?"

The woman begins to compare life within her flawed marriage to the lot of her single or divorced women friends—and she doesn't like what she sees. So she burrows even further into ambivalence. She may shop for one, then another, finally a third opinion (from a friend, therapist or lawyer); then—confused, guilty and "fed up with talking about it"—she gives up thinking about changing or leaving her marriage. In this stalled, denying and fearful state, she cannot rationally consider her options or do any costs-versus-benefits analysis, and cannot effectively prepare either to work on her marriage or leave it.

Attendant to each of the pro and con swings of her pendulum of ambivalence is vacant hope. Maybe the marriage will improve, she thinks one day—or one minute. Maybe Joe will stop drinking/playing around/being so hostile/insisting he doesn't want children. Linked to the opposite pendulum swing is the kind of vacant hope which triggers this naïvely euphoric "answer": Leaving Joe will free me, she thinks. I'll be rid of all the negative pulls in my life; I'll be able to be my best self!

Finally her ambivalence, which had been ascending like an arc, peaks. Then, when she finally decides to separate from her husband, the ambivalence begins to slope downward until, with the decision to divorce, it attains the form of a bell-shaped curve and is finished.

Now during the divorce it's guilt/grief/loss that become dominant. The woman feels either sharp grief at the loss she is experiencing (especially if the divorce was her husband's decision) or powerful guilt at finally doing the leaving (if the decision to divorce was hers). Because most decisions to divorce are not simple, she often feels both layers of this syndrome.

And regardless of the exact extent to which she initiated or resisted the divorce, her guilt/grief/loss finds a perfect companion in undeservingness. If she wanted to end the marriage more than her husband did, and particularly if she is a Haver, she feels morally undeserving of a good settlement and, using the respectable rationalization of "fairness," she actively goes about getting herself and her children less than they need.

If she did not want the marriage to end, and particularly if she is a Comer (with therefore fewer contacts and resources and less direct access to expertise), her damaged self-esteem will lead to an emotional undeservingness that manifests itself in a number of moves (choosing the wrong lawyer for the wrong reason, being afraid to ask questions, feeling she doesn't have the right to make demands) by which she passively goes about getting herself less than she and her children need.

Undeservingness can go on to color the post-divorce stage as well. When there's chronic discord and hostility between a woman and her ex-husband regarding the support payments and custody visits, it's often at least partly set up or fed by the fact that she unconsciously feels she deserves that kind of unpleasantness in her life.

But it's vacant hope that most characterizes the aftermath of a divorce. The vacant hope may be turned back on itself in the forms of regret and rumination. ("If only . . ." "Why didn't I . . . ?" "Instead I should have done . . ." she thinks, of her divorce and her marriage.) Or it may take the form of the fervent —and futile—wish to be completed, changed, rescued by the next prince that will come—or the next apartment, or city, or job. So instead of facing her real possibilities and capabilities, the woman either wallows in "why" and keeps herself stuck in the past—or waits to be acted on in some powerfully fantasized future.

These then are the broad brush strokes of the Divorce Poverty Mentality (Divorce PM). Taking the process more slowly and specifically through its course, we find there are fourteen major mistakes that comprise it. There is an alternative to every one of those fourteen mistakes. And those alternatives, taken together as a whole, comprise what I call Divorce that's As Positive As Possible (Divorce APAP).

Here are the fourteen mistakes of Divorce PM and how you can trade them in for Divorce APAP.

BEFORE YOU HAVE SEPARATED . . .

1. *Divorce PM is avoiding the realization that your marriage is headed for trouble—feeling that it would be sneaky, disloyal or just plain bad even to consider divorce as an option.*

Divorce APAP is acknowledging that your marriage is headed for trouble and taking action: inventorying your feelings and resources, collecting information, exploring possibilities, doing warm-ups—all within a reasonable time frame.

Women mistake lack of foresight and lack of contingency planning for virtue. We think that if we pretend a problem doesn't exist —if we go out of our way to avoid seeing it—we are somehow being loyal and positive; that if we face up to a problem and prepare for dealing with it, we are willing that problem to mature. "God forbid that should happen!" and "Don't even think such a thing!" are cries emitted from mostly female lips.

Men are not nearly so superstitious, so fearful. To them, contingency planning is smart and normal—not bad or sneaky, much less mystically causative. Women who have agonized guiltily for two years about whether or not they should consider divorce are often shocked, when they finally do so, to discover that their husbands have already talked to lawyers. And my own attorney tells me he does not know one divorcing man who didn't have money salted away in a place his wife couldn't reach—years before any papers were filed.

The first thing I tell an anxious, ambivalent woman who is afraid of holding her flawed marriage up to the light is: Remember, thought does not mean action. The act of becoming prepared does not itself push the prepared-for situation into effect. In fact facing a situation makes things not worse but better. You may actually be able to change and save your marriage if you attend to its tremors early on, instead of denying those tremors and thereby allowing them to escalate. Acknowledging that there's a problem in the marriage does not mean acknowledging that your marriage is coming to an end.

When you begin to feel the growing tremors in your marriage, take care of things. How?

a. First of all, calmly allow your thoughts to be there and pay attention to them. Start from the top: You're feeling badly. Consider all the possible reasons. Are you overwhelmed by your complex life, pressured by the demands of your work? Or is it, indeed, the quality of your marriage that's got you down? If you've narrowed the answer down to the latter, narrow it down even more: What do you feel when you're with your husband now that you didn't feel before? Sexual disinterest? Rejection? Hostility? Ask yourself: When? What? Why now? Are these negative feelings growing steadily stronger?

b. Explore, if you haven't done so already, the possibilities of saving your marriage—through marriage counseling or therapy, or simply a series of conversations and negotiations with your husband. But don't cling to the idea of saving the marriage if you know in your heart, or from experience, that it won't work.

c. Explore the other option, that of separation, remembering you are not necessarily going to act on what you find. Ask yourself: If you and your children were to live alone, what kind of special needs would you have that you don't have now—in terms of money, child care, physical and emotional support? To help arrive at a tentative answer, visualize a typical day for yourself without your husband. And go through a day with a divorced friend, preferably one with the same obligations, income, number and ages of children as you have.

d. Determine, specifically, from whom you could get this new and needed help. If from your friends: Which ones? For how long? And what could you give them in return? If the children's grandparents come to mind, don't forget to include your husband's parents as well as your own. Take them out of the "enemy camp" even before you set such a camp up; define them at the outset as valuable resources in your life, if separation and later divorce should occur. Would you have to hire a housekeeper or babysitter? If so, for how many hours a day or week? Check around to see how much such help would cost and how you would go about finding such a person if you should need one.

e. Find out exactly what you and your husband own—separately and together. Get copies of all bank books, CDs, deeds, stock certificates, documents, bills of sale and ownership. Know where all the safe deposit boxes are and make sure you have the keys to them. Aside from the obvious assets, what about any jewelry, art, crafts, book or record collections that may be of value? What are your cars worth? What is the assessment of his—and/or your—business? And if you have contributed, directly or indirectly, to the profitability of his business over the years (as so many wives have), consult an independent business manager or lawyer to determine exactly how you can prove the extent of your contribution.

f. Ascertain which, if any, of the following things you would have to change: your home, your job, your hours at the job, your children's school(s), the weekend routine, your personal habits and use of leisure time? Try to calculate the effect these changes would have on you and on the children. Nip your disaster fantasies in the bud by realizing that things you thought you could never do—sell the house and move into an apartment, for example—might not only be survivable but in some ways positive. And if you will have to move, either temporarily or permanently, start looking at the appropriate housing now.

g. Familiarize yourself with the terms, procedure and cost of divorce in your state. Buy a book on the subject. Go to a seminar. Interview a lawyer. Even if you should never need to use the lawyer's services, you must understand now what a matrimonial lawyer *is not* (namely, a marriage counsellor, psychotherapist, life planner or anyone who can spoon-feed you your rights)—and what he or she *is,* namely someone you hire to work on your behalf. In this latter role, the lawyer is only as good as the questions you are prepared to ask her or him. Know that you must know what the right questions are—all the questions whose answers you will need to get the kind of settlement sufficient to protect yourself and your children. Establish where you should go to research those questions.

h. Now that you have outlined the concerns you would have and the work you would have to do if you separated, set up a precise time line.

Using today as a baseline date, vow that: Within two months you will have inventoried the changes you will have to make after the separation, the cost of those changes and the resource people you will have to mobilize. Within four months you will know all the questions you have to ask a lawyer, you will have gotten the name of three lawyers who have good reputations in divorce cases and will know their fees, and you will have an accounting of your financial assets. Within six months you will either have decided on a separation or not and, if the former, you will have interviewed the three lawyers and hired one to negotiate your separation agreement; you will also have informed your husband of the separation plans, and you will have a place for him or for yourself ready to move into immediately. Finally, within one year, you will have decided whether to reconcile or to divorce—and, if the latter, you will have either committed your separation lawyer to the case or have hired one you prefer for the divorce—and that lawyer will be preparing to file.

If this seems like a threateningly rapid agenda, understand that more threatening yet would be lost time. The options a woman has to start a new life at forty are wider than those to start a new life at forty-five.

2. *Divorce PM means denying the fact that divorce always involves loss—and then finding yourself hit between the eyes with that fact.*

Divorce APAP means realistically appraising the risks, preparing for the sacrifice, anticipating the healing time—so you can plan your life around the dislocation and minimize its shock.

When two households replace what once was one, there is always less to go around. A second rent or mortgage must be paid, a second complement of furniture purchased—perhaps a second car. There are twice as many cleaning and repair bills, twice as many meals. Even the well-to-do experience some necessary belt-tightening.

"And no matter who's at fault or not at fault," noted matrimonial expert Julia Perlez told me, "no one is going to get a fair shake. The arithmetic just isn't there. A successful divorce is one in which the man feels he's given up a little more than he should have and the woman feels she's getting a little less than she deserves." A little is the operative term here. For the realistic hope is to equitably minimize the loss, not to deny its inevitability.

And that inevitable loss is not just financial—but emotional, spiritual and physical as well. It takes most people about three years to completely heal from the dissolution of a marriage, to fully adjust to a new life. This does not mean that your life must be miserable—or even deprived—during the process. It just means that the Camelot-style vacant hope of a "marvellous new life" is a dangerous delusion that will send you crashing into reality unprepared.

Knowledge is power. Internalize the knowledge and use it in assessing your needs, making your case and your plans.

3. *Divorce PM is leaving at a time and in a way that maximizes pain for the other person.*

Divorce APAP is leaving at a time and in a way that minimizes that pain.

The same cardinal rule that goes for relationships goes for their easeful termination: Don't go for the jugular. A wrenching and acrimonious leave-taking—timed to be a whammy to your partner—will only make divorce negotiations more difficult for you. Remember, you and the man from whom you are separating have a delicate bargain to strike in the months ahead, a settlement that may affect you and your children's welfare and quality of life for as long as twenty years. Creating unpleasantness now, for the sheer sake of recrimination, will only further cloud the process of communication upon which a fair divorce settlement is so crucially based.

When your desire to separate has been growing for some time, pick the moment wisely, with respect for your feelings and life circumstances—and his. This does not mean that you delay leaving for six or eight months because he's in the middle of a work project that would be hurt by emotional upheaval; but six or eight weeks is another thing.

AFTER YOU HAVE SEPARATED . . .

4. *Divorce PM is assuming your friends will take care of you.*

Divorce APAP is sitting down and figuring out, specifically and in detail, what kind of help you will need from whom, how often a week—and soliciting it.

5. *Divorce PM is breaking all contact with your inlaws, if you have children.*

Divorce APAP is taking the initiative now to keep communication with your husband's parents open and positive.

Immediately upon separation, spring into action on these two points on your pre-separation agenda. When your friend openly—and with fresh compassion—offers, "Is there anything I can do?", have an extremely specific answer, "Yes, thank you, there is. I'll need someone to pick Tracy up from kindergarten and take her to the park for an hour every day for the next two weeks, while I'm job-hunting. And when I get the job, I'll take you out for a great dinner." Knit your friends into the fabric of your recovery—and into your transitional life—while they're at the peak of their willingness to help.

And drop a note to your inlaws, saying: "As I'm sure Phil has told you, we've decided on a trial separation. But I want you to know my feelings for you are warm and, no matter what happens, you'll always be a part of the children's lives. I want them to see you and talk to you every bit as much as they always did." Set up the first of such visits or phone calls now.

6. *Divorce PM is going with emotions instead of with facts, preparing to negotiate from anger or victimization, and letting the past and the future bleed into the present.*

Divorce APAP is being careful not to let emotions cloud your decisions, knowing it is fruitless to try to get sympathy or a rise out of someone who is no longer in your life, understanding that "unfinished business" and "future business" simply do not exist at the end of a marriage.

Even before you select a lawyer and think about filing, you have to know that you are *not* going to walk into the court or mediation room like a wounded animal seeking sympathy or an angry one seeking revenge. Keeping your emotions on high wins nothing and may seriously skew all the decisions you have to make, starting now.

For example, the woman who has an emotionally charged attitude tends to pick a lawyer on the basis of her or his ability to "Go out and kill!" for her—or on her or his ability to soothe and mother her. Both criteria are inappropriate, and the lawyer who meets them is probably not a good one.

If you feel you've never been heard by your husband during your marriage, you may unconsciously leap on divorce as your "moment" to let everything out. But if he never listened to you while he was living with you, why should he do so now? If you feel he's been cruel and unfair to you, you may feel you can pull his sympathy strings. But he's formally separated from you; his conscience, never apparently particularly acute, is at an even further remove.

In short, divorce just does not work as a psychological battlefield, a place where you can resolve (or even effectively play out) the issues that have plagued a marriage. If you're carting around a lot of emotional old baggage from your days as husband and wife, drop it—right away. It's too late to take care of it productively.

And as the emotional past has no place in divorce, neither has the emotional future. In fact divorce literally severs the emotional connection between you and the man you were married to. Understand now that if you and he decide to divorce, obligations written into the divorce settlement are binding; any other "obligations" that are not written in simply do not exist.

Divorce is not a gentlemanly agreement, settled by a handshake and infinite faith; it is a finite termination of affairs and it is law. Resolve now that you are not going to leave room for emotional "pencilling in" on your divorce settlement, down the line, based on your husband's discretion, honor, changing circumstances, judgment, good will or conscience. This is not a hard-hearted or distrustful point of view. Rather, it is a pragmatic, accurate point of view and, as we shall see in Point 10, a critical one.

7. *Divorce PM is picking the wrong lawyer, often for the wrong reason.*

Divorce APAP is picking the most competent, suitable lawyer, for the right reason, and communicating with that lawyer until you understand everything.

A good divorce lawyer isn't a "bomber" and isn't necessarily expensive. But he or she is more likely to be a specialist in matrimonial law than a trusty general practitioner. A good divorce lawyer is someone with whom you can easily, clearly and trustingly communicate; who is fair and businesslike and listens to you —and who comes recommended.

You already know two things: (1) that you are going to approach your lawyer knowing what questions to ask, and (2) that you are not going to select a lawyer on the basis of his or her ability either to "kill" for you or to take care of you. Are there other mistakes left to make?

Yes, most frequently there are two.

First many women don't shop around enough. They hire the first lawyer they talk to who seems "good enough"—mainly because it's too painful to keep reiterating their story. But the two-hour discomfort of talking about your marriage is nothing next to the twenty years of discomfort a bad divorce settlement can bring. Be sure to follow the pointers outlined in the pre-separation time line: Do research to find out who the best divorce lawyers in your area are. Interview at least three before you make a decision to hire.

And don't necessarily limit those three to men. The second mistake women make in selecting divorce lawyers is: They disadvantageously narrow their choice to exclude good women attorneys. Why do they do this? Lawyer Babette Fleischman explains that they don't trust themselves as women, and this distrust extends to distrust for professional members of their own sex.

Interestingly enough, Fleischman says, more and more men are picking women lawyers these days. They think they'll "look good" in court ("How can I be the chauvinistic rat my ex-wife is depicting me as, if I've got a woman representing me?"), and they think they'll get nurturance. Neither stereotype-laden assumption is necessarily true.

Hire a lawyer on the basis of competence, not sex. And when you have hired your lawyer, ask the questions you need to ask as many times as you have to until you understand the answer. If you stop asking because you're embarrassed at not catching on fast, you may pay for protecting that embarrassment with twenty years of a bad settlement.

Now that you've hired a lawyer, you're ready to proceed.

DURING THE DIVORCE . . .

8. *Divorce PM is litigating.*
Divorce APAP is mediating.
Divorce lawyers will tell you it is always preferable to negotiate a settlement out of court than to bring the case before a judge. First of all negotiation is less expensive; secondly the outcome is more predictable. And possibly most important, negotiation carries the aura of good will; court settlement implies that you and your husband have become genuine adversaries.

Still, when children are involved and when the communication between the two parties isn't clear, simple lawyer-to-lawyer negotiation may not be entirely adequate.

What then?

Instead of rushing with your lawyer to your corner of the adversarial ring and preparing to fight it out in court, there is a gentler, more mutual and reasonable option. It helps deal with the over-load of feelings and it treats conflict in all its human—not just its legal and financial—dimension. It's called mediation, and beyond its interpersonal advantages, its tactical advantage is clear: In 80 percent of those court-settled divorce cases in which children are involved, the men stop paying child support. In only 30 to 40 percent of child-involved cases that are mediated does the same kind of eventual nonpayment occur.

In mediation a lawyer and a psychologist assist both parties in reaching an agreement with the children's welfare foremost in mind. There are separate, private sessions for the venting of emotion and for probing each parent's plans and goals. These alternate with joint sessions. For mediation to work both parties have to agree to full financial and emotional self-disclosure.

9. *Divorce PM is going for a lot of little wins.*
Divorce APAP is thinking big, as men do.

Here is a typical scenario: The divorcing woman announces in no uncertain terms that she wants: the heirloom silver service, the Persian rug, the collection of lacquered boxes and antique porcelain mugs—as well as the living room couches. Her husband and his attorney watch her amass this list of sentimental items—worth, say, $12,000 in all.

The husband's lawyer then says to the judge, "All right, she's won the rug . . . and the porcelain . . . and the silver . . . and the lacquered boxes . . . and the living room couches. That's five concessions we've made to her, Your Honor. My client asks for only one thing: the stock portfolio."

Five to one? The judge says, "Granted."

And before the woman and her lawyer know what hit them, the stock portfolio—valued at $20,000, $8,000 more than all her "wins" put together—is smoothly handed over to the man.

10. *Divorce PM is giving up money—through the neglect of your laches in the form of blind emotion, "fairness" and/or bread-winning pride.*
Divorce APAP is not only getting your full rightful fixed (not relative) settlement, but enforcing its prompt monthly payments in one of three possible ways.

"Let him keep the money!" the woman in my office says, with a deep sigh and an aggravated wave of the hand. "I'd rather have my peace of mind. I don't want a hassle; I just want out of the marriage."

Believe it or not, this happens again and again.

I always tell this woman that she is not going to have anything resembling peace of mind if she doesn't pursue her rightful settlement, that getting that settlement doesn't have to be a "hassle"— but even if it is, it's a very small one next to the permanent inconvenience she'll face raising a child or children alone, with much less money than she needs to get by.

That's one common example of blind emotion causing a woman to simply relinquish money that is due her. In this case the emotion is exasperation, and the mistaken "reasoning" beneath that emotion is that by giving up her rights—by neglecting her laches —she will somehow circumvent pain and simplify her life. (In fact what she is doing is inviting pain and complicating her life.)

In other frequent cases "love" is the blind emotion. It's fine to be in love—but not when that love, particularly when it comes without commitment, is costing you tens or hundreds of thousands of dollars in forfeited alimony. And that's what can happen.

I recently met a woman, divorced from a well-to-do dentist, with two teenage children. Her own income, as a photographer's assistant, was far from considerable. Yet she had relinquished her entire—sizable—alimony settlement by having her lover, a struggling artist, move into her home. (In the state of California a divorced woman who cohabits with a man automatically loses her alimony settlement. A divorced man who does the same thing loses nothing.) The lover didn't promise her marriage; he's still in fact having trouble with the notion of commitment. "But we're happy," the woman rhapsodized. To which I silently wondered: Yes, but given the circumstances you've just put yourself under, for how long?

It is absolutely inconceivable that a man would give up money like this. But large numbers of women do it every single day.

These are the glaring cases. There are subtle ones too. More and more Haver women who are exultantly proud of their new breadwinning ability, who as feminists disapprove of the idea of alimony and who feel guilt at wanting to leave husbands and marriages they've outgrown use the rationalization of "fairness" to deny themselves the settlements they need—and to make their ex-husbands' child-support payments relative rather than absolute.

"It's only fair," such a woman will say, "that as my income, as a professional, goes up, his obligation should be adjusted down."

This is subtle and devastating undeservingness. "I don't deserve to have my good professional income and the assurance of support for my children," this woman is as much as saying. "Somehow I have to keep it a struggle for myself. I'm only comfortable with the assurance of day-to-day, bread-and-butter survival. I can't imagine for myself an existence in which I'm able to leverage, to get ahead of the game."

But beyond making sure things are hard for herself, the woman who negotiates this "fair," keyed-to-her-income settlement is risking making things very bad for her children. Manhattan attorney and writer Carol Rinzler has seen "fairness" on the woman's part slide into nonpayment on the man's part again and again among her peers. I quote her at some length now because what she is saying is so important:

"There is no such thing as 'fairness' to your ex-husband when you are your children's provider and protector. By keying your husband's obligation to your income, you're gambling with the clothes on your children's back by putting faith in his 'honor' to continue paying.

"Honor comes with comfort. Men who might be perfectly honorable and decent when it doesn't tax their lifestyles are suddenly different when their child-support payments are cramping their style in some way. As we've seen from the statistics, they just stop paying. They become 'fond uncles' to their own children. Their attitude becomes: 'I love these kids. Gee, if I had any money, you know it would go to them first.' And I am not talking about late-blooming middle-aged hippies who throw off their neckties and go to New Mexico to throw pots. I'm talking about so-called solid, upper-middle class providers. By my casual survey, doctors and lawyers are the worst."

It all comes down to laches. Hardly typical deadbeats or shirkers, these men have simply been given reason to believe they can get away without paying. Their self-sufficient, resourceful, "fair" ex-wives have agreed to divorce settlements which make their fatherly support obligation not absolute but relative. Relative then to what? If it's relative to the woman's income, it might as well also by extension be relative to the man's ability to buy a weekend house or not (after all, he'd be entertaining clients there, so it's important for his work)—or to take that trip to Europe.

"Relative" is a dangerous concept to attach to a man's support obligation. It puts the foot of nonpayment securely in the door.

For these men know that somehow their ex-wives will not let their children starve. That these women are knocking themselves out to keep the kids clothed and fed and schooled when the support checks start coming late (and eventually stop coming altogether) is beside the point. The men don't have to see their ex-wives' exhaustion and personal denial and fear. And even if they saw it, they would not be obliged to care.

The more a woman takes it upon herself to personally compensate for her ex-husband's real or potential neglect, the more reinforced the man is to do nothing.

So you will want to act on your laches and negotiate for an absolute, not relative, amount of support—fully enough to cover your children's needs. Beyond this are there any ways you can help guarantee prompt payment by your ex-husband? Yes, there are three.

a. First, if possible, take a lump sum settlement instead of monthly support payments.

Because of the high incidence of nonpayment, it's wise to consider taking, for example, your husband's half of your country house (appraised at $144,000) instead of six years of $1,000-a-month support payments (which amount to the same thing, $72,000). This way you're choosing the bird in the hand instead of the monthly ones in the bush—a bush you're asked to believe will still be standing, branches and leaves intact, years from today.

And the bird in hand is worth well more than those in the bush. For the principle of the discounted value of money means that money to be paid in the future is *a priori* worth less than its equivalent paid in lump sum now. So if there is property valuable enough to take in exchange and if the tax ramifications still make it worthwhile, the lump sum settlement is the best assurance you can have that your child support needs will be met. (It goes without saying, of course, that you should not use the rent or resale revenue from the settlement property for anything other than what it was intended to replace: the fixed, steady, adequate support of your children.)

b. Second, if a lump sum settlement is not possible, have it written into your agreement that each child support payment must be backed by a promissory note.

The note might say, "I have just made my January child support payment of $500. I now owe $5,500 more for the year, payable in monthly units of $500 and receivable by the fifth of each month." It is easy to sue for late payment or nonpayment when a promissory note has been violated.

 c. Third, set up a bank trust to collect and administer your child support payments for you.

The logic is simple: A man will be quicker to reach for his checkbook if the Bank of America, rather than his ex-wife, is calling him up to ask him about his delinquent payment.

AFTER THE DIVORCE . . .

11. Divorce PM, if you have children, is regarding your ex-husband as an enemy, retaining your ego involvement in dealing with him.

Divorce APAP is understanding the necessary continuity of your relationship with your ex-husband, staying focused on the children's best interests whenever you deal with him and leaving your own ego out.

A child cannot shuttle back and forth between two enemies without being damaged. No matter what your personal feelings about the man, if you continue to think of your ex-husband in negative terms, no one—not him, not you, and certainly not the children—is going to win.

If you harbor leftover anger at the man you were married to: Take care of it. Deal with it, vent it, discharge it—through therapy, journal writing, talking to women friends. Just get it out and explored and over.

And in all of your dealings with your ex-husband, stay focused on the child's best interests. Keep your ego, your memories of his past behavior toward you out of it. In this new stage of your relationship, you are repartnering with your ex-husband in a clean, limited, single-focus/single-issue way. What counts isn't you or him. What counts is the child you have made together. That is all. And that is everything.

And because it is, it might help for you to:

a. Take a little time, at the outset, to understand your ex-husband's point of view.

Most men, even if they directly or indirectly caused the breakup of the marriage, suffer the shock of dislocation after divorce. Men like a feathered nest, a lair. They get used to being taken care of. Even after they became unhappy within the marriage, the sheer routine and amenities of that marriage often continued to satisfy a need they didn't know had existed until the marriage was over. So if your ex-husband's attitude seems unfathomably martyrous or resentful, it might be caused by the sheer, powerful dislocation he is experiencing.

"Ha!" you might say. "I'm supposed to sympathize with him—him with his money and his girlfriend, while I'm knocking myself out as a single working mother." No, you are not being asked to sympathize or to empathize or to approve. But for the sake of your child, it does help to know the things that affect him, the rationale for his actions as well as that of your own.

b. Use positive reinforcement for your husband's involvement with your child.

When I asked my colleague, psychotherapist Dr. Dick Varnes, why he thought ex-husbands stop honoring their child support obligations, he answered with another, provocative question, "What, after all, do they ever get for paying?"

Well . . . give him something.

If your ex-husband's payments have been prompt, you might send him the original of your child's report card (not the Xerox copy, which so clearly indicates the secondary parent) with a note saying, "I knew you'd want to keep this. I'm sure you're as pleased with Jessica's improvement in math as I am. I know that your helping her with her homework every week was instrumental. Thanks too for getting the check to me by the third of the month. I really appreciate it."

If his payment had been several days late and, this month for a change, it is several days early or even just on time, you might drop a note that says, "Thanks for the prompt check. Getting the payments on time makes things much easier for me—and directly benefits Jess. Last Tuesday, for example, right after the orthodontist removed her braces, I was able to take her out for a special dinner (full of formerly forbidden food). If the check had been late, we'd have had to postpone the celebration. I know you agree that it's important for Jess's sense of security for her to be able to count on things coming at their appropriate and promised times."

This kind of occasional communication is not pandering, not ingratiation. It is simply reinforcement. It is also a good way to keep a father involved in daily events that he no longer directly experiences with his child. Most experts say that the more involved the man is in the child's daily life, the more likely he is to continue paying. And, it goes without saying, both the payment and the involvement make things better for the child.

But what if reliable involvement does not occur?

c. To protect your child's feelings and to assure that you are not inconvenienced: negotiate upfront on visitation; when he doesn't keep his bargain: deal logical consequences, while continuing to keep the lines of communication open.

If he is supposed to take Jessica for every other weekend, you specify the time and tell him at the outset why the time is important. For example, you might say to him, "We'll expect you at nine. Jessica's looking forward to it. She'll be dressed for the day—and I have a finance class at nine forty-five."

If he is late more than once, you might say, "Since I have to be at my finance class across town at nine forty-five, I've had to hire a neighbor to sit with Jess while she waits for you. Here is the babysitting bill."

If his tardiness continues, or if he cancels out on his date with the child: "This is the third week you've been late or have canceled. Jessie, of course, is disappointed and confused. And I have things I've made appointments to do. Is there some other day of the week that is more convenient for you—and, if so, can we firm it up now? [Always give him the opportunity to make a counter-offer.] No? Well then, I'm going to assume you're going to honor your commitment to seeing her Saturday at nine o'clock. If not, I'm going to assume that you don't want to see her, and I'll make a commitment to have a babysitter for her all day Saturdays and send you the bill."

If in fact he is late or cancels the next Saturday, hire the sitter and promptly send him the bill for the next three weeks of sitters in advance.

But, keeping focused on the interests of the child, remain reasonable, continue to extend him the opportunity to make a counter-offer, and keep communication open.

12. *Divorce PM is leaving yourself vulnerable at critical times.*
Divorce APAP is covering yourself—and your children—by taking care to plan for custody visits, holidays, weekends.

What exacerbates the Poverty Mentality is not being equipped for the beginnings and endings of your ex-husband's visits with your child. Here you are, packing the child's weekend suitcase, feeling fear of the loss of her, guilt at her dislocation between two parents—and feeling undeserving of getting any pleasure from the weekend.

Plan in advance to ward off these debilitating feelings. The weekend should be seen as your vacation. Get tickets to a play, a concert, an art exhibit. Make a date for a movie and a nice meal. Buy a book you've been hearing about for months and spend the weekend lazily reading. Don't leave the time open-ended and yourself bereft.

And when your child returns, be careful not to interrogate her, no matter how curious you may be about your ex-husband's new life. Questions such as "What's his new apartment like?" and "What does his lady friend look like?"—no matter how casually dropped—are only a way of using the child and beating yourself up until you feel all the needier.

Plan ahead for holidays—more than ever before. First, ascertain clearly in advance whether you or your ex-husband are to be with the child for each holiday. And whether you make firm commitments for festivities. Don't wait for invitations; create them.

13. *Divorce PM is letting time go by or making empty threats when his payments are late or when they stop coming.*
Divorce APAP is going into fast action.

I know a woman who is finally suing her ex-husband for nonsupport after two whole years. And it took me most of those two years to help her to see her right—and her need—for action.

Women wait much too long. First they vacantly hope for the checks—and before they know it, that vacant hope has turned into full-fledged hopelessness. They're convinced that they'll never get anything from their ex-husbands, so why knock themselves out trying? Or they're so desperate that their ex-husbands can "starve them out" and offer them half the monthly amount, which these women then gratefully take.

When people feel like victims, they can't do anything. Action helps diffuse your sense of victimization. You're moving, talking, doing—acting. So when the checks are late, snap into fast action.

Mention should be made to the ex-husband the first or second time a check comes late, depending on the man's prior record and how late the check is. If it's been late three months in a row, act on your laches: pick up the phone and call your lawyer and instruct him to call your ex-husband's lawyer and request prompt payment, suggesting that action will otherwise be taken right away.

Even if it costs you $50 to have that phone call made, it is worth it.

If the check has stopped coming altogether, instruct your lawyer to take full legal action. Contrary to what many people think, you can sue for your husband's contempt of court immediately and you can have his wages attached.

14. *Divorce PM is living in the past and waiting for your life to be transformed.*

Divorce APAP is putting the past behind you and taking full charge of your future.

Not long ago a divorced woman wrote a letter to the editorial page of the Los Angeles *Times.* Under the headline "The Grass Is Always Greener," the letter cautioned middle-aged women to think twice before divorcing, even if their marriages were unhappy. There are, this woman said, a lot of sadder-but-wiser divorcees out there suddenly shocked that the supply of single men is so low, suddenly exhausted by their poverty and their diminished options: suddenly, in short, regretting their divorces.

I wish I could tell these women that they—not "circumstances," not the supply of men—are acting as their own worst enemy. Regret is the worst self-sabotage of all. It keeps you trapped in a past you can never return to, in a mode of inaction, in a mind set of anger and defeat. Feeling sorry for yourself, feeling rudely awakened to facts you were unprepared for, feeling the "odds" (of making more money, of remarrying, of being happy) are against you: all of this keeps you the victim; all of this keeps you stalled.

And all of this means you are stubbornly waiting for something or someone to come along and transform you, just as you thought divorce would transform you . . . and just as you probably thought marriage would, years before.

Acting on one's laches is a responsibility, finally, that pertains not just to a woman and her ex-husband—but to a woman and herself. After all the divorce papers are filed, and the property is divided and the physical adjustments have been made, you have the obligation—not the option, not the opportunity, but the obligation—to positively and passionately get on with your life.

IV

HAVING IT ALL

CHAPTER 10

Lust Is Not a Dirty Word

"Greed," "Never enough," "Obsessed," "Ravenous," "Driven," "Haunted," "Heated," "Feverish," "Fixated," "Seething."

Those were some of the words shouted back to me when I wrote L-U-S-T in big block letters on a blackboard in front of a seminar audience of Comer women and asked them for the first flash associations that sprang to mind.

Yes, there were a few positive words piped in—"Passion" and "Zealous" were contributed from far corners of the room. But these were quickly drowned out by the din of negatives: "Lascivious," "Trampy," "Salivating," "Groveling," "Groping," "Grunting" and on and on.

That powerful experience drove home what I had come to believe over years of other seminars and numerous private counseling sessions: To women, but not to men, lust is a dirty word. It's "not nice," not gracious, not ladylike, to want something so badly that all of your heart and your energy and your fire go out to that particular goal. It's gauche, women think. It's primitive. It's desperate. It's masculine, uncouth, uncivilized, crude, raw, vulgar.

It is, in a word, dirty.

It is this attitude that freezes us. For, far from being a dirty word, lust is exquisitely clean—like the pure, elegant ascent of a rocket. Lust (and by lust I mean the passionate, wholehearted, unapologetic longing for something) impels. It empowers. It energizes. It thrusts. When we act without lust, we act listlessly, halfheartedly, rotely. Very often, we don't get results. Very often, too, we don't even notice or care. We're treading water, not coming away with anything learned from an experience, without anything changed or pushed a notch forward. Without lust, we're simply marking time, breaking even on our lives.

Lust is our fuel, the blood in the stream of the acting self. And, like any blood, it can be too watery or too thick. It can come forth in an ineffectual trickle or in a driving, excessive rush, dealing destruction and, ultimately, self-defeat. The lust that gives lust a bad name is this latter, and we will explore in a moment how and why women, once they've become Havers, find it hard to modulate lust, to come to balance with it. It is lust-in-balance that makes purposeful action possible with satisfaction and nourishment, without any negative side effects for the actor or anyone else in his or her path or life. It is lust-in-balance that can lead to courageousness. And it is courageousness that makes us soar.

But I am getting ahead of myself. For the moment, instead, in order to go forward, let's turn around and recap. In Part I of this book, we discussed the four components of the Poverty Mentality, and how the stem feeling of each of them can spark an attitude that leads to behavior that is ultimately self-sabotaging. You learned how to recognize those components in the various ways they operate in your own life, and what to do to reverse them. In Part II, we discussed some of the chief ways that Poverty Mentality can penetrate your relationships with men, and you learned how to change that, too.

We've cleared the path of the brambles. Now we get to the path itself: you getting for you. This is where the challenge lies. In the next chapters in this part, you'll find blueprints for action in the present and in the medium- and long-range future; plans for networking and for maximizing your assets. But no one can adapt and revise and breathe life into these blueprints but you. You cannot mold another person, push her on, make her take responsibility for her own life. You can help her find the gate, but you cannot walk her through it. That she must do for herself.

And she starts that process with one ingredient: lust.

COMERS AND HAVERS, NOURISHMENT AND EXCESS: COMING TO BALANCE WITH LUST

When we think of lust, we usually think of sex. But for women, the far more useful and appropriate metaphor for lust is food.

Food is a loaded symbol for women. Not only are the making and serving of meals so central to the traditional idea of "women's work" and so symbolic of fulfillment on so many levels (from the bodily to the emotional to the domestic-obligatory), but eating itself has become a crucible for women today. Dieting is a preoccupation, thinness a desperate goal. Eating too much, wanting to eat too much, gaining weight, thinking constantly about food, are sources of shame—secret vices that we hide. We fake a casualness about food to mask our true obsessiveness. Among young women, anorexia nervosa and its sister illness bulimia (gorging, then vomiting) are almost epidemic.

It is food, in short, that we lust for most—and food that is the area of our physical lives with which it is hardest to come to balance. On the one end of the eating-disorder arc, women keep a tight lid on their hunger: masking it through diet aids and amphetamines, denying it through an obsession with thinness. They don't eat healthfully or naturally so they don't get well nourished. On the other end of the arc are the women who gorge and grab and eat gluttonously but who have created a physical insatiability through the use of vomiting and laxatives. They are never full; they are never nourished. They eat with a literal version of the proverbial hollow leg.

In the middle—the crest—of the arc are the healthy, balanced, nonneurotic eaters. They relish food but do not obsess with it. They eat—and think about eating—neither too little nor too much: according to a natural hunger, not an unnaturally suppressed or psychologically bloated hunger. They use food as a pleasurable fuel for energy and for nourishment.

As food is physical fuel, lust is psychological fuel. And what goes for women and food goes, in an almost precise analogue, for women and lust. At one extreme end of the arc of lust are the women whose lust is so deeply denied that further nuanced description of their condition is meaningless. They are simply numb to any experience or perceptions that might change their state. Next to them, and far more receptive to change, are those women who haven't allowed themselves to acknowledge or develop their true appetite for accomplishment on their own. They may be wives/mothers who deflect all their lust into the needs and goals of their husbands and children. Or they may be Comers who will tell you they want careers and distinction and satisfaction independent of the men in their lives, but whose every action belies that claim—and who operate, instead, out of a mild hunger that will not fuel them enough to get them where they think they want to go.

On the opposite end of the arc are the overamped Havers who have retained their Poverty Mentality despite their accomplishments, who have set up an emotional system like the bulimic's intestinal tract, whereby no matter what they take in they cannot get filled up. Competing with everyone they know and feverishly feeling they have to somehow make up for "lost" time, they go and do and grab and get and push and collect and acquire. They lust indiscriminately. And yet they remain ungratified. They remain, in their hearts, undernourished.

At the center—the peak—of the arc are the women, be they Comers smoothly ascending or Havers who've arrived, who have their lust in balance. These women use their lust as fuel, their life experience as nourishment. They want a lot for themselves, but that wanting doesn't run away with itself, doesn't become an end in itself. Just as the healthy eater is uncomfortable feeling stuffed with food and knows when to restrain herself from eating more, so the woman with lust-in-balance knows when it is time to stop taking in and start savoring. Just as the healthy eater knows when she's nibbling junk food out of boredom and can stop herself in time, so the woman with lust-in-balance knows when she is starting to crave a mere image or superficial symbol—and she, too, will stop herself in time.

What distinguishes the woman with lust-in-balance from the women at the other two ends of the arc is, indeed, this consciousness. Women in mild hunger and in indiscriminate lust are usually not nearly so aware of their states. "I really want that promotion," said a young Comer I know whose boss tailored a training program to help her earn it. Yet she often called me, complaining of boredom, during those training sessions; she overslept through a Saturday seminar that would help her in her field; and she directed most of her energy not to doing the optional work that could stand her in good stead with her firm but to fixing up the kitchen of her new apartment into a marvel of country French warmth and there cooking dinners for the man in her life.

And "I'm so happy! I have everything!" exults another woman I know—while gulping her sandwich, consulting her watch, sneaking sidewise looks out the corners of her eyes for work "contacts" at the restaurant she entered, for our lunch appointment, breathless and half an hour late. Overdressed, overjeweled, overeating, she's just expressed envy at one friend's wardrobe and another's salary, scribbled a note in her pocket calendar about an event that won't be taking place for another two months, and has asked me three times in five minutes: "What was it you just said?" This woman is suffering from indiscriminate lust, but she doesn't know it.

Watch this woman at work, as I have, and you'll see the waste, the tail-chasing futility, the sheer destruction of the indiscriminate luster. As director of promotion for a perfume house, she wants a new Christmas brochure to turn out better than any the promotion department ever produced before. (Like most indiscriminate lusters, she is constantly competing: "bigger," "better," "best" are leitmotifs in her talk.) To that end, she fights with the art director, insults the copywriters, wastes time and goes over cost having pages rephotographed again and again, and alienates her own staff with her single-mindedness and her insensitivity. She wants! wants! wants! (her lust bangs like a fist on a tabletop) so hectically and insatiably that she miscues on dozens of decisions, big and little, of aesthetics, diplomacy and budget. The brochure, needless to say, does not turn out well. And neither does her standing in her company or her reputation in her field. Ironically, yet with perfect logic: She wants so much that she cannot have.

The first step in taking lust out of the dirty-word closet and learning how to let it fuel you in a balanced way is to know where you stand in relation to it. Take a little time reading Table 9 and, as truthfully as you can, locate yourself on the arc of lust that curves from ineffectual mild hunger to self-destructive indiscriminate lust—and peaks with effective, life-enhancing lust-in-balance.

If, having done so, you've found that your lust is out of balance, how can you correct it?

DEVELOPING APPETITE FOR COMERS WITH MILD HUNGER

1. *Ask yourself: Is there something I want to do more than what I am doing now?*

Maybe it's not the energy that's low but the goal that's insincere, the activity that's inauthentic.

If so, why not stop putting low lust toward one halfhearted goal and find the goal that will bring out your strong lust-in-balance?

The young Comer in the training program I just spoke of eventually decided, with some help from me, to use her two weeks' vacation from work to take a gourmet cooking course. On the basis of that experience, she realized that her lust lay in the direction of making, displaying and serving food not just to please a man and prepare herself for marriage but as a creative act in its own right. She's decided to change fields: go to work for a caterer, with a view to eventually opening her own gourmet takeout shop.

2. *If you feel there's nothing you want to do more, turn back to Chapter 2, "Ambivalence," and take the fantasies/skills/assets exercise again.*

3. *If you still cannot work up enthusiasm, take some time off from the pursuit—and the consciousness—of lust.*

Perhaps you're burned out from a long stint at any unsatisfying job, or all your passion has been drained by staying in the fray of an emotionally consuming relationship. Rest. Take the pressure off yourself; let your mind, body—and lust level—recharge and replenish on its own.

At a certain point in this process, when you feel ready . . .

4. *Follow the thread of your daydreams and brainstorms.*

Let your thoughts and yearnings flow, and watch them. Keep a journal and record your changes of mood, from day to day, week to week, even hour to hour. What makes you happy? curious? What do you find yourself going out of your way, even a little out of your way, to do? What makes you sit up and pay attention? What gets you out of yourself? What bobs in the back of your mind as the small but significant reward after a long, perhaps tedious day?

Pick up the thread of that clue and follow it where it leads. One young woman, a listless secretary in an insurance firm, discovered by this process of self-observation and self-sleuthing that what got her through her day was the thought of going home and playing her records. She's now an infinitely more gratified—and higher-lust—secretary in a law firm that represents recording artists. And she's taking a business school course at night to equip her for the work she eventually hopes to do, as a performer's manager.

5. *Surround yourself with those things and people that stir, provoke and stimulate you.*

Go back and reread the poet whose work felt so profound to you in college. Call the old friend who always turned your neat assumptions upside down. Revisit the woods where you walked by the lake years ago and reached that crucial decision, that clarifying insight. See the paintings, listen to the music, read the biography of those creators who have engrossed, elevated, even disturbed you. Artists, writers and composers themselves place great store by inspiration, by being jolted to the depths of their senses. They know where they must be and what they must have around them in order to call forth those inner stirrings that enable them to create. Be as conscientious in inducing those inner stirrings as any of these artists. For those stirrings are lust.

6. *Find your "noble lust" and transfer that energy to yourself.*

Noble lust is passionate, wholehearted, unapologetic longing in the interest of loved ones. I have talked to many women with ostensibly only very mild hunger for their own goals and have asked the question: "But don't you have lust for your husband's career? For your children's welfare?"

Their heads snap back, their backs straighten. "But of course!" they say, in word or demeanor. "I would kill for them!"

Imagine this noble lust applied to yourself. Understand that you *can* make such an energy transfer without depriving others.

PUTTING INDISCRIMINATE LUST BACK IN BALANCE FOR HAVERS

1. *Don't try to fight time.*

Many women rev up to indiscriminate lust out of the furious attempt to "make up for" all the years they missed as housewives, as secretaries, as underlings. They end up blurring their priorities, burning themselves out, and doing twenty things badly instead of seven things well.

What you can do is make the most of your time now and operate with appropriate speed, directness and focused purpose. (We'll have more on this in the next chapter.) There is a difference between exhilaration and desperation, between concentration and combustion. The woman with lust-in-balance has the first; the indiscriminate luster courts the second.

When you feel you are going over the line from the one to the other, stop; listen to your body; look at your motives; and alter the course. Above all, look forward on the calendar, not back.

2. *Break out of the "lust traps" of anger and jealousy.*

Many women only feel empowered when they're angry or angrily avaricious. "I'll show him!" or "I'll outdo her!" they think—and the motors churn. A self-fulfilling prophecy is set up: Because lust is such a dirty word to them, they associate it wholly with negative motives and impulses. Pretty soon, they can't want unless these motives and impulses are present. As most women who get caught in this trap soon find out, the gains are short-term, the satisfactions are the grim ones of retaliation and revenge. If you have to stay angry and envious in order to feel lustful, you are paying a price for your energy with every ounce of your being and you are slowly destroying your emotional and personal life.

To start detaching lust from these negative emotions, first of all, very simply, try not to take things personally. Most women never learned how to separate aggressive empowerment toward a goal from moral judgments of those empowered. In other words, they never learned (as boys *did* learn) that you could knock someone down on the playing field, according to the rules of the game, but remain, afterward, best friends. They never learned how to sift personal feelings—and notions of goodness and badness—from lust.

Women go through their lives dropping all their desires, energy and action into the general bucket of their personal lives. (It is sometimes said that we *only* have personal lives, while men only have professional lives.) We know now, as we discussed in Chapter 5, "Guilt as a Smoke Screen," that our valuing of relationship is a good and strong thing. But one of the caveats attached to our proud valuing of relationship over goal orientation is that we must be careful not to so interlace personal energy with personal feelings that, in confusion, we render all that energy "bad"—and we end up, ironically and painfully, having to feel bad in order to feel energized.

3. *See yourself as a "student of balance." Understand that you have to master desire in order to transcend it.*

"You have to know how to draw the human figure before taking off into abstraction," art students are told. The message is clear: As impatient as you may be, to go on to individual creativity you have to absorb and digest and master the basic foundation of your discipline.

Havers who find themselves in indiscriminate lust often put the cart before the horse just as impatient devotees of these disciplines do. They do not stop, absorb, learn from and feel gratified by one accomplishment or acquisition before going on to the next. Emotionally and productively, they cannot transcend that original level of fierce, vain, unrequited wanting because they have never really achieved the satisfaction of having. In their personal and their professional lives, they are as underdeveloped, disadvantaged and doomed to secretly "fake" status as the painter who never learned drawing.

Only you can know if you're missing that crucial mastery/transcendence step, if you're bypassing the process of your action in your hurtling lurch toward its product. The clues are a puzzling, probably escalating sense of meaninglessness with what you're getting and doing; the sense that you're still competing, still angry, still insecure; even though you've been doing and getting successfully for some time now, the hunch that despite all material evidence and despite your on-top-of-it-all attitude, something is missing from your life.

If you suspect you have these feelings, make the brave decision to let them come to the surface of your consciousness. It is time to stop and reassess. Part V of this book, "Beyond Money," is of particular relevance to you.

COURAGEOUSNESS

Several years ago, Perdita Huston, the first woman director of one of the three global divisions of the Peace Corps, boarded a plane and embarked on the task of flying to remote areas of the world to find and interview Third World women for a book she knew she had to write. Though she had never written a book before, she felt compelled to reverse the wrong-minded assumptions of the mostly male study groups of the United Nations on the subject of women in developing countries.

"I distinctly remember being halfway across the Atlantic," she says, "and realizing that I had just turned forty . . . and all of a sudden being hit with the thought: 'My God, Perdita, how do you know the women will talk? How do you know you can write? How did you get yourself into this thing?' "

She was thinking rhetorically. For she knew what had gotten her into the brave—and eventually policy-influencing—pursuit: lust-in-balance, accompanied by a well-planned strategy (for financing the project, securing publication, contacting the right women in the right places, making travel plans). The third quality is one she might not acknowledge in herself but one that she always felt inspired by in other women all over the world. And that quality is courageousness.

You don't have to travel to exotic places or have an impressive title to summon—and move with—courageousness. I hear examples of this quality, coupled with lust-in-balance and planning, transforming the lives of women everywhere. Some examples:

■ An eighty-year-old writer refuses retirement, revives a journalism career at a pace that would leave many women half her age exhausted and, between yearly trips to Mexico, starts a lucrative second career on the lecture circuit.

■ A woman in Ohio decides, upon the birth of her eighth child, that her marriage is bankrupt and that she wants a challenging, meaningful career. She divorces, raises her children alone and still finds time to go back to graduate school and get her M.A. Today, ten years later, she is a director of the office of job training in one of the most unemployment-ravaged regions of the country.

■ A young woman filmmaker finds an ingenious way to support herself, leverage her capital and buy time for her own creativity. She forms a strong partnership with a colleague and friend and tackles the usually long, long odds of writing an uncompromised film that will be produced in a way that reduces those odds considerably.

These are just a few of the many women who have taken their lust-in-balance, fleshed it out with a firm, well-considered, creative plan for action and suffused the whole process with courageousness: that inner resolve and resourcefulness that makes it possible to fly in the face of safety and probability and make the dreamed-for happen.

We'll talk about the spiritual and emotional predispositions for *courageousness* in Part V, "Beyond Money." But first, let's take a long, useful look at the part of the process that lust makes possible and courageousness enhances: the formation of a personal plan for action through conquest of time and money (Chapter 11), demystification and interactions with the people we assume "control things" (Chapter 12), and support-networking with the people in our daily lives (Chapter 13).

TABLE 9
WHERE ARE YOU ON THE ARC OF LUST?

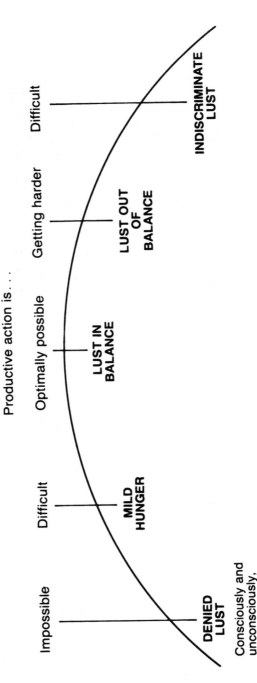

Productive action is . . .

Impossible	Difficult	Optimally possible	Getting harder	Difficult
DENIED LUST	**MILD HUNGER**	**LUST IN BALANCE**	**LUST OUT OF BALANCE**	**INDISCRIMINATE LUST**

Consciously and unconsciously, lust is such a dirty word that you are ashamed of it, and you suppress it completely.

Dealing with those four out of the five points on the arc where some level of lust is operative (it is not operative in DENIED LUST), let's go through ten signs and criteria. Circle the answer in each row that best describes you. This will give you a good idea of where you stand on the arc of lust.

(Continued)

	MILD HUNGER	LUST IN BALANCE	LUST OUT OF BALANCE	INDISCRIMINATE LUST
Wanting	Diffused, halfhearted wanting	Clear, focused wanting	Extreme wanting	Insatiable wanting
Digestion of Experience	Chewing but not swallowing life experiences	You take in events and experiences at a pace and in a way that allows you to relish them, allows them to nourish you.	Eyes bigger than stomach: you want more/take in and take on more than you can handle well.	Compulsive ingestion, low nourishment, hasty excretion of experience; your emotional system is overworked, overwhelmed, underfueled by doing/wanting too many things at once.
Image and Trappings vs. Process and Substance	The former, not the latter, are the objects of value and desire ("The fur coat means success; I want the coat")	The latter is valued ("I want the great feeling of doing the work well/relishing the experience. The fur coat is nice but has nothing to do with it.")	The image, once arrived at, and the trappings, now affordable, are disappointing payoffs; satisfaction seems elusive ("I have the title and the fur coat; funny, I still don't feel filled up.")	Obsession with wresting value out of image and trappings until they finally pay off the way they're "supposed" to. ("I want another fur coat and another promotion; then a third fur coat and a corner office; then an even better coat and ....")

(Continued)

	MILD HUNGER	LUST IN BALANCE	LUST OUT OF BALANCE	INDISCRIMINATE LUST
Planning	Low degree of planning for future.	Appropriate planning for future while enjoying and living in the present.	Getting ahead of oneself; mentally jumping ahead from present to future event, losing focus.	Inability to concentrate on the moment; excessive planning is beginning to self-destruct.
Concentration	Inability to concentrate on task at hand because of constant interruption by others and/or lack of internal purpose.	Life arranged so that concentration on task at hand is optimal; interruptions from within and without are minimal.	Concentration is fierce, even a little desperate, tension and do-or-die spirit beginning to interrupt effectiveness in task at hand.	Hell-bent-for-results attitude leads to frequent miscues, bad decisions, alienation of others.
Competition	Competition with others on basis of symbols and acquisitions.	Healthy competition with appropriate peers spurs and inspires you, is undertaken and expressed in such a way that neither party takes it personally.	More and more of self invested in more and more competition with others.	Everything is a contest, everyone a potential subject of envy.
Relaxation Is . . .	. . . an aim, sometimes an alibi, but often (and incomprehensibly) hard to achieve.	. . . a welcome reward for a good stretch of work; a valued source of energy replenishment.	. . . accompanied by guilt and unease, is more and more difficult to do.	. . . is impossible and senseless.

(Continued)

	MILD HUNGER	LUST IN BALANCE	LUST OUT OF BALANCE	INDISCRIMINATE LUST
Movement Toward Goals Is . . .	. . . ambling, listless, aimless.	. . . firm, smooth, straight.	. . . lurching, restless.	. . . pushy, grabby, stalking, often blindly singleminded, sometimes helter-skelter.
Things are Thought Through . . .	. . . when they absolutely have to be.	. . . most of the time.	. . . less and less these days.	". . . . . . What? There's no time to do that anymore!"
If You've Been Told You're "Missing" Something (A Trip to the New "in" Resort, A Promotion, Work Satisfaction, The Thrill of Hot-Air Ballooning . . .)	". . . then maybe it isn't for me."	". . . I'll have to think a bit to see if / really want it, despite its being touted by somebody else."	". . . then I have to have it! (And what's wrong with me that I don't?)"	"Give it to me—now!"

CHAPTER 11

Tailor-Making Your Agenda for Abundance: The One-Year Time Line for Real Results

All of life is arithmetic.

Barbara, a successful Minneapolis businesswoman, I met at a seminar, didn't know this not long ago. She earned $150,000 and spent $150,000 in the same year. She had just gone through a divorce and, she kept saying, was "in no condition" to "get around" to sitting down and concentrating on the details of her financial life. She did not have any emotional energy "left over" to learn how to manage her assets—to "go out of her way" to educate herself enough to know how to maximize, even perhaps double, them.

Those phrases I just wrapped in quotes lost Barbara thousands and thousands of dollars. By automatically relegating finance to the bottom rung of her agenda, she was shooting herself in the foot. She could go on forever making earnest, plausible-sounding excuses for not digging in and learning how to creatively harbor her money from runaway taxes; how to make aggressive, appropriately risky, high-payoff investments instead of safe, unimaginative, low-return ones, she could have made those excuses, but whom would she have been fooling? They would never have protected her from her own losses or changed the simple fact that all of life is arithmetic.

All of life is arithmetic.

This statement comes not from the lips of a banker but from those of a marvelously cultured and life-loving seventy-four-year-old woman. What she, my friend Lillian, meant by it—and what I mean when I repeat it—is not that money is the be-all and end-all of our lives. Such blindered obsession with money is Poverty Mentality at its utmost.

No, what is meant by that statement is that money—like air and love—is an absolutely essential, and at its best invisible, medium through which life is lived, and which determines our freedom and comfort in that life. Having money allows us to own our own time. It allows us to stop being preoccupied with survival—to stop being panicked about next week, next month, next year. Having money frees us from money: it allows us to get on with our lives without fretting about money on a day-to-day basis at all.

Think of it this way. When you have a toothache, all the other sensations and experiences in your life are shoved into back seats behind that nagging pain. Your whole range of options—your very consciousness—is at the mercy of that one throbbing nerve. All you can think of is your tooth. Your tooth becomes your whole world.

When the toothache goes away, life opens up again.

Having money is like not having a toothache.

Men have always known this. No man I know would dream of making those demurrals Barbara made when she got and spent that $150,000 those years ago. Men go for money. They put it where it belongs: at the top, not the bottom, of their agenda. They make career choices and changes, strategize for raises and promotions on the basis of the fact that all of life is arithmetic. When it's wise and appropriate for them to do so, they make present-for-future trade-offs, enduring long and expensive training and apprenticeships that will pay off in big careers later. And when it's wise and appropriate to do so, they make future-for-present trade-offs, deliberately going into debt in order to free up a cash flow to invest at high return now.

They know that the IRS is not God but is rather a bulky machine full of fallible nine-to-five workers. They know that good tax planning, like good gourmet cooking, requires sophisticated and deftly measured creativity. They know that accountants, bankers, stockbrokers and insurance agents are people you hire and direct. They watch their investments like a parent watching a child step off the curb. Crossing guard or not, they do not turn their backs until that child has safely reached the other side of the street.

Men are not smart at all things. But they are smart at this.

Let's get smart, too.

But first, let's get conscious; let's set our attitude right, so that we can better and more enthusiastically do what most of us are already—but apologetically and haphazardly—doing.

Just the other day, I was talking to a divorced Haver with a seventy-thousand-a-year media job, a fourteen-year-old daughter and two mountain properties which she rents out to supplement her income. She had just spent an hour telling me about her financial life when her face took on a look that told me she was growing uncomfortable and faintly guilty with the conversation. "I don't want you to get the wrong impression," she said. "The things I really care about have nothing to do with money."

This is absurd! And yet it is so maddeningly typical. Everything she cares deeply about has to do with money. The leisure time in which she is able to tend her herb garden, read her Proust, circulate petitions for arms control, listen to Mozart over fine wines with her friends; her daughter's health and happiness; her excellent education and devoted supervision by a first-rate caretaker during those hours when she is not home—all the quality and sensitivity, idealism and grace in this woman's life are not inimical to money but are made possible by it, advanced by it. In other words, not just some but all of life is arithmetic.

If only she knew that, she could have so much more. And so could most of us.

We cannot afford to feel ambivalent about, disinterested in or ignorant of our financial lives anymore. We cannot afford to blindly delegate. We are only begging exploitation when we do.

We also can't continue dwelling on the minutiae and ignoring the big picture. An accountant I know tells me that women are much more conscientious record keepers than men are, but that women don't analyze those figures they meticulously write down. And without analyzing, we can't get the larger projection we need to determine what to do next.

Neither do women challenge. A man will take a look at any amount of money on a bill—taxes, service charge, specialist's fee—

and think: "Hey, this is a rip-off!" or "What did this guy do to earn this from me?" or "How can I get around this, now or next time?" A woman takes the opposite tack. Oh, such a small amount . . . , she will think. Or: It's on my bill; I assume there's a good reason for it to be. In other words, the bottom-line thought is, Who am I to question the experts?

We have to stop taking this servile, scared, lazy and losing way out.

Barbara stopped and she's been seeing the changes. After a lifetime of delegating her financial affairs to others, she turned herself into a person who is in direct control of her financial team: the people (insurance broker, tax analyst, accountant, stockbroker, bankers) she hires to supply herself with additional expertise, not to do the work or make the decisions for her. Yes, it requires more work on her part. But everything, from her portfolio to her energy to her confidence, has shot up with this shift of perspective and action.

When women educate themselves to take control of those processes and institutions they once felt so beholden to; when they stop asking, "Who am I to challenge the experts?" whole systems change in their favor. We have all seen this happen twice in the last five years—overwhelmingly and nationwide: First, women changed mastectomy from a one- to a two-stage operation because enough of them got smart and said, "I refuse to let a doctor cut off my breast before I have been told the result of the biopsy. I demand to be conscious and alert when informed of his finding so I can make the decision about what he does next." And second, women changed hospital childbirth from the doctor-led, drug-accompanied process it used to be to a parent-orchestrated, natural procedure. "This is my body and my baby," the women said. "I know how to give birth; I will be in charge."

Imagine what will happen when we do with money what we just did with medicine. No more being hoodwinked by hidden-charge credit cards; no more passovers by employers for promotions or by headhunters for job opportunities. No more feeling intimidated by —and getting humored and talked down to by—financial institutions and the IRS, or by accountants, specialists, stockbrokers, brothers, fathers and husbands. No more staying in financial maintenance year after year after year. No more mere, plodding survival.

All of life is arithmetic. And you are the one standing at the blackboard adding up the figures, sitting at the computer terminal, punching the keys. Only you. You alone:

The most qualified person to be there.

THE AGENDA AND THE TIME LINE:
COMERS AND HAVERS, AND MOVING FROM WAITING
TO ACTION

Strategizing for more—making your agenda for abundance, as I call the process—means different things to Comers and to Havers. For Comers, the main challenge is getting enough to get more with: starting to save, leverage, invest, and bust out of the living-from-paycheck-to-paycheck cycle. For Havers, the task is to be smart and tough and creative with what you've got: not to siphon your savings or idle your career but to keep building both, while also keeping an eye on your emotional and spiritual abundance.

But whether you're a Comer or a Haver, you're probably what I call a *lady-in-waiting.* You wait. And wait and wait (often without knowing you're doing so) for opportunity, recognition, "word" to trickle down from some monetary Mount Olympus on what and how you should be investing. Comers—even the smartest ones— wait for some mystical hoist from the weekly circle of brute maintenance. ("I do what my friends do," says Chris, a witty, vital young woman you'll meet in more detail in a moment. "I love my work and my life and my freedom, and I have no interest in living through or being rescued by a man. I have all the intellectual answers to my psychology down pat." A pause. "And I'm still waiting for something to come along and magically pull me out of my financial panic.") Havers—again, even the smartest ones—wait to be taught or forced to do better what they could have been doing better all along. (A forty-year-old advertising executive named Donna, whose time line we'll explore later, says: "I can't believe it took me twenty years of my working life to realize: (a.) that I wasn't being promoted as fast as the men I work with and (b.) that despite the fact that I own a country home, I was giving a large chunk of my income to the federal government every year. It took my younger brother to look me in the eye like I was crazy and say, 'You mean you aren't tax-sheltering any of this?' before I saw the light.")

To get out of waiting, I've devised the time line. And it's a one-year time line because, I have found that when people make strategies for more than a year ahead of time they usually do not act on them. Only when you really have to start now to do now will you get things done. (Then, next year, those accomplishments will be the groundwork for your second one-year time line. Your long-term plan will be built, brick by real brick, instead of rendered, in full detail, on exquisite but vulnerable parchment.)

Here's how it works.

Starting with today as Day 1 and one year from today as Day 365, draw a year of your life as a straight line and crosshatch it at equally spaced intervals, to indicate months. You may also want to subdivide the year into four separate time lines of three months each, in order to be able to make your agenda in more detail. The basic timeline, and the four subdivisions, appear here as tables 10 and 11.

TABLE 10
THE ONE-YEAR TIME LINE

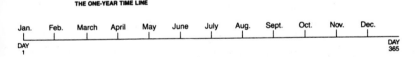

Establish your goals for the year. Do you perhaps want to (A.) receive a promotion, (B.) learn a foreign language so you can transfer or travel abroad and thus become more marketable and well-rounded, and (C.) move to a better apartment in a more desirable neighborhood?

Under each lettered goal, list every action, tactic and strategy you need to reach that goal. For Goal A, for example . . .

A. *To receive a promotion,* I'll have to:
1. Start attending more company meetings.
2. Take an executive training course.
3. Present memos on a regular basis—one every other month —to my unit supervisor, suggesting improvements.
4. Research the length of time and productivity of others who have recently been promoted from my current job to the one I want:

Table 11

THE ONE-YEAR TIME LINE BY QUARTERS

JANUARY	FEBRUARY	MARCH
APRIL	MAY	JUNE
JULY	AUGUST	SEPTEMBER
OCTOBER	NOVEMBER	DECEMBER

    a. Check with personnel.

    b. Take colleagues to lunch.

    c. Check with professional associations.

5. Be familiar with all the details of the job I want to be promoted to.

    a. Cultivate _____ as a mentor.

    b. Do research through professional associations.

    c. Subscribe to specialty publications and read books on the subject.

6. Demonstrate to my employer a familiarity and skill at that job by volunteering to do extra work on that department's projects.

    a. Get the schedule of that department's projects.

    b. Decide the one I want to volunteer for (and arrange my workload around it, accordingly).

    c. Do research on what that specific project entails, how it fared in the past, what its goals are, etc.

    d. Request the volunteer work in such a way that my knowledge of the project and my value to it will be recognized.

7. Ask for a promotion in the right way, at the right time.

Now, commit yourself to one day within your year—a logical, realistic day—when you will take each of these actions. With a large dot (•), schedule each of your strategies; make clear deadlines and appointments for them. (It is best to write the actions and strategies out beneath the dots; but in this example, to save space, I'll just code the strategy/action according to the preceding outline. See table 12.

TABLE 12
THE ONE-YEAR TIME LINE

Jan.	Feb.	March	April	May	June	July	Aug.	Sept.	Oct.	Nov.	Dec.
DAY 1	1 / 2 / 3	4a	5a / 3	4b	5b / 3	4c 6a 3	6b	6c	6d	3	5c	6	DAY 365

Finally, indicate, above the line, the changes you project in your income over the intervals. You can indicate this in real dollars or, if your income is derived from a combination of sources (salary, commission, rental revenue, stock dividends, etc.) that are in constant flux, by notations such as "down 10 percent" or "up 25

percent" from your monthly average income as of Day 1. In the
example we've been using, since the goal is promotion (and attendant raise) and since, for simplicity's sake, we're assuming this
person has no other income but her salary, the figure stays steady
until the very end, as illustrated in Table 13.

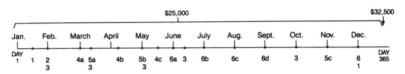

TABLE 13
THE ONE-YEAR TIME LINE – PROJECTED

With other agendas and time lines, though, there may be projected financial upgrading within the year. In still other agendas,
particularly of Havers, a woman may well choose and plan to go
into debt in the present, to make some divestiture or other trade-
off in order to go after a gain which won't be realized, in dollars
and cents, during the time-lined year. In this case, it's particularly
important to write these figures—"down 20 percent," "down
$400/month" (however you wish to indicate it) above your time
line—and look at them, and get used to them, and strategize to
make room for them in your budget and life-style. Only by under-
taking them with calm design and foresight will you stop being
scared by financial risks. And only when you stop being scared by
such risk-taking will you finally begin to make more.

This, then, is your PROJECTED TIME LINE: your map for action
and income for the year that starts today.

Now you have to follow that map.

So beneath the Projected Time Line, draw another line, as
shown in Table 14.

TABLE 14
THE ONE-YEAR TIME LINE – ACTUAL

Jan.	Feb.	March	April	May	June	July	Aug.	Sept.	Oct.	Nov.	Dec.

DAY
1
DAY
365

This is your ACTUAL TIME LINE.

Keep both time lines together in a drawer where you will not forget or overlook them. On the first day of every month, take them out and mark your actual progress with the strategies and actions you've outlined for yourself against your projected course. See if you've kept your deadlines and appointments for action.

Shelly, a corporate consultant I counselled, made a time line in June 1983 with the aim of relocating from Detroit to Atlanta, a goal that represented abundance to her on a number of levels but which would entail her trading-down financially for that first time-lined year. (She would be disbanding most of her projects in the Midwest in order to take on new ones in the Southeast.) She faced the financial trade-down and wrote and strategized around it in her time line. The time line itself consisted of actions and strategies that would enable her to eventually reap high returns, financial and otherwise.

On the next page—table 15—is what the first six months of Shelly's PROJECTED TIME LINE looked like:

TABLE 15
HALF-YEAR PROJECTED TIME LINE FOR SHELLY

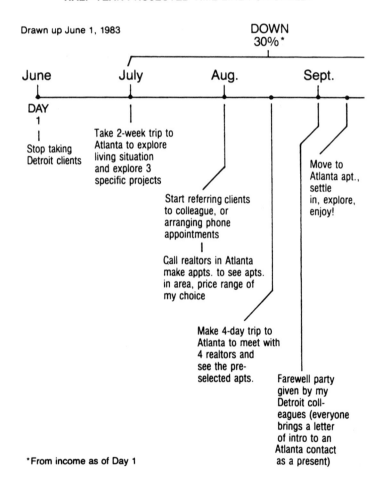

Drawn up June 1, 1983

DOWN
30%*

| June | July | Aug. | Sept. |

DAY
1

Stop taking
Detroit clients

Take 2-week trip to
Atlanta to explore
living situation
and explore 3
specific projects

Start referring clients
to colleague, or
arranging phone
appointments

Call realtors in Atlanta
make appts. to see apts.
in area, price range of
my choice

Make 4-day trip to
Atlanta to meet with
4 realtors and
see the pre-
selected apts.

Move to
Atlanta apt.,
settle
in, explore,
enjoy!

Farewell party
given by my
Detroit coll-
eagues (everyone
brings a letter
of intro to an
Atlanta contact
as a present)

*From income as of Day 1

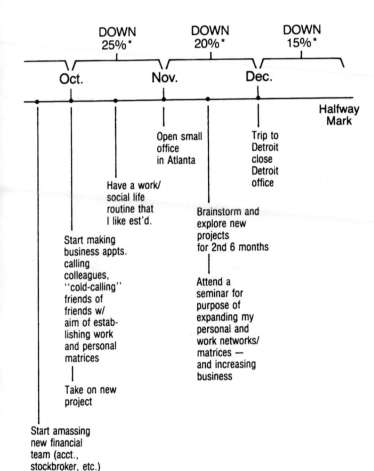

DOWN
25%*

DOWN
20%*

DOWN
15%*

Oct.   Nov.   Dec.

Halfway
Mark

Open small
office
in Atlanta

Trip to
Detroit
close
Detroit
office

Have a work/
social life
routine that
I like est'd.

Brainstorm and
explore new
projects
for 2nd 6 months

Start making
business appts.
calling
colleagues,
"cold-calling"
friends of
friends w/
aim of estab-
lishing work
and personal
matrices

Attend a
seminar for
purpose of
expanding my
personal and
work networks/
matrices —
and increasing
business

Take on new
project

Start amassing
new financial
team (acct.,
stockbroker, etc.)

Shelly kept the time line in her desk drawer, consulted it every month and filled in her ACTUAL TIME LINE just beneath it. By the end of that first half year, Table 16 shows what the two lines looked like.

TABLE 16
HALF-YEAR TIME LINE

PROJECTED

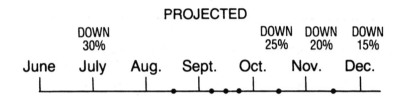

ACTUAL

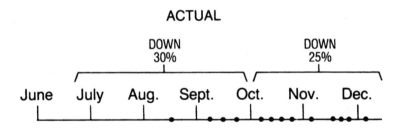

As you can see, Shelly stayed pretty much on course. Financially, she fell a little behind of her projection (moving to a new city always entails expenses hidden from even foresightful planning) but added some strategies and actions (those dots toward the end of the ACTUAL line) to bring her back to her projection in the second six months.

You can learn a lot by comparing the dots on your two time lines. Try, for a moment, to see nothing but those dots when you look at the time line. If the length of line between dots on both lines is short, you are probably in Hope rather than in Vacant Hope or Hopelessness. You take action. You strategize and follow through with appropriate speed and with a realistic sense of self and possibility. But if there's a disparity between the lines—if there are

TABLE 17
TIME-LINE MARKING

PROJECTED

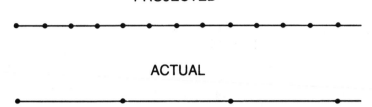

ACTUAL

short lengths between dots on the PROJECTED line but long lengths on the ACTUAL—you may well be in Vacant Hope. You unrealistically expect to do more things, and faster, than you are actually inclined or prepared to do. And if your ACTUAL line is virtually uninterrupted, you may be in Hopelessness: unable to muster any but the most minimal energy to plan and take action at all.

In helping dozens of Comers and Havers make their year-time-lined agendas for abundance, I have come to identify 19 guidelines. Some apply more to Havers, others apply more to Comers, some apply across the board. Of these 19, by far the most universal and constantly applicable are what I call:

THE BIG THREE GUIDELINES TO ABUNDANCE

1. *Start with your satisfactions; let them determine your Lifestyle Priorities and make trade-offs on the basis of that.*

"What do you love?" Remember when I asked that question of the ambivalent Comer in Chapter 3? At the time, I was using the question, as I often do, to force up some passion—some lust—through the thick ice of apathy.

Now I'm asking it in a different way. "What do you most love and need in your life?" I want you to consider. Think about it. Because you will never fulfill your agenda for abundance—on time or even behind time—if you're setting about to do something you don't want to do in the first place—or if, in the process of strategizing for something you do want to do, you're sacrificing one of your most essential gratifications.

Very simply, you have to start by listening to your feelings. Is getting this promotion something you really desire or is it something you feel you "ought" to want (when, in fact, what you're really yearning for is to change careers, or to take a year off and have a child, paint, travel)? Before we embark on a course of action—any course of action—we must be careful not to cut off the one barometer, our feelings, that tells us if something is right for us or not.

Your satisfactions, translated now into your life-style priorities, are important in guiding the course of your agenda. Take something as relatively small as taxis versus walking and public transportation. Some women I know find taxis indispensable: they can get ten minutes of work done in the back of a cab; or they can kick off their shoes, close their eyes and get the same amount of refreshing relaxation or meditation in; and, while in taxis, they regularly do both of these things. So for them, the money spent on taxis is not a frivolity but a valuable investment, a priority that feeds directly into their productivity and, hence, into their abundance.

But for other women, taxis not only are a needless expense but also deprive them of the energization they feel from walking and from the direct contact with the public that they need so much for their work. The money that these women save by not taking taxis is doubled by what earning-power advantages walking and public transportation indirectly provides them with.

Once you begin to see things this way, you can strip your life of a lot of dead-weight, outgrown or false priorities and take a faster path to abundance.

Shelly recently liberated herself from two outgrown priorities, the need to buy expensive silk shirts and the need to live in a large apartment. At a certain point over the last few years, Shelly started feeling comfortable enough with who she was and what she had achieved not to need the status value of both of those things, and not to want the nuisance and expense of their maintenance. So she's changed her shopping habits and scaled down her living quarters (to a much more manageable studio) and funneled her profits, in time and money, into the move to Atlanta and those services (housekeeper, taxis, secretary, hairdresser) that feed directly into her agenda for abundance.

2. *Break through the concrete wall and educate yourself.*

Sometimes it feels like a concrete wall: your conditioning against money-consciousness, your lack of interest in finance, your fear of math, your thirty-year-long neglect of the stock market columns, your hewing to a schedule that honors such leisure-time activities as exercise, novels, quiche-making and crossword puzzles but has absolutely no place for a course on tax shelters.

Push through that concrete wall and, against all habit and alibi and inclination, educate yourself about money: how it operates in your life and in your world. Quite simply, you will never get anywhere in your pursuit of abundance until you do.

Start reading the financial page of your newspapers and the financial columns in news magazines, even if you have to rise an extra half hour in the morning to do so. (You'd relinquish that half hour's sleep to go jogging or to squeeze in an "essential" hair appointment or to take an early plane to a resort, wouldn't you?) Take courses at your local high school night school, nearby college's continuing education programs; attend the seminars so frequently sponsored now by women's groups, brokerage houses and banks. Buy books. Some of the best and clearest are mentioned in the next chapter.

Arrange a mentorship from the one person you know who is the smartest and most conscious about money; trade a skill or service of your own in return. Or pay the person for these lessons. (Staying in the Poverty Mentality is thinking you don't have to pay for the services you receive.) Work at developing your money articulateness as you would at learning a new language. Fight the slideback to money ignorance and apathy as you would fight the urge to take "just one puff" once you've just kicked the nicotine habit. Ignorance of money *is* a habit you can kick.

And it's a widespread habit, affecting both Comers and Havers. Chris, whom I mentioned before and whose time line is coming up momentarily, speaks for many Comers when she says: "At about age thirteen, I started assuming money was something *les outres*— the others, the money experts and the hired money servants— would do. I was elitist in two contradictory senses: in acting as if money were too banal and boring for me and in mystifying it to such an extent that those who did take care of it came to constitute an elite in my mind.*

And many women who have made it to Haver status practice what I call selective ignorance of money. Phoebe, an investment banker whose time line appears later in this chapter, gave a seminar on tax shelters to a high-powered group of businesswomen. "When I told them they were in the 50 percent tax bracket, most of them were dazed and incredulous," she reports. "They knew everything else about life except *that!*"

Education has a special importance to the partnered woman. To her I say, push past the inclination to lean on your husband for advice, to do what he says with your money. Get yourself so educated that you can say: "I know we can get a better return on our investment by buying a house instead of by buying bonds, as you are proposing we do. Listen to me and I'll explain my strategy and how we can put the money here instead of there."

3. *Follow the money.*

That was the advice Deep Throat kept giving Washington *Post* reporters Woodward and Bernstein, until they uncovered the Watergate coverup. In other, broader ways, it's good advice for all of us. "Follow the money" means several things along the Comer-to-Haver continuum:

- "Follow the money," according to my friend financial consultant Russell Pearson, means, for the Comer, "making your career choices starting from the outside." He explains: "Find out where the money is—in what fields, what industries, what subspecialties, what parts of the country. Then look to your interests and try to make a 'good marriage' between them. Those are the two things you need: the likelihood of high payoff and your enthusiasm. Training, the third component, you can always buy."

How do you follow the money this way? Do research. Send for state and federal labor department brochures and surveys which define growth industries and promising fields five and ten years from now. Call professional associations and read professional publications to understand salaries and employment supply and demand. Read futurist magazines: *Omni, The Future* and others, and financial publications such as *Forbes, Fortune* and *The Wall Street Journal.* If this seems like a lot to do, stop and realize that we are

---

* We'll get to the *de*mystification of these "moneylords" in the next chapter.

talking about the path you will take for the rest of your life and in what degree of comfort or discomfort you will live. Isn't that worth a broad, energetic canvassing of possibilities?

- Once you've followed the money in this way and have located a field you would like that is promising, follow the money further by following the top people in that field. Go to the library and read about your chosen field, industry, career. Make a list of the top ten people or companies in it and write them each a persuasive letter asking for an apprenticeship position, an internship, an entry-level job. That's how many people get jobs with dynamic creative people and teams. You have nothing to lose—and even if you don't get a job, you acquire some wonderfully encouraging rejection letters.

- Once you've become a Haver and have some money to invest, "follow the money" means watch your money move and direct that movement. Adopt a hands-on approach to your finances. Sit down with your accountant and do the arithmetic together. Select a stock on your own, not on the basis of your broker's advice; invest in it, and follow it *daily* for a month. If you come out ahead, do it again, putting a higher amount of money on the line. Necessity breeds attention: the more indispensable your concentration on the stock market becomes to your own monetary welfare, the more you will concentrate. And the more you will learn. Once you get going, you might even want to take the courses offered by the Securities Training Institute, which, though it caters to professionals in training, also admits the lay public.

Now that we've covered the three universal guidelines, let's move on to the seventeen further ones and see how they apply in real life. Here are the cases of four individual women—from low-income, starting-out Comer to high-income, starting-to-reassess Haver. One of these women is probably not unlike you.

COMER I, 28 YEARS AND $23,000: WRESTING SOME LEVERAGE POTENTIAL OUT OF A BARE-BONES BUDGET

Chris is an assistant to a top lecture-tour booker. She has a warm wit, a sophisticated sensibility, a joy for living and exquisite literary

and musical taste. Unfortunately, with a take-home income of only
$1,200 a month, she is almost always broke.

This didn't bother Chris too very much until, last spring, she
bicycled through Greece with a friend. She fell in love with the
experience; it became, quite suddenly, essential. She wanted to
bicycle through other countries, regularly. For this, of course, she
would need money.

That's when she came to see me.

We started by making the two crucial lists that everyone making
a time-lined agenda for abundance should start out with:

SATISFACTIONS/LIFE-STYLE PRIORITIES	BUDGET
1. The Life of the Mind (intellectual stimulation and activity, access to culture)	Monthly income: $1,200, net Savings accounts: None Property, stocks, assets: None
2. Eventually starting my own lecture bureau	$ 450 Rent (her share of a $900 apt., w/garden)
3. Closeness to nature: a garden to tend and enjoy, frequent trips to the country	150 Credit card payments 300 Food and entertainment 50 Dental and medical 100 Transportation (mostly public)
4. Close friendships	100 Clothes and makeup
5. Bicycling through various countries	50 Books $1,200 TOTAL SPENT

The challenges were clear. Since her satisfactions alternated
high-idealism pursuits (Nos. 1, 3 and 4 on the list) with pursuits that
depended on money and ambition (Nos. 2 and 5), we had to demonstrate that the two sets of goals were not unrelated but were
rather actually interindependent, making each other possible. We
had to forge an agenda that laced the two sets of goals together in a
cooperative pattern that would not only work for the short term
but drive home to Chris the "friendliness" of money and ambition
to her other aims and desires.

And we had to break into the closed circle of no-savings, no-investing, no-leveraging that her budget constituted and find some way to begin to build.

Taking the second challenge first, we moved on to abundance guideline No. 4 and worked to:

4. *Find the most elastic expense on your budget, and tighten the reins.*

"Rent" and "Books" were not elastic, because having a garden and establishing a personal library were key satisfactions (Chris's life-style priorities Nos. 2 and 1). But food and entertainment, a roomy one quarter of her monthly expenses, looked promising. By analyzing a typical month's expenses in that area, Chris found she could save forty dollars a month. At last, a start!

But because it was a small-scale start, and one accomplished at some sacrifice, I suggested that Chris take that forty dollars a month and—

5. *Practice transparent money leveraging and play "tricks of the mind."*

Transparent leveraging means making money on your money in such a way that you can't interfere with the process because, in a sense, you "forget" about it. The monthly, recurrent "decision" to save is taken out of your hands. Having the designated amount automatically deducted from your checking account every month and deposited into a savings account is one good way now offered by many banks.

Well before banks started offering this service, canny people did it on their own. My friend Lillian calls this procedure "playing tricks of the mind," and she swears by it. For example, when she had just moved out on her own after college, she bought a radio on installment payments of $33.13 a month. The figure had such a sonorous ring that it stuck in her mind long after the radio was fully paid for. So she continued to write a monthly check in that amount. But this time, she put it into her savings account. Fifteen years later, she opened the Pandora's box of that effortlessly afforded, "forgotten" account and got a trip to Paris out of it.

Still, cleverly saving money goes just so far. High-potential, tight-budget Comers like Chris have to increase their incomes. And can—much faster than they think. To this end, I worked with her to strategize four steps, the first of which is guideline No. 6.

6. *Practice job leveraging: negotiate for a raise or promotion by expanding an expandable job.*

Many professions, particularly those in the service and media areas, offer great, though sometimes hidden, opportunity for expansion. You simply find a way to move the company's business upward or outward, while at the same time getting yourself credited and remunerated according to the new work and responsibility such expansion creates for you.

Chris's speakers' bureau booked authors, musicians and academics to speak at colleges and at civic and women's groups, at conferences, forums and the like. There were always more available speakers than venues. Why not create more demand for the abundant supply by following the money? I suggested. Might there be a new, untapped audience for these speakers in the burgeoning, and very wealthy, high-tech industries? The newspapers had recently featured stories on stress and burnout suffered by the highly competitive, one-dimensional workaholics in places like Silicon Valley. "Ah," Chris laughed back. "Culture soothes the savage computer executive's breast. 'Living Software for Hard-Lived Lives.'" Then she stopped laughing. Her face filled with surprised delight as the brainstorm, improbable as it had sounded only seconds before, began to take deeper and more logical hold.

She began to map her strategies for educating herself on the high-tech industries, for fashioning a successful appeal to them, for finding out who were the people to go to in the major companies, for drawing up a proposal on the idea for her employer. The deadlines for all of these tasks would be written into her projected time line.

We'll discuss job leveraging in more detail in Chapter 12, "Interindependence: Negotiating for Help." But the important thing to remember right now is, it all starts with creative brainstorming, with going back to guideline No. 3 and following the money, and with the conviction that your idea can make the company better.

But along with leveraging through her workplace, I thought Chris could leverage on her own. We explored ways that she could, following abundance guideline No. 7:

7. *Develop a dormant skill into a money maker.*

Chris could write and think very concisely, thoughtfully, ironically. And she had access to famous and important thinkers. What if she went along with one of these speakers on a particularly dramatic, controversial or touching engagement: a left-wing economist to a Moral Majority–affiliated debate, a flutist teaching music to handicapped children? Might not the event and her skill combine and ignite, producing a piece of reportage that could be the beginning of a sideline or second career as a writer?

Finally, we turned to the last important task on Chris's agenda:

8. *Strengthen the weak link in your mastery chain for long-term career leveraging.*

Chris's strengths in her job were in dealing with people, dealing with ideas, writing and nurturing. She could skillfully match a speaker to an audience, clearly and provocatively synopsize that speaker's work in brochure form and make sure she was happy when she traveled to the engagement.

But, particularly in light of her new plan to expand the business, she had to get better at money. Strategizing toward this end became an important part of her time line, which appears on the following page (Table 18).

COMER II, TWENTY-NINE YEARS OLD AND $35,000: CAPITALIZING HER OWN PROJECTS, BALANCING OPTIONS, STAYING OPEN TO CHANGE

Mindy is an independent filmmaker with a successful low-budget documentary to her credit and a specialized skill in film production with which she can market herself, to the tune of five hundred dollars a week, even though she loathes the work.

Like Chris, Mindy is of the generation of women who grew up not expecting to lean on or live through a man. Like Chris, she's idealistic, intellectual, full of up-to-the-minute taste. But unlike Chris, she incorporated money consciousness into the mix of her life right after college. She knew she wanted to make films, and she knew it took money to do so. Out of this knowledge, she did several important things, all of which constitute the next several abundance guidelines, starting with:

9. *Allow yourself to sight—and strike—Targets of Opportunity.*

During wartime, when a bomber pilot is unable to strike his planned target because of weather or other conditions, he is given a choice of secondary targets to strike, for similar tactical results. These are called Targets of Opportunity.

I'm not usually fond of the language of war, but when my friend business strategist David Stone mentioned this phrase—Target of

TABLE 18
PROJECTED TIME LINE FOR CHRIS

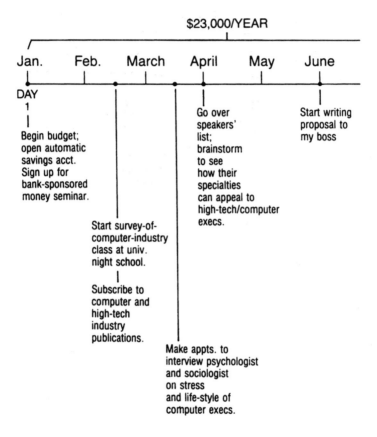

$23,000/YEAR

| Jan. | Feb. | March | April | May | June |

DAY 1

Begin budget; open automatic savings acct. Sign up for bank-sponsored money seminar.

Start survey-of-computer-industry class at univ. night school.

Subscribe to computer and high-tech industry publications.

Go over speakers' list; brainstorm to see how their specialties can appeal to high-tech/computer execs.

Start writing proposal to my boss

Make appts. to interview psychologist and sociologist on stress and life-style of computer execs.

ACTUAL TIME LINE FOR CHRIS

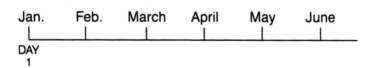

| Jan. | Feb. | March | April | May | June |

DAY 1

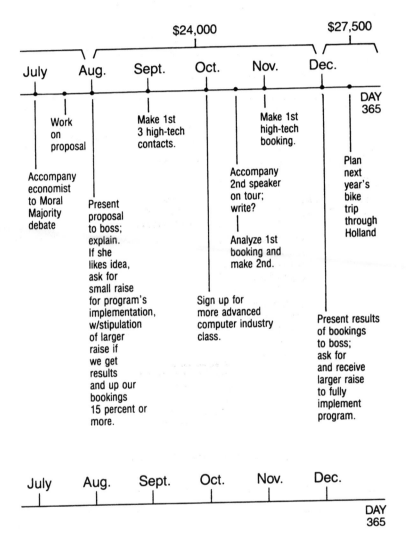

$24,000

$27,500

July Aug. Sept. Oct. Nov. Dec.

DAY 365

Work on proposal

Make 1st 3 high-tech contacts.

Make 1st high-tech booking.

Accompany economist to Moral Majority debate

Present proposal to boss; explain. If she likes idea, ask for small raise for program's implementation, w/stipulation of larger raise if we get results and up our bookings 15 percent or more.

Accompany 2nd speaker on tour; write?

Analyze 1st booking and make 2nd.

Sign up for more advanced computer industry class.

Plan next year's bike trip through Holland

Present results of bookings to boss; ask for and receive larger raise to fully implement program.

July Aug. Sept. Oct. Nov. Dec.

DAY 365

Opportunity—I realized how perfectly it adapts to describe those serendipitous events that pop up in our lives and our careers which, with just a little work and nerve and imagination, can comprise perfect detour routes to a goal whose achievement has just been thwarted.

When Mindy and her college filmmaking partner left the Midwest to move to Los Angeles, their efforts to start financing a film of their own were met by expectable adversity: they were young, unknown, untried, unconnected. Their efforts at finding a nice, cheap apartment on the city's desirable West Side were similarly thwarted.

Then, through a conversation they happened on at a party, they heard that the downtown industrial area bordering Little Tokyo was just beginning to be inhabited by a few hardy artists, who were converting the large spaces for mixed professional and residential use. Loft leases in these forlorn buildings on these unimagined-as-residential streets could be purchased for extremely low key money and the rents on these still bare and unlivable quarters were low.

But a little renovation could make them habitable; and a lot of renovation could make them attractive, should Los Angeles ever go the way of Manhattan, where industrial areas were gentrifying at breakneck speed and quadrupling (sometimes even septupling) in worth. Most people guessed that essentially suburban/outdoors-oriented Los Angeles would never go the route of industrial-chic New York. But Mindy and her partner knew they had nothing to lose, and everything to gain, by making the opposite, long-shot guess.

So they turned from two thwarted targets—film financing and good, cheap housing—and struck one Target of Opportunity that provided them with just what they wanted from those first two: they borrowed money to buy one loft to fix up and live in; then, two years later, borrowed more money to buy a second, adjacent, loft to fix up even more and sublet for profit. Two years after that they borrowed more money to buy and sublet a third.

The result? Just last year, their unlikely area took off as a newly desirable residential neighborhood for adventurous, space-seeking young professionals. Mindy and her partner now have ample living and working space and enough revenue, as landlords, to help finance a second film. (The interim revenue, over the past six years, helped them finance their lower-budget first film.) To do all of this, of course, they had to learn quite a bit about Los Angeles real estate law and practice, construction, maintenance and the fine art of landlording, but it was well worth it. There are Targets of Opportunity in every woman's career path. It just takes determined vision to sight them, and a little effort and research to strike them.

Interpreted in a broader sense, Targets of Opportunity exist everywhere in our lives, as tributaries off the river that rushes us along to our main goal. Make an effort to see and seize those tributary opportunities, those little trickle shoots off the principle course you have struck for yourself. Too many women, their noses earnestly (sometimes nervously) to the grindstone of new careerism, mistakenly dismiss such offshoot opportunities as "distractions." They think they're being focussed when they're really just blindering their eyes, as a farmer would a plough horse, to ways of getting to their goal faster.

So look out the sides of your eyes. Understand, too, that opportunity can be hidden from you by your pride. One Haver credits her leap from low-level managerial job to the high six figures to the simple act of abandoning pride to take an opportunity with high learning potential. An executive in her company came into her office one day, said that a major meeting was starting in a few minutes and that his secretary had just taken ill. Would she take the minutes instead?

She could have called him a chauvinist, gotten indignant and stayed, for the next ten years, at her thirty-five-thousand-a-year job. Instead, she was intrigued by the opportunity to sit witness at a meeting of the company's top executives—to eavesdrop, as it were, on power. Refusing to let her ego get in the way of success, she agreed: she took the minutes, then did all the attendant research involved in making sense of the financial jargon. The educational process—and the access to power—was worth its weight in gold. Armed with her new resources, she propelled herself on a course of action that eventually took her to where she is today.

Getting back to Mindy now: in buying and subletting the lofts, she was also doing two other things, which can be summarized in the next two guidelines:

10. *Maintain cross-leverage with other Comers.*
Mindy and her friend from film school went out into the world

thinking of themselves as full business partners. They collaborated artistically and technically on their own films, using their different but compatible skills and viewpoints to make a better film than either could have made on her own. They shared rent as roommates and coinvested in the lofts, thus leveraging together at half the cost it would have taken them to leverage separately.

They negotiate smoothly with each other for their mutual tradeoffs of privacy versus revenue (e.g., sometimes living as roommates in one loft while the second is sublet for profit that's funneled back into their film; at other times, when it works better for their work, they opt for the privacy afforded by separate living spaces). They take turns free-lancing at their respective film-related crafts, one bringing in outside money while the other spends her days working full time on the film.

This is sophisticated, complex partnership and collaboration that works for both of them on four levels: the artistic, the commercial, the financial, the domestic.

Men have always known how banding together as partners during early Comer years is a key ingredient to success: for the partners as a team and, later if they wish, for them individually. Look at Martin and Lewis, Woodward and Bernstein, Simon and Garfunkel, Lennon and McCartney. Look at almost every law, advertising and public relations firm in your phone book.

Women are just beginning to see and make use of the tremendous tool of cross-leveraging with a trusted Comer partner, particularly one whose strengths and contacts augment your own. One woman I know was helped in getting a college scholarship by her roommate, and later dealt that roommate into a new division of an advertising agency she was heading up. Last year, each woman— at twenty-six years old—pulled a $150,000 salary out of their remarkably successful joint venture.

11. *See yourself as your own company—and invest in yourself.*

Free-lancers such as Mindy come to this realization more naturally than others because it is literally rather than figuratively true. But *all* women—all people—in the marketplace (or, in fact, at home) should realize: I am my own company because I am selling my own time.

Once you see yourself as your own company, you see things more pragmatically, more clearly. You take courses and seminars, read books, make contacts, select your wardrobe and maintain your person, take your vacations on the basis not just of your satisfactions but on the R.O.I.: return on your investment—in yourself. You stop sighing, "But all that computer hype bores me, and you start saying, "If it's true that using a word processor can double my output and earnings, then it's certainly worth looking into."

Seeing herself as her own company, Mindy is going to take classes in film editing, a more reliably marketable skill than that of the public relations with which she now makes her money. Seeing herself as her own company, Mindy refuses to rest on her laurels, to be lulled into complacency by Fans who think it's so terrific that she's gone so far so fast. Seeing herself as her own company, Mindy bought the third loft partly because, with the adjacent other two, it could eventually serve well as a small film studio.

Still, the final crucial guideline that Mindy illustrates is her pragmatic willingness to let that last dream go.

12. *Be willing to let go of what you love, to "trade up" for greater gain.*

Although Mindy is now living in this third, and her favorite, loft, and she has it furnished to her taste, she would consider selling it within six months if it would be in her greater interest to do so. "Right now," she reasons, "my partner and I are property-rich and cash-poor. If I want to get financing for the next stage of our film, the fact that we're able to sublet this loft for seventeen hundred dollars a month means nothing to a bank; but our having fifty thousand dollars (the resale value of the loft leasehold) in cash in a C.D. would qualify us for a loan."

Trading up, Mindy knows, means making certain trade-offs. With the same logic with which you throw things over the side of a lifeboat so it can get to the shore faster, you have to forget sentimentality and scuttle attachments (as long as they're not critical attachments) fast when the opportunity for long-term gain arises.

Given this consideration, Mindy's time line reflects her contingencies, her options and her well-worked-out partnership (Table 19).

TABLE 19
PROJECTED TIME LINE FOR MINDY

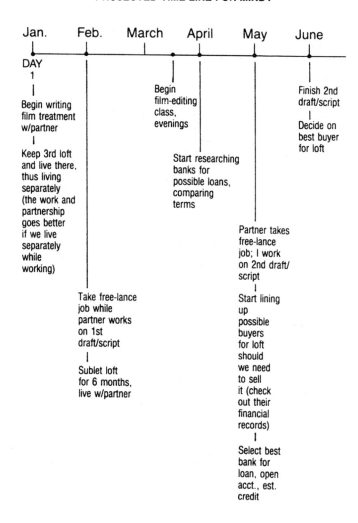

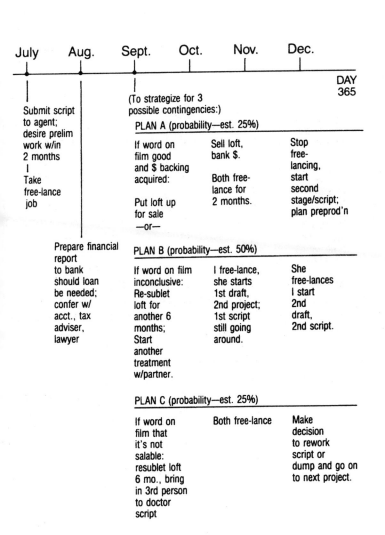

July	Aug.	Sept.	Oct.	Nov.	Dec.

DAY 365

Submit script to agent; desire prelim work w/in 2 months

Take free-lance job

Prepare financial report to bank should loan be needed; confer w/ acct., tax adviser, lawyer

(To strategize for 3 possible contingencies:)

PLAN A (probability—est. 25%)

If word on film good and $ backing acquired:

Put loft up for sale
—or—

Sell loft, bank $.

Both free-lance for 2 months.

Stop free-lancing, start second stage/script; plan preprod'n

PLAN B (probability—est. 50%)

If word on film inconclusive: Re-sublet loft for another 6 months; Start another treatment w/partner.

I free-lance, she starts 1st draft, 2nd project; 1st script still going around.

She free-lances I start 2nd draft, 2nd script.

PLAN C (probability—est. 25%)

If word on film that it's not salable: resublet loft 6 mo., bring in 3rd person to doctor script

Both free-lance

Make decision to rework script or dump and go on to next project.

HAVER I: FORTY YEARS OLD AND $70,000 A YEAR: CATCHING UP, MOVING FASTER, TAKING RISKS

When Donna's brother made the incredulous remark I reported several pages back about her ignoring the 50 percent of her income that went right to the government, the shock of her inaction changed her life. "All those years I was so good at making money for my ad agency," she realized, "but I never thought of doing the same for myself!" Like so many women, she had separate financial agendas—an aggressive, informed one for business; a passive, uninformed one for her personal life.

She vowed to put an end to that disparity. From that day forward, she steeped herself in financial books and courses, determined never again to give that kind of money away, never again not to know where the money was going. Now, two years later, she's holding on to more of her money, the initial phase of her catch-up has yielded her 20 percent more per year, just from smart tax sheltering. (Tax shelters, as we will learn in the next chapter, range from a simple IRA or Keogh plan to municipal bonds to investments in certain commodities—natural gasses are one—that allow you to defer your tax on gains.) She did this by taking steps that comprise the next two guidelines:

13. *Get out of the caution zone. Don't be afraid to go into debt.* Playing it safe is not playing it smart.

The way to get ahead of the game—once (a.) you are not jeopardizing your own or your family's immediate interests by doing so, and (b.) you have educated yourself enough to make good, discriminating decisions—is to go into debt so you have a cash flow to invest for higher return than you'd get if you didn't go into debt.

Take risks appropriate to your circumstances, your responsibilities and your goals.

Donna is single, does not and will not have children. She owns a country house; her job is secure. Her goal is to build a strong capital base and to continue to educate herself in money and experiment, in order to make increasingly exciting, creative and lucrative investments.

Donna recently dismissed an accountant who used to caution her, "But you could get audited for those expense account write-offs," and hired one who says, "So what if you do get audited? All you have to do is pay what you owe, plus a penalty, that's all." She agrees with this second man's attitude; just two years ago she timorously agreed with the first.

All the very high incomed Haver women I've talked to say they got where they are by, as one puts it, "getting out of the caution zone," by very informed risk-taking.

14. *Maintain cross-leverage with other Havers.*

Donna bought a country house with a good friend five years ago; it's doubled in value now.

Donna formed a professional women's network with friends and colleagues in related fields, then broadened it to include women in disparate fields. The trading of expertise, contacts and favors, the consolidation of power and clout, has helped everyone many times over.

Buy a piece of real estate with one or more other women in your position, if you can afford it. Even if you have only five hundred or a thousand dollars to invest, round up several others who have the same amount available, decide on the right investment and go to a lawyer to draw up limited-partnership papers. Watch your money grow, as Donna has. In addition, as she did:

15. *Get bored with being grateful. Don't let loving your job keep you from having more.*

"But I love what I do," women reason when someone tells them they've been underpaid or have stayed at their level longer than necessary. "I'm so grateful to have my job/an agency that is so pleasant to work for/to have had the opportunity, four years ago, to have come up from assistant. I'm so grateful . . ."

And I am so bored with all that gratitude!

You get bored with it, too. Because, really, after the first time you say it or think it, it has no further use in your life except to keep you down.

It's wonderful to love and appreciate your job.

But you can always love and appreciate it a little more at a higher income level.

As she began educating herself about money and making smart investments and sheltering arrangements, Donna did a logical mental segue: just as it suddenly seemed so sensible to make more money with her money, it also seemed sensible to make more career with her career. Yes, she enjoyed—and was respected as excellent at—her account executive position. But why stop there?

"I want a vice-presidency," she came to me saying. "If I had realized that five years ago, I would probably be only two years away from that position now."

"You can still get there, almost as fast," I told her. To that end, she would need to take Step 16.

16. *Focus squarely on your Purpose with the help of the four D's.*

Donna's purpose was to attain the vice-presidency as quickly as she could. For that she needed not to be more competent or effective in her current post (she was already that, and praised for it) but to be more political, to attain more visibility in her field, to demonstrate her value as a figurehead as well as an administrator. All of this involved altering her off-hours life (whom she entertained, where she summered, what committees and organizations she joined and how active she became in them) as much as, if not more than, her on-the-job life. The challenge was to do this in a way that didn't violate her privacy, her own personal style or her time.

And the answer, as it often is, was to hack away at misused or runaway hours in her week, hours she spent doing burdensome and needless errands instead of using for her enjoyment and career advancement.

I suggested that Donna start each week with a four-column list—

DELAY   DELEGATE   DUMP   DO

moving from left to right—and slot tasks, errands and obligations into whichever column made the most sense in terms of moving toward her purpose of attaining the vice-presidency fast (with care given not to slight her life-style priorities and satisfactions). She "got rid of" most of what turned out to be her unnecessary, time-wasting tasks by the time she got to the DO column.

Donna's projected time line for the year focused on this, her main goal, as well as on two other goals: (1) establishing wider personal and business matrices; and (2) working toward a capital base with which to do creative financial investing.

(For the sake of moving along faster, and because I think you understand the time-line concept by now, I'm going to dispense with the time lines in this and the following case.)

HAVER II: FORTY-SIX YEARS OLD AND $350,000 A YEAR: PLAYING HARDBALL WITHOUT BEING HARD

Two and a half years ago, Phoebe lost her senior vice-presidency at a brokerage house because, as she puts it, "I ran a $30 million business and the man above me was stupid—and I let people know I thought so." She assumed that her sheer skill in maximizing assets would protect her from reprisal. She was wrong. She was, she sees now, doing what so many Haver women do: talking hard instead of playing hard—unnecessarily (and undiplomatically) telling what her sheer actions could have been far more effectively showing.

That firing and her subsequent regrouping illustrate the next three abundance guidelines, starting with:

17. *Learn to be graciously strong.*

Playing hardball means conducting business with what I call "gracious strength." This means cleanly, clearly, confidently doing —instead of shuffling, whining, cajoling for, bragging about, fuming over, bitching about, threatening or planning to do. Gracious strength is saying, "We are going to do it this way," with a strong voice, a straight spine, no question mark at the end of the sentence or search for approval in the eyes, a firm handshake, a calm, gracious smile and a prompt turn on the heels.

Gracious strength is a crucial part of playing hardball, and playing hardball is the business equivalent of dealing logical consequences, which we discussed in Chapter 5. It's speaking softly but firmly and carrying, via your demeanor and strategy and results, a big stick.

Phoebe was determined to use gracious strength at her second job. After her first eighteen months of hard work, she presented her growth figures to the president. She calmly and undefensively requested a raise—and promptly got it. She's been doing the same at six-month intervals ever since.

In order to make her quick recoup after the firing, Phoebe had to:

18. *Understand it's all right to let life be lived in the Balanced Imbalance for a while.*

We all want balance in our lives. But sometimes you have to go out of balance for a while in order to get what you want now, the getting of which will allow you to strike a better long-term balance later. This form of life planning is what I call the Balanced Imbalance. By its design, the texture of life is seen not as a static, here-and-now proposition (each day is 50 percent work, 25 percent relationship, 25 percent play) but is extended over time (these twelve months are 80 percent work; 20 percent relationship and play; the *next* twelve months will be a gradual re-equilibration in the other direction). In the Balanced Imbalance, you're arriving at well-roundedness over time.

For the year and a half it took her to reach her two-year-marked goal, Phoebe was mostly work, little relationship and play—just as, in reverse, some (though by no means all) women strike the opposite proportion—mostly relationship, little career—when they take time off from work to be with a newborn. But living in the Balanced Imbalance brings with it the responsibility to yourself to:

19. *Diligently watch for signs of imbalance.*

Phoebe came to me right after those eighteen months of career recoup. Her raise was secured. She had doubled her company's business. "I won," she said. Her voice was triumphant. Her face looked depleted.

Now it was time to recoup what that winning had lost her.

I had Phoebe buy red, green and blue felt-tip pens. For a week, she would keep a detailed daily journal, listing everything she did on lined legal pad. The items for a typical day took up two sheets of the paper, twenty-four inches in all.

At the end of the week, she was to strike a column-length vertical line (/) to the left of each item in the applicable color: red for things related to work; blue for things related to relationship; green for things related to creativity or play.

She was to add up the inches of red, of blue and of green.

Of her total of 170 inches of colored line, a full 87 of those inches were red. She was, in other words, giving twice as much time to work as she gave to play and to people combined.

"Reverse the ratio," I told her, "and we have the beginning of your agenda for the next year."

We fashioned a time line for Phoebe that started with this radical shift of balance for the first three months, to give her immediate relief from impending burnout; then gradually re-equilibrated her life to end up with a 60 percent work/40 percent people and play balance by Day 365. The projected net income loss (in commissions) was 15 percent, but it was well worth it in peace and sanity. She was trading off money for emotional, mental and physical gains. (As a high Haver, the trade-off was reasonable and affordable.)

You see, all of life is arithmetic—not just "including" but especially pleasure, replenishment and play.

We'll get to all of this in the last part of this book, *Beyond Money.* But before we can get beyond it, we have to make money's various technicians and processes comprehensible and masterable, to shear the money "experts" of the power we give them (a power most of them do not ask for) to intimidate us.

CHAPTER 12

Demystifying the Moneylords

Not long ago, I walked into a busy New York City bank as an unknown newcomer. In twenty minutes, (1) I knew that this bank, and not the three others I had "shopped," fit my specific needs, (2) I had a checking account and a money market checking account and (3) I had the beginnings of a promising relationship with a banker I liked.

Just nine years ago, the same information and services would have taken me several hours to attain. (And just a few years before that, going on the familiar premise that "all banks are alike," I wouldn't have even known how to seek them at all.) Just nine years ago, my interview with the banker would have been riddled with my remarks that "Yes, I'm sure my accountant has that document filed somewhere; I'll get it to you."

Most important, just nine years ago I would have left the session wondering what the banker thought after he interviewed me.

Today, I leave such sessions concerned about what *I* think of the banker and the bank, now that *I* have finished interviewing them.

My nine-years-ago self was reacting (not acting; *re*acting) as so many women do: by unconsciously shrouding the bankers (and stockbrokers, insurance agents, accountants/tax advisers) in a film of mystique. Yes, to be sure, as a psychotherapist and negotiation expert I would have seen through this man's insecurities and understood his negotiation style (probably, in fact, better than he himself did), so I wouldn't have been intimidated by him personally. Still, I would have erected an invisible screen between what I viewed as his competence and preparedness and education in one area of life, and mine. Without knowing it, I would have glorified his mastery of something that I was still insisting was a half-comprehended language to me: money.

And with all of that, I would have given him a power over my life that only belongs to me.

Women do this all the time. We mystify finance professionals (even at the same time that we may be smugly and silently condescending to them, for example, thinking, "That poor guy in his polyester shirt and plastic pen holder . . ."). We allow ourselves to be distanced from and intimidated by their esoteric knowledge and judgments. We react to them instead of acting freely, with the help of their information and resources. We defer blindly to them instead of confidently delegating to them. (The truth is, they don't want such responsibility, such power. It handicaps not merely their client's self-sufficiency but their own work on that client's behalf.)

We view these people as the *Moneylords*.

Changing all this—bringing the finance professionals to proper eye level and to their appropriate, more effective place in your life —begins with three things. They are:

DEMYSTIFICATION STEP I:
REALIZE THAT YOU HIRE THE FINANCE PROFESSIONALS ON YOUR TEAM

When Donna, the advertising executive you met in the last chapter, realized she was giving 53 percent of her money to the government, she made what she thought at the time was a humorously presumptuous retort: "Well, then the government should be working for me!"

Today she doesn't think it's so funny—or so presumptuous. It's simply true: the people and institutions to whom you give money should be answerable to you.

If you give your money over to a finance professional (accountant, stockbroker) or to an agent of a financial institution (bank, insurance company) for purposes of protecting and leveraging it, these people and companies are profiting from your trust and relying on your guidance and approval. Make the former real by stepping in and doing the latter. Simply put, the reins are there for you to hold. Take them.

Start by adopting a critical interviewing mentality toward all the finance professionals and institutions you're already signed up with, as well as toward those you're considering. Go through your entire portfolio of papers and contracts and policies (and if you don't have all these documents clearly organized and filed in a safe but accessible place, now is the time to do so) and ask yourself:

1. *Which of these agents and agencies and institutions did I "inherit"?* (Did the insurance company you still have a contract with "come with" the group plan policy you had with your last job? Is the stockbrokerage you're using the one that's been in your family for years?)

2. *Which did I fall into for sheer convenience?* (The bank is so close to home. The insurance agent solicited you by a mailed brochure; all you had to do was supply your credit card number and you had a policy.)

3. *Which were recommended by people who are not necessarily very knowledgeable or discriminating about money?* (The secretary you share your coffee break with; your neighbor.) And, as opposed to all the above:

4. *Which did you carefully select, from a field of several, to meet your specific needs?*

All but those that fall into category No. 4 should be candidates for reappraisal. At the same time, you are going to appraise competing agencies, agents and institutions. Take some time to acquire a list of the best. From this field of contenders, you are going to select those truly most suited to you and assemble your personally tailored financial team.

Of course, it's easier to join a preassembled team, and today such teams are readily available and aggressively courting your business. Large brokerage houses offer multiservice accounts, whereby you can do long- and short-term, low- and high-risk investing, buy life insurance and even real estate in the same office. Even large stores offer financial services.

It's seductive to hand over your financial life to these large umbrella groups. But once you do so, you lose the ability to control the individual parts of your team—to fine-tune the instrument that is working for you, exactly to your specifications. It's the difference between playing a record on an old hi-fi, with its simple HIGH/LOW volume control and LEFT/RIGHT speakers, and playing that same record on a state-of-the-art stereo, with twenty different switches for precise fidelity and nuanced modulation.

DEMYSTIFICATION STEP II:
COME FULLY PREPARED

If you enter a classroom for second-semester Spanish, the teacher will say, "I am assuming that all of you here have taken and passed first-semester Spanish. If not, what I have to teach you will be incomprehensible and of no use to you."

In the very same way, if you go to see a finance professional without having educated yourself in basic personal finance, acquainted yourself somewhat with the workings of the financial world and without having prepared a complete and up-to-date personal financial statement, then the value of the exchange will be nil.

Before you set about assembling your team, give yourself a full four months of the following education. (This may seem like a lot of reading and studying, but it is important, when you call on the finance professionals, to know the language of their domain. You don't want to sound naïve or uninformed, and you can't ask the kind of questions that will get you the information you need if you don't know the language to ask it in.) So:

■ Read at least one basic money book, such as Jane Bryant Quinn's *Everyone's Money Book* (hardcover, Delacorte, 1979; Dell trade paperback, 1980), cover to cover.

■ Take one personal finance seminar sponsored by a bank or a women's group or available through the local high school adult education or college continuing education or extension program.

■ Read the financial page of the newspaper daily.

■ Read *The Wall Street Journal* at least twice weekly. (You can find it at the library if not at a nearby periodicals stand.) Better yet, take a trial subscription.

■ Read the financial column of one of the three newsweeklies (*Newsweek, Time, U.S. News & World Report*) every week along with the business news therein.

■ Read one issue of *Forbes, Fortune* or *Business Week* per month. Better yet, take a trial subscription.

■ If you are going to interview a stockbroker, read *How to Buy*

Stocks by Louis Engel and Peter Wycoff, hardcover Little Brown, 1976; Bantam paperback, 1977.

■ If you are going to interview an accountant or tax adviser, read Publication No. 17 of the Internal Revenue Service (available at any IRS office).

■ If you are going to see a venture capitalist, or if you have a business or business idea you would like to capitalize, read *How to Raise Venture Capital,* edited by Stanley E. Pratt and the staff of *Venture* magazine (reprinted by Scribner's, 1982).

Prepare a full personal financial statement. (You can find the form in most money books.) Type it up and make several photocopies. If you are an owner or co-owner of a business—a service, agency, company or shop—you should prepare a business financial statement as well.

Now that you're prepared, move on to:

DEMYSTIFICATION STEP III:
KNOW HOW YOU MYSTIFY WHOM—AND WHY

"My insurance agent doesn't intimidate me!" you may say, in no uncertain terms. Or: "My accountant? He's not anyone I'd have lunch with, much less fear."

You may well be wrong. Mystification is a much more subtle and various process than you might think. We see, and mystify, each of the moneylords in a different way. Here is how.

THE BANKER

Most women don't even think they have a banker. They know they have a bank—the place where they withdraw and deposit their money, the institution that sends them a monthly statement. And they know they have a teller at that bank. And that's the person with whom they develop a relationship, as in, "Hi, Katy, you're looking great. I like your new haircut."

They regard the men and women sitting at the officers' desks (one of whom, months or years before, opened their account) as people to go to for occasional special service—approval of cash withdrawals over a thousand dollars, for example. They assume that since they have no current business to discuss with an officer

—the acquisition of a loan, the opening of additional accounts—there's no point in "bothering" the officer. They do not think to cultivate a relationship with him or her.

They are very wrong. The officer at the desk—not the teller at the window—is your banker. You must establish a relationship with him or her from the outset.

Why is this so important?

By far the most important element in getting what you want out of a negotiation is the quality and strength of the relationship that you have evolved, over time, with your negotiating partner. Such a relationship is not started on a dime, nor in a crisis, but is slowly and trustingly nurtured, and enables both partners' best selves to show.

Especially because banking in the future is going to be so aided by home computers that you'll be able to do all your routine transactions without getting out of your bathrobe, the relationship you establish with your banker is a crucial human connection to an increasingly impersonal institution.

The potential for establishing such a relationship with your banker should be the first thing you look for in a bank. For every bank you consider (and you should have at least three in mind), find out:

1. *Does this bank aggressively pursue and welcome accounts the size of yours, or is their main interest larger and corporate accounts?* Study the bank's brochures, its newspaper ads and television commercials, its promotional campaigns. Whom is it trying to appeal to? Whom is it trying to woo?

The bank that gives new depositors free toasters and irons, and the one whose TV ads feature the bus driver father of four having a warm exchange with the banker, is aggressively going after the small-to-middling account. "You don't have to be a millionaire to be treated well here," is the message these banks are loudly sending. The bank whose newspaper ad shows two Fortune 500 types shaking hands over expensive briefcases in a mahogany-paneled boardroom is sending the opposite message and clearly courting the kind of business you aren't going to be able to give them.

2. *How easy or hard is it for a person in your financial position to secure a personal, auto, business or home improvement loan (pick the form of loan you are most likely to need in the next two years) from this bank? A down payment loan on a home, a cooper-*

ative or condominium? A mortgage? Some banks woo the small depositor for bread-and-butter assets, while also keeping these same customers at arm's length by making other services, such as loans, very difficult to obtain. You don't want such a bank. Any relationship you forge with the banker here will be useless.

Even though you do not need a loan now, it is well worth your while to investigate the bank's terms and specifications for getting one. Do you have to take out a life insurance policy for a loan? Have a cosigner? How long do you have to be employed at your current place of business? Think ahead. The ease of obtaining that loan that you're most likely going to need is one of the main things to look for in selecting a bank.

Now that you've checked on the policy of the bank, turn your attention to important specifics of the particular branch of that bank that you will be using.

3. *Do the officers at the branch of the bank where you will be banking have longevity there, or is this branch a "training-ground" outpost with a built-in high turnover of the best and most competent officers?* Many small, residential neighborhood branches of major banks are used as training grounds for new officers. The branch serves as a low-pressure breaking-in place where those new to the organization can learn the ropes. Once they learn them, they're transferred to the more challenging branches.

These branches have a comfortable, personal, even small-town feel to them that can be initially appealing. And the new officers there may be eager to please. But if you are going to take the time to build a relationship with your banker, you certainly don't want him to be transferred away right at the point when that relationship can begin to pay off for you. And you don't want to have to build a new relationship every six or ten months.

Find out from someone who has held an account at the branch for several years if the officer turnover is high. If it is, consider the fact a very strong minus.

4. *How busy is the bank during the hour that you can most conveniently do your banking? And what is the ambience between customers and officers?* Are there long lines of impatient customers waiting to see the officers, or is there a good flow to the service being given and received?

Do the officers look courteous and involved with the customers they're talking to? Or do they seem distant and officious? Harried and distracted? Dismissive? Are the customers relaxed in one-to-one conversation with the officers? Or do they seem taut, defensive, combative?

While you are observing this interplay, make a mental note of the officer you feel you could relate to best. If you end up selecting this bank, go to him or to her.

All right. So far we've been talking about you auditioning and selecting the bank and the branch and the banker; you making the decisions and the judgments. But there is, as we all know, a time when the banker does the appraising and judging, and makes a decision upon which your future hinges.

And that is when you are applying for a loan.

Because the loan application process is so intimidating to so many women, I enlisted the help of Larry Peterman, the vice-president and manager of the West Los Angeles office of Security Pacific National Bank in role-playing with Felicia Babcock, an author and colleague, a typical loan-negotiating session (with me coaching and commenting).

Here's how we played it, and here are the asides and critiques that we made on those plays:

We are pretending that Felicia has arrived at Larry's desk at the bank with her personal financial statement and photocopies of her last three years' income tax returns.

BANKER: What can I do for you?

CUSTOMER: I'd like a twenty-five-thousand-dollar loan. [She really wants fifty thousand but doesn't have the courage to ask for it.]

BANKER: What do you want the loan for?

CUSTOMER: To buy a computer.

BANKER: How do you propose to pay me back?

CUSTOMER: As you know, my private practice is now at a minimum because I'm in the process of writing a book. The paperback rights will be sold in six months. By that time, I'll have an additional advance payment of twenty thousand dollars, and I'll be able to pay you back principle and interest.

BANKER: But Dr. Babcock, according to your three years' tax returns, you don't show the kind of income to support this request. You're asking me to make the loan based on the fact that this book will be published and will sell well, and I can't do that. [LARRY: *You have to realize—and this is important—that, to the banker, every loan applicant is guilty until proved innocent. Accept this adversarial questioning process as part of the game. Try not to be thrown by it. Be relaxed, prepared and undefensive.*]

CUSTOMER: Yes, but if you'll look at my last three years' tax returns, you'll see that though I functioned in the red, there was less and less red and more and more black as time went on. I've been catching up over the last three years. However, there are specific things down the line: videotapes, a possible TV series, seminars and other offshoots of the book. In fact, if you'd like to have a letter from my publisher outlining their commitment to the book and telling you what their print order and publicity budget are, I'll be happy to provide you with this evidence that the book will be published and is expected to sell very well.

[TESSA: *She should have deleted that last sentence. As a loan applicant, you shouldn't talk too much. This is a common mistake of women. If she'd gone on trying to educate the banker on those specifics of the publishing industry that would have made her future income predictable, she would have appeared naïve and would have risked making him impatient by taking up his valuable time.*]

[LARRY: *That's right. It's our job, as bankers, to know all that. So I would have replied to her last sentence with:*]

BANKER: What if for some unforeseen reason the book does not get published, how are you going to pay me back?

CUSTOMER: In the highly remote event that that happened, I would double my seminar schedule and rush into production the two videotape projects I now have pending. I would also—

[LARRY: *Whoa. If you keep talking about how you're going to go out and make money to pay me back, you're going to bury yourself.*]

[TESSA: *Exactly. You see, women have to learn to play the balance between giving too little in the way of an answer and doing what Felicia has just been doing to make the point here—explaining, and justifying—all in a way that shows a lack of understanding of the basic tenets of banking—*]

[LARRY: *—one of which is: The secondary source of income to pay back the loan* must *be something concrete, not something potential.*]

[TESSA: *Felicia has slipped into a "Comer" attitude, when, indeed, she is a "Haver." What she should say, instead of that last answer, is . . .]*

CUSTOMER: In the highly remote event that the book isn't published, I have—as you know from my personal financial statement —an antique porcelain collection valued at a hundred thousand dollars. I've already taken a second mortgage of my home, as you know. In fact, I've brought you the real estate appraisal, done just two months ago, as well as the authentication papers on the porcelain collection.

BANKER: Good. Let me take a look at these. *[Pauses to look at documents.]* All right, Dr. Babcock. We'll arrange for your loan.

[LARRY: *You must be prepared. If you aren't prepared, don't start faking it. The banker will only see through you. Simply terminate the interview at this point. Say: "I'll go back and work on it and come back in a few days." Secure a sound, convincing secondary income source. Get copies of all the papers you need. And come back to the banker with that added horsepower.]*

While your banker handles your day-to-day checking and basic savings account (which, these days, means a higher- and fluctuating-interest money market account, often with checking privileges), you go elsewhere to vary your portfolio with stocks, bonds and other more creative investments. You go to the next finance professional,

THE STOCKBROKER

"Stockbroker." Quick: what image leaps to your mind?

Nine out of ten of you reading this book probably conjured up a granite-jawed young man in a crisply tailored suit radiating razor-edged confidence, emotional invulnerability and professional cool, who lives in an exclusive suburb with a tennis-playing wife who's active in the Junior League.

The same nine out of ten of you may well have been using that intimidating stereotype as an excuse not to go to a stockbroker.

And that's a shame, as well as a misconception.

Today's stockbrokers are of both sexes, all backgrounds, diverse life-styles. Many of the best of them bear no resemblance to that Central Casting stockbroker at all. Take Patricia Murphy, for example. She's twenty-eight; she's a broker with the New York office of Merrill Lynch; she's approachable, enthusiastic, unaffected.

And far from the buttoned-down cliché, she works sensitively, with the clients' needs and hesitations in mind. ("If a person has never invested anything before, advising her to go immediately into a speculative stock would be traumatic. I'd start such a client off with a blue chip and then, when she was ready for it, we'd move on to greater risk. Or, if I know a couple want to buy a house in two years, I'll want to maximize their money while still protecting it so that in two years they're ready to make the purchase. For these people, I'd probably select a utility.")

It is this attitude—this sensitivity to you, the client; this concern with the trust that the two of you need to build into your relationship; this factoring in of your long-range plans—that is the first thing you should look for in a stockbroker.

When interviewing stockbrokers, also ask:

1. How long have you been in the business? (You do want experience.)

2. Are you a regular stockbroker or a discount broker? (Discount brokers do not give you investment advice. They simply trade for you, according to your orders, and, as such, are not recommended for the small or beginning investor.)

3. Are you just a stock trader or does your company offer full service? (Bonds, utilities, treasury bills, cash management accounts, money markets, etc. Whether or not you want to avail yourself of all these services, it's nice to know they're there.)

The stockbroker isn't a genie or a therapist. You have to sit down and do some hard thinking before you go to her. Realize, first of all, that investing in the stock market is a prime example of not being able to have your cake and eat it, too. You cannot expect maximum returns with minimum risk. You cannot be safe and rich at the same time—at least not on the same stock.

You have to be honest and candid—first, with yourself. And, second, and just as important, with the broker you eventually select. The temptation, for many new brokerage clients, is to want to inflate or keep vague the extent of your ability to risk. (Who wants to seem poor in a rich man's playground? Or consistently cautious on the slick fast track?) This embarrassment or bravado serves neither you or the broker.

Tell the broker what your income is, what your life-style is, the real (not idealized) extents to which you need access to your money now, to which you can tie your money up long-term, to which you can gamble.

"The broker has to have this information," Pat Murphy stresses. "I follow from what you tell me. If you say, 'I don't want any of my principle at risk,' then I'll put you in something extremely safe—say, a money market or a treasury bill. If you say, 'I want to double my money,' I'll consider you an active, speculating trader who is willing to lose the entire amount."

How much contact and interplay should you have with your broker?

This depends on where your investments lie on the low- to high-risk continuum. If you've instructed your broker to go for long-term gross, she'll put you in growth-oriented stocks and you'll need to make only monthly contact. But if you're an active speculative trader, the contact may be daily.

And if you do become an active, speculative trader—with, say, a five-thousand-dollar investment—how much do you do, and how much does the stockbroker do?

Pat Murphy answers: "The investor doesn't have to do anything. She's hired me to find and trade the stocks for her, and to keep her apprised of what I'm doing, when I'm doing it, and why. Still, she may want to be more involved."

Do become more involved. Take the hands-on approach. (And by all means, steer clear of any broker who says, "Give me two thousand dollars; I'll double it for you in a week; don't ask any questions," or who otherwise discourages your participation.)

Read the stock market pages in your newspaper to see where your stock is daily. Ask your broker to provide you with materials, from the brokerage house's research department, for every company in which she's recommended you invest. (This is called *fundamental research,* and it consists of corporate reports, earnings estimates, outlook on the company, and the brokerage house's research analysis.)

As your expertise increases, you might also ask her to supply you, verbally, with the *technical-approach* information (answers to such questions as What is the stock's trading range? Does it have support or resistance at the current level?) that she culls from the many reports that she reads. (Subscriptions to these reports are too expensive, and the information within too specialized, to be worthwhile to the lay trader.)

Then, when you really know what you're doing, pick a stock of your own and use her as a discount broker, merely to make the trade, on your orders. You call the shots. She doesn't coach you this time out. But do listen to every bit of Monday-morning quarterbacking she gives you.

As worthwhile as it is (once you can afford it) to take risks through stock trading, it's even more important to reduce other risks. Which leads us to the next finance professional—

THE INSURANCE AGENT

"You can never be overinsured," goes the false common knowledge particularly subscribed to by women. Having lived for so long lives that were utterly dependent on their husbands' earning power and Decision Monopoly—and having given up their own earning power outright—it's no wonder that women have wanted to cling to the one apparent life raft in their sea of financial vulnerability: the insurance agency.

That agency looms in our minds as a grand and beneficent temple. The agents who come forth from it are pictured in advertisements and commercials as kindly, caring men (they're never pictured as women; that would dampen the aura of paternalism) who are deftly interjected into scenes of idyllic familial warmth, as if to whisper: "Never forget: All this could shatter any minute."

To be sure, insurance agencies are among the most vital institutions in our lives, absolutely irreplaceable in crisis. But they do capitalize on fear, insecurity, ignorance—and on a blind trust in patriarchy. And which sex has always been the more vulnerable to these things? I don't have to tell you the answer.

The truth is, you can be overinsured. And you can have the wrong kind of insurance policies. You can also be missing the right kinds, leaving yourself bereft of the protection most valuable to you, despite your fat portfolio of contracts and big quarterly payments.

Before you start interviewing insurance agents, sit down and carefully assess your needs and vulnerabilities, and those of your spouse and your children. And know, and avoid:

THE FIVE MOST COMMON INSURANCE MISTAKES THAT WOMEN MAKE TODAY

1. *The single woman with no children needlessly takes out life insurance.* If you have no dependents and you own property or otherwise have enough assets for your debts to be taken care of in case of death, there is no reason for you to have life insurance (except, in some instances, if taking out such a policy is a condition for getting a bank loan, and in that case, it should be term insurance). Instead, the money you've been wasting on a life insurance policy could be funneled into more appropriate and higher-earning investments. And make sure you aren't making the second mistake, which is:

2. *The working woman doesn't have adequate disability coverage.* Full disability insurance is what you should be concentrating on. It is the crisis blood transfusion of the working person. It compensates you for your loss of income if you can no longer work. When you bought your car, your television set, your washing machine, you probably took out a warranty to protect you in case of mechanical breakdown, didn't you? Well, take out the same full-sized warranty on the very earning power that enabled you to buy those machines—and everything else in your life—in the first place.

3. *The nonworking wife and mother takes out "homemaker's insurance," spending on that policy money that could be much better spent augmenting her husband's policies.* The homemaker's insurance that some big agencies have come up with (ostensibly to protect a family in case of the loss of services of the nonworking wife-mother) is judged by many finance writers and consumer authorities as a smoke-screen policy that hides the family's real vulnerabilities.

The way to keep this family protected against such a loss is to make sure the breadwinner husband's policy is large enough to cover the consequences of his wife's disability or death as well as his own. In all too many cases, the working husband of the nonworking homemaker-policied wife is woefully underinsured.

The homemaker's policy is at best a luxury, but never should it be construed as a substitute.

4. *The woman in her twenties, thirties and early forties doesn't take out, and annually keep up, a Keogh or an IRA.* Individual retirement plans are forms of insurance, too. And they are vital ones, particularly to women in this age range. Because there are so many members of what is called the baby boom generation (people born right after the end of the Second World War), they—and those younger than them—stand a good chance of never receiving Social Security benefits when they come of retirement age: there simply won't be enough money to go around.

The 30 percent of your income that you currently pay into Social Security is enabling today's older citizens (who themselves paid only 6 or 7 percent of their income to Social Security) to collect full benefits now. The Keogh and IRA are ways of guaranteeing recompense for what turns out to be this social "good deed" (with the added advantage of providing tax shelter). Right now, they're the *only* guaranteed retirement fund you have.

5. *Women who go into business with one another do not protect themselves by taking life insurance policies out on one another.* When one partner in a business partnership dies, the partnership is automatically, legally disbanded. This means that banks can stop extending you credit and that they, and *all* creditors, can immediately demand payment on the spot, effectively closing you down.

Too many women going into small businesses with one another do not know this. And they leave themselves and their children tremendously and unnecessarily vulnerable.

Each partner should take out a policy worth exactly half the net worth of the business, naming the other as beneficiary and including a "buy-sell" agreement, enabling the survivor to buy the deceased's share. If one or both of you have children, you should specify, in writing and through a lawyer, that in the event of death the insurance payment be turned over in full from the beneficiary partner to the deceased's children (this is, of course, in addition to the payment those children will get from their mother's separate life insurance policy, in which they were named beneficiaries) in exchange for the right to take over their mother's share of the partnership.

This protects everyone.

All right. Now that you've assessed the protection you need, and now that you know the major mistakes to avoid, how do you find the right agent?

First of all, never buy insurance through the mail. Consider only reputable agents who come recommended by knowledgeable friends who have used them for years. When you go to interview each agent, bring your personal financial statement, your will (if you don't have one, make one immediately), all your insurance records and a complete list of your employing company's benefits.

Look for integrity (someone who has your interests, not his or her commissions, at heart); aggressive pursuit of new information, offerings, changes of laws; and experience.

Is an independent agent better than an agent who works through a large company? There are advantages and pitfalls with each. The former can offer you a wider range of choices (what is known in the trade as a smorgasbord portfolio of policies) since he or she isn't committed to just one company. But the à la carte prices on some of these policies may be higher than they would be had they been secured with the package-deal discounts agencies offer. And since these agents collect their commission from the various companies, some practice what is known in the industry as churning (selling you a new policy instead of renewing your still appropriate old one, because the sale will give them a bigger commission than would the renewal). By the same token, company agents have a vested interest in selling you as much of their company's policies as they can—even some you may not need. And many are always "selling" the company.

Good, principled agents—whether independent or company—resist all these temptations that come with their particular territory. They're honest; they care; and their satisfaction and challenge come not from picking up a few extra dollars of commission but from making just the right fit of person to policy and in servicing you as fairly, thoroughly and creatively as they can.

How do you test for such an agent? There's one good way to start.

The insurance industry has graduate degrees that are voluntarily taken by some agents and do not at all necessarily result in a higher salary for the agent. An agent does this extra work for one reason alone: to be better at his or her work.

In life insurance, the equivalent of a master's degree is the Life Underwriters' Training Council (LUTC) license, and the Ph.D. equivalent is the Charter Life Underwriters' license (the CLU), which is granted after a ten-part qualifying exam and usually takes five years. In health insurance, the Ph.D. equivalent is the Registered Health Underwriters' license (the RHU), which involves one year's preparation and a big final exam.

If the agent you're interviewing has these degrees, you're on the right track.

Incidentally, many insurance agents are now going into financial planning and real estate, too. You might consider going with a trusted agent who is long familiar with your needs—if you're impressed that the agent has genuinely broadened his or her expertise and has the sufficient education. But be careful not to fall into the umbrella-service trap I described earlier.

As much in awe as we tend to be about insurance agencies, we're even more in awe of one overwhelmingly intimidating institution. And this mystification leads us to a distorted relationship with our next finance professional—

THE ACCOUNTANT

Oh, how we fear the IRS!

We interpret computer-printout bills and notices from this agency as some voice from above, whispering, "You're not cheating—or thinking of cheating—are you?" Most of us dread the specter of a tax audit as one would dread a police interrogation.

The government helps foster this mystification. Watch your newspapers around April 15 and you will see lots of stories about "illegal" uses of tax shelters and pictures of people just convicted of tax fraud. The IRS has an active public relations department that makes sure these stories appear with the right force, the right moral to the story—and at the right time of year.

It is often at the dreaded tax audit that many of us unmask the true face of the IRS. Like Dorothy finally, and timorously, approaching the Wizard of Oz, we see that there was a mere mortal behind the booming voice and imperious façade. My favorite demystification story is of the auditor who arrived at an appointment with a nervous client and her accountant. The auditor seemed twice as nervous as the auditee; after clearing his voice and shuffling his feet he confessed: "This is the first corporate case I've ever done!" "Don't worry," the accountant beneficently offered. "I'll walk you through it."

Because we fear the IRS so, we take an attitude toward those, our accountants, who buffer us from this agency that may seem paradoxical but is, in fact, quite logical. On the one hand, we view accountants as infinitely unmystified: dronelike, dreary, uncharismatic, reliably sensible. On the other hand, we view these same people as miracle middlemen to whom we can hand over a jumbled file of old receipts and forms and, presto!, after forty-five minutes, our tax account will be settled. Of all the moneylords, accountants are the ones it feels safest to overdepend on because we can do so with our sense of superiority and our self-image intact. They're not glamorous like stockbrokers or our image of stockbrokers, not paternal and all-protecting like insurance agents or our image of insurance agents, not powerful like bankers or our image of bankers.

They don't threaten us as these other moneylords do, so we can lean on them without feeling one down or bettered. Because they intimidate us so little and the institution they're shielding us from intimidates us so much, we can collapse on them entirely, without even knowing we've collapsed! A Manhattan accountant tells me: "I have one client, a woman who writes magazine articles about self-reliance, who presents me with a stack of unopened bank statements and IRS forms every month; another who won't make a move without me—and she's a finance writer for a national magazine."

Guard very carefully against this invisible abdication of power. Take a hands-on approach with your accountant, which means:

1. *Do the arithmetic together.* Don't just let the accountant in the door and come back when the checks are ready to be signed and the envelopes sealed. Sit there and participate in the accounting, step by step.

2. *Ask a question as many times as you have to, until you understand the answer.* Don't just give up after three queries and assume the answer, and subject, is "too technical." Press for an explanation that makes sense to you. You may have to help the accountant bring it down to layperson's language and you may have to work on yourself to stay interested. Remember: they're not poets or teachers; they're CPAs.

The accountant who genuinely meets you halfway—who doesn't just answer questions but intitiates educating dialogue—is particularly valuable. My own accountant, Andrew Watkins, is such a professional. He knows it is to his advantage to help with the demystification process. "If the clients don't understand, they don't trust," he says. "And if they don't trust, we can't leverage and move forward."

3. *Don't follow your accountant's advice or instructions by rote; understand the logic behind it.* A woman I know set up a corporation with her husband, as a tax shelter. She and her husband also had separate checking accounts and a couple of money market accounts. When her accountant told her, in the fall, that she could be funneling more money through the corporation, she began changing the money market accounts from individual to corporate. By the middle of the winter, the accountant told her he was having trouble justifying all the expenses she was now accruing through the corporation; could she set up a little "slush fund," not corporation-linked, on the side?

She couldn't—because by now all the major accounts had been changed to corporate accounts.

She didn't understand the delicate, and shifting, balance that had to be struck between corporate write-off and plausibility. She took the accountant's one-time remark as a permanent instruction, and because she didn't understand the subtext of that remark (and because he didn't understand that she didn't understand it), it cost him more work and her and her husband less write-off.

4. *Prepare for tax time throughout the year by keeping an expense diary.* Buy a four-column analysis pad at the stationer's and break down your daily expenses into the major tax deduction categories you and your accountant agree are most relevant (for example, research, travel and entertainment, transportation, misc.). Enter the daily total outlay of funds in the appropriate category. Buy an expandable accordion file and file the receipts that back up each daily entry according to month.

By the end of the tax quarter, or year, you won't have to wrack your mind for a complete list of deductions. You'll have all the totals on paper; all the receipts in a chronological file.

5. *If your income is over thirty-five thousand dollars a year, by all means, get a tax shelter.* A tax shelter is anything from an easy-to-get individual retirement account (IRA, which we discussed under "Insurance Agent") to a limited-partnership oil investment —a much more sophisticated venture, to which not everyone is privy. What these diverse and differently affordable investments have in common is that, through them, the investor is buying a tax

write-off and getting her investment back via tax savings. If you have a lot of money to shelter, you find the investment through tax-shelter specialists (stockbrokers, lawyers, investment bankers) that a good accountant can put you in touch with.

If you are self-employed, the best tax shelter may be self-incorporation. An attorney draws up the actual incorporation papers (at a straight fee that ranges from $500 to $1,000, depending on state and circumstances); the accountant keeps your corporate books on a monthly basis. The fee for the accountant's services, including the filing of annual returns, is anywhere between $1,500 and $5,000 a year, depending on the complexity of the corporation and its principals' financial and business situation. The tax savings are usually well worth the expense.

How to select an accountant?

Start, of course, with three highly recommended men or women. Look for personal rapport; trustworthiness; ease and clarity of communication (this is very important; however excellent the accountant, if he can't convey to you what he's doing and why, you'll never get your hands firmly on your financial affairs); and a risk style that matches your own (don't hire a cautious, conservative accountant if you've finally geared yourself up to make imaginative investment, or a bombastic hipshooter if your situation dictates caution).

Never ask the accountant if he or she will cheat for you, not even kiddingly. ("Cheat" is a word accountants don't use. But someone who says, "If you're creative with your expense diary . . . ," is willing to help you make all the savings you can. "Creative" is a word accountants do use.) It's all right to ask the accountant what percentage of his clients have been audited. A good accountant will be proud of his record.

You can test an accountant by asking a few questions about your specific case:

Bring your own salary checks and tax forms and ask, "Is too much being withheld?" "How can I maximize greater tax flow?" and so forth. His spontaneous response to your case can tell you about his risk style and communication talent and whether you feel you can have a rapport with him.

THE VENTURE CAPITALIST

Yes, I know: this feels like quite an improbable leap—from the bread-and-butter life-management moneylords to a sophisticated executor of millions of dollars of capital. But the leap I've just made is consonant with a leap that so many women make: as much as they tend to be intimidated by even the most basic finance professionals (as we've just seen), the minute they get a great idea for a business, they emotionally leapfrog over months, if not years, of preparation and research and a good deal of sober, savvy reality, and fairly shout: "This is an idea whose time has come! No one has thought of it before! Why, it'll make millions! Now all I need is someone to finance me."

"Women who want their businesses capitalized," says venture capitalist Joy London, "exhibit the flip side of the coin of being undeserving. They have the unrealistic expectation that they should get something, often for nothing. Their level of under-standing of what they have to do to get what they want is very low. Their understanding of the probability of getting it is low. They are very naïve. They think that because they've put together a couple of pages of some kind of prospectus on a service business the venture capital community should drop dead to put their money in."

Rather, the road to capitalization is slow and tough and specific. Few are chosen to follow it through to the dispenser of funds at the end. As euphoric as it makes one feel to have come up with a good business idea, it's crucial to stop and clearly see that road for exactly what it is.

But first, just what is a venture capitalist firm?

Venture capital firms raise large pools of capital to invest in new companies by going to institutional investors (pension funds, cor-porations, endowment funds and the like) and there soliciting a small percentage of the hundreds of millions of dollars that these investors raise for venture capital, which is characterized as high-risk, illiquid investment.

Since venture capital firms have gotten a lot of play in the press these days, a lot of people approach them—people who believe in their businesses and their products and for one reason or another can't get bank financing. "Our firm sees hundreds of deals a year," says Joy. "Only about three out of a hundred get funded. And the great majority of those other 97 percent shouldn't be financed because they can't possibly be worth enough money down the road for a venture capital firm to take them on. (We're looking for big returns, and a five- to ten-year horizon on returns—meaning return on investment beginning to show in five years.)"

What must a woman with a business idea know to determine if hers is one of those ideas, and she one of those entrepreneurs, who can fit through the eye of the venture capital firm's needle?

1. *Understand which businesses are candidates for venture capital funding and which are not.* Most women's business ideas are service businesses. These, unfortunately, are rarely candidates for venture capital funding. Businesses in the technology field—educational software, for example—and in other high-growth fields are good candidates.

Find out exactly which, if any, venture capital firms specialize in funding your kind of proposed business.

2. *Do your homework—thoroughly.* Research. Research. Research.

Find out not just which venture capital firms have funded ideas like yours, but when, why, for how much and with what results? What were these businesses' strengths? Are yours similar, equal, superior?

What kind of money do you have to raise for each stage of your business? What will it take from the principals, the management, the talent, the distributors, the marketplace? How feasible is this idea, and are you willing to do what has to be done? What is the competition, and why are you better? Has anyone tried what you want to do before, and what was the outcome, and why?

Educate yourself not just to your specific business field and the supporting business environment, but to the venture capital community. Talk to lawyers who deal with the community, and to other entrepreneurs.

Forget about the idea of getting "just enough working" financial background and coasting on your creative contributions; that kind of division, while it may work in other aspects of business, does not work when you are going for capitalization. Joy says: "In my five years in this business, I've seen about a dozen women entrepreneurs. Unfortunately, none of them got funding from my firm. (Of course neither did 97 percent of the men.) They just hadn't paid their dues yet."

3. *Realistically evaluate what you're "bringing to the party."
And if you're not bringing enough, team up at the outset with
someone who is.* As women climbing up the ladder from well-
remembered positions of exploitation, we've been so geared to
defend against having our ideas ripped off that it's hard to drop
this posture once it no longer serves us. But in venture capital, it
no longer serves.

"It was *my* idea, after all!" is not enough to qualify you as the
sole, or even the major, principal in the business you are proposing. Realistically assess: What are my qualifications for leadership
in this business. What is my background? What should my role in
the business be? What am I bringing to the party—and if *I* can't
supply it, *how* is it going to get there, before we try to convince
someone to put up the money?

Possession may be nine tenths of the law in many situations, but
not here. Two examples: A few years ago, I had a great idea for
turning my first book, *Winning by Negotiation,* into a board game,
à la Monopoly. I had the game all worked out; the idea and the
book were no one's but mine. I was introduced to someone who
had the unique experience and contacts to take the business part
of the deal over, but he wanted 50 percent of everything. "No
fair!" I responded. "I've worked on this material for eight years!
You're asking much too large a cut on what is mine." That was it—
for the potential partnership and for the project.

And: A woman recently came to Joy with an idea for a women's
tennis club. "She was aggressive and confident and had a good
idea," Joy recalls. "But her background was in something entirely
unrelated to tennis club management. I offered to put her together with a woman I knew who did have that experience, but
she flatly refused the introduction. She would not team up with
that woman." Her venture capital proposal stopped there—not
just at Joy's desk, but at the desks of three other firms' capitalists.

In short, it is unrealistic for you to say: "It's my idea, so even
though I don't have direct experience in this field, I'll be vice-
president of marketing and I'll hire a financial manager and a
software developer when I need them." You need them now—
before you go one step further.

Still with us? All right; the next step is to:

4. *Hire a financial adviser, an accountant, and draw up, in
about six months' time, a solidly convincing, irrefutable business*

plan. Is this a truly viable business? Do you really understand the specific need the product or service will fill? The market? The competition? The margins of error? What does it take to distribute the product? What's the downside? What's the payoff? And when will it start? How do you know?

Interrogate yourself, knowledgeably, toughly, again and again. Spend about six months asking and answering these questions, and write those answers up.

The business plan should be concise, intelligent, well thought through and extremely well documented, and it must display a very realistic understanding of the market. Address all possible risks and drawbacks. Face all exigencies. Don't leave a question begging. Submit the plan for careful and tough-minded critique to colleagues in your field before you submit it to the venture capitalist.

What is the venture capitalist looking for in the plan? "To be convinced," answers Joy, "that you know exactly what you're getting in for, that your business has merit, that you've met and assembled the right people and that the probability is strong that you can pull it off. Your plan has to convince me that it and not the other 1,599 that I've read, is the one I can most successfully and profitably fund."

If the venture capitalist is interested enough in your plan to call you in, you then have to:

5. *Convince her, in a face-to-face meeting, that you're sufficiently entrepreneurial and that your plan is sound.* "If you're called for a meeting," says Joy, that means there's serious interest, jump. If they ask you to meet them in Alaska day after tomorrow to talk about your proposal, get right on the plane."

Bring with you a list of references that vouch for your background and experience and, more important, for the viability of the business you're proposing (these latter, from experts in the field). Prepare these people to be called. "Make it as easy as possible for the venture capitalist to find out what she needs to know," counsels Joy. "I want to be able to pick up my phone and, within a couple of hours, have confirmation of what you're proposing."

Also: Be prepared to back up every claim you make—immediately, on the spot. Joy says: "Your plan is going to be dissected on the cellular level. Don't ever assume the take-my-word-for-it position. You're guilty until proven innocent. You have to be extremely persistent in convincing the capitalist that your business will make money. I'm looking for persistence in the people I fund, because you have to have that quality in abundance to be a successful entrepreneur."

Ask the right questions, which are: What role does your firm play in its investments? (Does it play a passive role, or do you prefer to occupy board seats?) How much time do you spend with the companies you're invested with? and Does your firm typically lead a deal or do you prefer a secondary position? Do not ask, How much equity do you want?

Convey your sense of enthusiasm. "When you find someone who really enjoys what she's doing as well as someone who knows what she's doing, that's a big plus. What it really comes down to is the venture capitalist asking herself, 'Do I really believe in these people? Am I willing to bet money on them?' We are looking for winners. We are looking for those very rare people in this world who can really pull off a successful company."

Pulling off a successful company is one thing; pulling off a successfully run life is another. Beyond demystifying the world of finance and the finance professionals lies the woman's often (and deceptively) much harder task of getting the sheer help she needs to push herself singularly forward through the thicket of obligations that is her life.

Let's turn to the next chapter to learn how to do just that.

CHAPTER 13

Interindependence:
Negotiating for Help

A few years ago, I appeared as a guest on a TV talk show, along with actor Dennis Weaver. As we were sitting in the Green Room, where guests wait for their turn before the camera, Weaver remarked—offhandedly, yet not without pride—that he and his wife had been married for thirty-five years. "That's got to be some kind of record for Hollywood," I said. "How have the two of you done it?"

He thought for a moment, and then he replied: "We've always remained useful to each other."

Useful. I loved that true, yet unexpected, word. With it, Dennis Weaver was restoring to honor an idea that has become so terribly maligned over the last twenty or so years. And that is the idea that two people using each other is a good and binding and loving thing; that instead of discrediting the utilitarian—the pragmatic—dimension of relationships, couples (and all partners, in whatever enterprise) should celebrate it.

What he was saying, in essence, is that "use," like "lust," is not a dirty word.

Indeed it is not, as people who lived during the centuries and centuries before the technological revolution knew. In those times, "love" and "use" were intensely intertwined. Help in surviving the hardships of life was the greatest gift of love that husbands and wives and parents and children could give to each other.

Today, we feel differently. "He doesn't love you; he's just using you" is one of the dozens of remarks we make to one another that pit "love" and "use" against each other in enemy camps. The kind of deceitful, exploitive behavior to which "use," in these contexts, refers is really abuse; but somewhere along the vernacular route, the prefix was dropped and we were left with the idea that people who get utility from one another are selfish, malevolent and underhanded—particularly if they are women.

No wonder, then, that so many women watch their best laid plans for getting more crumble. Even if they've gotten as far as we've now gotten in this book—they've corrected their Poverty Mentality feelings/attitudes/behaviors; they've worked out their abundance-linked problems with the men in their lives; they've gotten in touch with and acted on their lust, made one-year agendas and learned how to see the money establishment clearly—taking the next step leaves them at the edge of a sharp cliff. Their goals are across the chasm, on top of the opposite cliff. And the chasm is the void left by their inability to negotiate for help.

These women need to marshal the necessary assistance to manage their lives (and, in many cases, their family's lives) and their careers at their current full-time levels while at the same time putting their singular plans for abundance on fast, uninterrupted forward. That's the edge of the cliff. The chasm between the cliffs echoes with these sounds:

"I know I could do twice as much creative work if I didn't have to make my own Xerox copies and phone calls and do my own correspondence."

"If I don't plan my husband's birthday party, and make sure the kids don't watch more than an hour of TV a night, and make certain the vegetables aren't overcooked and the gardener doesn't cut the hedges too short, who is going to do it?"

"I have a great idea for a business. But who has time to do all the research, hunt up the contacts, and do everything else when you're working five days a week?"

"I do want to make vice-president, but I also want a nice life. How could we have possibly remodeled the coop, and entertained Phil's clients with any bit of style, and gotten Jimmy over his math problem and Sarah into the junior gymnast finals, if I had put in the extra work hours needed to really go for that promotion? Oh well, maybe next year."

"All the secretaries in my office stay late and go out of their way for the male executives. But no one will do it for me."

"I'm sick and tired of hearing that a woman can have a career and a husband and a child. You can't do it all—unless you're an octopus!"

Vaulting that chasm means getting help. If you're a Comer who has responsibilities to people (husband, children or both) other than yourself, it means getting digging-out help—household help and childcare—as well as the starting-out career help that single Comers need as well. As you move toward Haver, it means getting pushing-upward help: the promotion from the boss that gets you the secretarial help you need, then real help from that secretary. It may also mean getting career-leveraging help through forming a collaboration or a partnership with a peer. When you become a Haver, you move on to those higher levels of delegation that protect you and your good life from burnout. At this point, getting help means getting loyal and effective aid (that is not redundant with the work you do, or the strengths you bring to a project) from an increasingly responsible staff and taking on a trusted adminis-trivial assistant for your personal life.

Getting help on all of these levels means you are getting help from people while at the same time you are giving help to them. It means being a partner in an acknowledged reciprocal flow of use that is beneficial to both people's agendas, satisfying to both peo-ple's spirits and positive to the relationship between them.

Negotiating for, and receiving, help in this way is the essence of interindependence. In relationships of interindependence, each person is her best independent self not despite but because of her reliance on others, who also, in turn, rely on her. The interlaced mesh of these positive reliances forms a matrix of trust and support that cushions us and springs us forward.

All women need that cushioning, springboarding web of sup-port, but women who are wives and mothers need it most of all because they're always being called on to give of themselves with time and support. For this reason most of this chapter is directed at this woman. And since being a single mother requires a higher outlay of time and support with a lower intake of the same, what goes for the partnered mother goes double for the unpartnered one.

So let's move on and learn how to get the help you need, as a Comer or as a Haver, on the home and the work front.

NEGOTIATING FOR HELP—THROUGH INTERINDEPENDENCE—ON THE HOME FRONT FOR COMERS

Jane is a twenty-eight-year-old dancer who suspended her career to have a baby. When the baby was a year old, Jane wanted to get back to work, but she couldn't do so on a dime. She had to get back in shape in order to go out on auditions in order to get the first of the hoped-for series of jobs that would bring in the cash flow that would justify the childcare she needed to be able to work.

But she also needed childcare to start the whole process. Where was she to start? Her husband worked full time as a video engineer, and the high rent on their new apartment, the loss of her salary for the past year and his new-father anxieties all combined to make him intensely resistant to their dipping into the very small nest egg they had in order to fund her practice time and dance lessons. He didn't see the payoff. She did.

Jane had two choices to break the circle. The first was:

1. Working around your husband (until the results start to show), by creatively using your marketable skills.

Jane knew that pursuing the issue with her husband would only waste time, drain energy in ugly quarrels and result in constant tension that would be destructive for the baby. Instead of staying stuck in inaction while she tried to change him, she wisely gave up the Vacant Hope that he'd see the light and put her energy into looking for a solution elsewhere. Jane had two marketable skills: dancing and needlepoint. She would use these to break the circle.

She drew her start-up agenda as a six-month time line: The first three months, she would take fifteen hours of dance classes and practice per week; the next three months, six hours of classes and as many auditions as she could attend, until she got a job. She counted two advantages in negotiating for help to finance the first three months: the dance classes she needed to take were given several times each day, and her baby took a regular, two-and-a-half-hour afternoon nap. Thus, she had time options for what she needed to get—and time certainty for what she was able to give.

Seizing these advantages, here's what she did:

She approached the owner of a neighborhood needlepoint boutique and offered to do whatever had to be done—stock work, sales work, needlepoint advice to customers—three days a week for two and a half hours, while her son napped in his stroller by her side. The owner, who usually staffed the shop alone and needed a lunch break, agreed. The small salary Jane got paid for a babysitter to cover her fifteen hours of dancing and transportation time.

Next, she approached the dance studio and offered to design and teach a daily one-hour stretch class for nondancers in exchange for free enrollment in a two-hour advanced class right before or after the stretch class. They agreed. (Jane had shrewdly figured that the popularity of physical fitness was bringing nondancers to the studio, which did not yet have a proper class for this potentially large clientele.) Now her bar workout and the price of her lessons were covered.

The second three months of her time line presented a challenge. The scheduling of dance auditions being wildly unpredictable, Jane needed childcare more flexible and on tap than her present babysitter could provide. She needed someone who was available on twelve-hour notice and who was sure to be free any three of four hours of the day Jane needed her. She also needed to continue financing—and having time for—her lessons. By now, though, she had three interindependent relationships thriving:

1. The needlepoint shopowner saw her as a personable, knowledgable worker, and one who brought with her a unique asset. (Having a sleeping baby visible through the window brought in a lot of young mothers with strollers, who then became customers.)

2. The dancing school was profiting from the stretch class and planned to expand its program for nondancers. And:

3. Jane's husband was delighted and impressed with her ingenuity, and couldn't help soften his resistance to her overall plan. He was ready to cooperate and help.

Here's how she used these interindependencies to put her second three-month agenda into action:

1. The dancing school continued to give her free lessons and found for her a beginning dancer whose evening waitressing job left her entire days free to babysit—which she agreed to do, as needed, in exchange for private lessons from Jane that would be given during the baby's nap.

2. The needlepoint shopowner commissioned from Jane a large window tapestry which Jane would work on during the long waits that are such a maddening part of dance auditions. The money she made on the tapestry would start her childcare savings fund.

3. Jane's husband agreed to take over the baby on those late auditions that cut into the sitter's restaurant hours (even when it meant giving up his weekly softball game) and to take care of the baby when Jane got her first job, dancing in an evening theatrical revue.

Eventually, after that first job, Jane and her husband worked to come up with a joint six-month time line. Together, pooling their skills, they would produce a videotape of Jane's stretch class and another of the process of making a needlepoint tapestry. The first they would try to market in conjunction with the dance studio; the second would be the focal point of a series of weekend lessons that Jane would give at the needlepoint shop (splitting the proceeds with the owner).

If these projects were successful, Jane and her husband would each have a second career under way, one that would bring them together to offset those hours apart that their her-nights, his-days work schedule necessitated. The proceeds would pay for the nearly full-time childcare and, if they were really successful, could make their dream of buying a home come true.

Now that's successful interindependence.

Jane chose to start negotiating for help from her husband only after she'd negotiated successfully with others. The alternate way to break this same circle involved bringing her husband in at the start. I particularly recommend this method to older Comers who want to start or reenter careers after their children are in grade or junior high school. This way, the children—flattered, as they are at this age, by being given responsibility—also become partners in the interindependent negotiating. This is a ten-point plan by which you:

2. Negotiate with your husband and your school-age children for the help you need to get the training to do the work you want.
    a. Define the situation to yourself.

To take classes toward a master's degree in social work, Lee, thirty-seven, knew that she'd need more help around the house from her family; that she'd eventually need a three-day-a-week housekeeper instead of just the weekly cleaning woman; and that her husband and children would have to become more self-sufficient and less dependent on her.

    b. Again, to yourself: assess the trade-offs for the whole family, and do a costs-benefits analysis.

On the minus side: Lee's husband and children (an eleven-year-old daughter, a nine-year-old son) would lose a little time with her, time her husband depended on and time the children, facing the turbulent teen and preteen years, might very well need. And their tight budget would be strained by the housekeeper's salary. On the plus side, her income, in two years, would more than make up for the financial sacrifice and would start bringing more in to the family coffers just as the specter of college costs began to loom. And Lee's going back to school would give her so much greater identification with her children's lives that the quality of mother-child communication would greatly improve (to more than compensate for the loss of time she'd have to give them). Feeling more fulfilled and confident, Lee would also have more of substance to bring to her relationship with her husband. The verdict: In terms of money and relationship, the plusses outweighed the minuses.

    c. Present the situation, the trade-offs, and the payoff to your partner in a way, and at a time, that is conducive to successful negotiation.

Lee waited until her husband Bob was relaxed, after a workday that included a triumph for him, and the children were asleep. Rather than jump right to the proposition, she did a negotiating warm-up by talking about her increasing feeling that she had more to offer to the outside world and to her family than her current limited role as homemaker was letting her develop.

Then, briefly, clearly and assertively, she told Bob that she wanted to go back to school to get her master's degree and then to pursue a career as a social work administrator.

    d. Attend and observe.

Lee watched Bob look away, clench his teeth, reach for and light a cigarette. Bracing herself against his obvious tension, she listened to his counterargument: the children would be neglected; they would spend more money; his own life would suffer.

She silently recorded her disappointment in his attitude, and she geared herself not to be thrown by it.

    e. Keep focused.

Despite her dismay, Lee held to her agenda: she wanted an M.A. and a career. And there was help she had to have in order to get these things.

    f. Be alert for your partner's hidden agenda.

"But I count on you—not some maid—being here," Bob said. That was the real issue.

    g. Restate the payoff as the answer to his anxiety.

"But I will be here," Lee responded. "What time you'll lose from me will be more than made up for by the new qualities I'll be able to bring to my relationships with all of you. The housekeeper will just free all of us to enjoy those relationships more. Why don't we see how it goes for one semester?"

    h. Get direct help from partner and children by attaching importance, fun and ceremony to that help.

Lee enrolled in the master's program. Two of her weekly classes were scheduled so that she would get home in time to dine with her family, but not in enough time to prepare the meal. A third class wasn't over until 10 P.M.

To take care of the dinners on the earlier nights, she gave each of her kids the assignment to choose and cook and serve one meal every week. Good china would be used for these special events. The kids could ransack her cookbooks and shelves and do their own food shopping from a list they prepared. (They would be responsible for keeping to the food budget and for cleaning up after and putting everything away.) The rest of the family would rate the chef's masterpiece on a scale of 5 to 10 (no discouraging low numbers); an over-8-rated meal would be encored for company.

The children loved the idea.

To take care of the late night when she wouldn't be able to be with her family at all, Lee came up with the idea of a Forbidden

Delights Night Out for Bob and the kids. They would make a weekly ritual of going to a fast-food restaurant and relishing the junk food Lee disdained; then top it off with a movie of the action-adventure genre.

The children loved that idea, too, and Bob, presented in the deal as the Good Guy parent, liked it, too.

    i. Celebrate, reward and reinforce that help, and call attention to its positive effects on the family as a unit and on the individual members.

The children's meals were served to company, who remarked later to Lee and Bob on the new self-confidence the youngsters exuded. The successes spurred them to want to cook and to shop more.

The Forbidden Delights evenings brought Bob closer to the children.

Next, to heighten the new similarity in their three lives, Lee and the kids all did their school homework in the same room together at night, and took turns quizzing one another. The children's grades improved.

    j. After these first signs of payoff appear, present the case for secondary or additional help.

Once Bob saw how his wife's new agenda was enriching, not threatening, the family, he agreed to hire the housekeeper for three days a week.

That was two years ago. Today Lee has her master's degree and her career. The family has more money, a full-time housekeeper and four members who are more self-sufficient as individuals, yet also closer to each other, than they ever used to be.

That, too, is successful interindependence.

NEGOTIATING FOR HELP THROUGH INTERINDEPENDENCE FOR HAVERS: LEARNING TO LIVE WITH YOUR DELEGATIONS

Every strong, successful, busy woman I know saved her life in the same manner: she finally learned how to delegate. And I mean "finally" with all the bell-ringing emphasis I've implied—for, as we talked about earlier in this book, women have a terrible time letting go of unnecessary tasks. As we discussed in Chapter 5, we get struck with guilt (that great, revered excuse for inaction) and with the wrongheaded feeling that by giving away the drudgery work involved in keeping up a home, we're also somehow giving away the human work.

Or, having made it to Haver status, we secretly long for those earlier, innocent days when we could spend an hour looking for just the right birthday card for a friend; when we could hand-select every single outfit for the children; when we could make pesto from scratch. And in an attempt to wrest just those small, specific pleasures from the thick soup of housework that we now delegate to somebody else, we dive back into the soup pot itself—and come out barnacled with a lot of extraneous, unenjoyed tasks as well. We're stuck in a syndrome I characterized in Chapter 3, as the Two Faces of Undeservingness: In a panicked attempt to be both our past and present selves, we turn ourselves into the delegator and the delegatee.

Most working Havers, particularly those with children, know that they must have help on the home front, and they elicit that help, or hire that help, or both. But the relief that they actually derive—in sheer hours of freedom and in emotional and physical ease—is not nearly what they thought they were bargaining for.

They know how to delegate. They just don't know how to live with those delegations.

Here is how:

1. LET GO! (Phase One):
Realize that you alone cannot be responsible for your entire family's well-being.

"Bill doesn't care what the kids eat. If it weren't for me, they'd have pizza six nights of the week."

"The last time I let our thirteen-year-old do the laundry, everything white turned gray."

"Send my husband to the market and he comes home with the hardest pears, the mushiest bananas and the scratchy brand of toilet paper."

As hackneyed as these sentiments may be, women do feel them and they won't let them go. Bite the bullet and make yourself relax your standards; let your husband and kids learn by doing (and finally become self-sufficient, as you want them to be). Force yourself to look the other way. In the same way that a dieter wouldn't sit down in front of a piece of chocolate cake, close the door to your son's unmade bedroom—and to the kitchen, after your husband has just finished making chili. Throw a large towel over the dishes in the sink that await tomorrow's visit from the cleaning woman. And if you have a dinner meeting at seven-thirty, don't dash home from the office "to shower and change" (translation: to check up on things, pick up after everybody, get embroiled in the household's tempest-in-a-teapot of the day—and not even have time to freshen up, after all). Instead, arrange to meet the kids outside of the home, and sit with them through an early hamburger-restaurant dinner—or use the interim time to sit at your desk and do extra work, or visit a museum, or read a novel over a glass of wine at a nearby café. When you walk in your front door at ten, your household will have survived your absence.

2. LET GO! (Phase Two):
Find a childcare person you absolutely trust.

For the working mother of a baby or young child, here's the paradox: You hire the most loving, experienced caretaker you find, so you won't have to spend a moment worrying about your baby's welfare, only to wind up spending a lot of time worrying, instead, about your maternal competence. How come this woman can get your child to eat strained peas and you can't? Can dress him without his screaming? Can lay him down for his nap at noon and have him asleep by twelve-thirteen?

No, of course you're not going to fire her and hire someone less excellent just so you can look better to yourself, but maybe, you tell yourself, you should work on developing her skills. Now confusion and self-flagellation set in. Do you alter your child's dinner hour (and cancel your business drink dates) so you can go home and feed him and thereby become as good at the feeding as she? Do you spend both days of the weekend you counted on for love and replenishment "working on" getting him to nap for you, and ending up feeling both tyrannical and impotent (hardly the shape you want to be in when you waltz through the office doors Monday morning to try to make a confident bid for a project)? Should you not take the nursemaid along with you on your much needed week at the resort and do twenty-four-hour-a-day, hands-on mothering instead?

Relax. Rather than trying to imitate and match your caretaker's very well honed talents with your child, focus on and rejoice in your own. No one can approximate your love or substitute the unique things you give your child. Delegation is wasted when skills are duplicated. Delegation is successful when two people bring slightly different, supplementary strong points to a task or to a person. Who wants to unwrap two boxes and find identical gifts?

Recent infant research tells us that an emotionally healthy baby will forge a different interactional fit—write a different script—with each of the major adults in its life. Be glad of your child's power of discrimination, his smooth fit with his caretaker—and congratulate yourself for taking the time, and the money, to have provided for him so well.

3. Ask yourself, What do I love to do?

Anyone who has ever separated eggs for a recipe know how exacting this small act has to be. If you don't carefully lift the yolk out whole, it breaks and bleeds into the surrounding white, and the recipe is done for.

It's the same thing with qualifying a delegation. You have to be very exacting in lifting out, whole, the little thing you love to do from the surrounding mass of work you don't have time for. If you let that one task bleed into the doing of others, your agenda is done for.

Don't exceed your self-promised limit; keep your boundaries clear. The housekeeper is to do all the supermarket shopping, but you buy the fresh fruits and vegetables. She puts everything away (you've taught her exactly where, and exactly how you like produce washed, so you don't have to do anything over again), but you cut and arrange the flowers. She does the laundry, but you do the sweaters your own special way, by hand. The whole family chips in to make weekday dinners, but you give yourself one gourmet touch at each and, on weekends perhaps, a full-scale meal. The housekeeper picks up the kids from school and takes them home each day—except Tuesday, when (by negotiation with your boss) you leave the office early in order to take them, and support them through, their piano lessons, and every Friday in spring and summer, when you get off work early (again by negotiation) to play ball with them in the park.

To stop and savor the richness of life without breaking stride

toward your goals, you must be very specific about just what acts
and tasks comprise that richness for you. Do them—only them.
Enjoy them to the hilt. Then let go and move on.

4. Delegate! Hire a trusted person to help you organize your own life and your family's life.

Household administrivia is the organizational work that goes
beyond the basic survival work of cooking, cleaning and childcare.
And what a lot of work it is. There's comparison shopping and
option-investigating for everything from vacation homes to vacuum cleaners to oral surgeons to wineglasses. There are repairs,
remodelings, renovations; inquiries about everything from extending service warranties to getting or not getting a new kind of
telephone or cable TV service. There are dinner parties to plan,
theater tickets to buy, travel timetables to secure, restaurants to
make reservations at—and phone calls to check and recheck the
taste and convenience of all the parties involved. There are four
seasons of clothes to buy for each family member (and to clean, put
in storage, reline, alter, change buttons on, etc.) There are garden-
ers, auto mechanics and salespeople, and other service people to
deal with. There are trackdowns that can take a whole day: which
store has this brand of ski wear, that line of makeup, a certain type
of dishware in a certain color, a glass globe lamp to replace the one
that just broke?

No one can do any of this but you—right?

Wrong.

Someone you trust very well can.

One top woman executive and single parent realized, after her
last promotion, that if she didn't get help in this way she'd be
constantly frazzled. She thought of her sister, a recent widow
whose one child was off in college. This woman had a wealth of life-
organizing talent but no place to use it. She could also use some
money and contact with people. And no one knew better this
executive's taste, temperament, style and quirks, and those of her
family.

So the executive approached her sister about going on salary
and becoming "Someone in My Corner"—an affectionate job title
that might also be called that of life manager, first lieutenant,
household contractor, aide-de-camp or, for these purposes, personal administrivial assistant.

"I hold the reins," the executive says, "and I make the decisions. But my sister does the research, makes the phone calls, does the ground-level investigating to bring me the options to make the decisions from—and then she does the legwork to expedite those decisions."

You can find people to do this job everywhere: a neighbor with time on her hands, a college or high school student, or any of those people who advertise themselves as babysitters/housecleaners/dogwalkers on laundry and supermarket bulletin boards. You can hire this person to be your administrivial assistant for however many hours per week you need to lighten your load. Do so. And when you do:

5. Keep in mind the important distinction between lovework and legwork.

Lovework is glimpsing an adorable party dress for your daughter as you dash from a store to an appointment. *Legwork* is sending your administrivial assistant out to buy it so you can present it to her.

Lovework is thinking how tickled your husband would be if a group of musicians turned up to serenade him with his favorite Dixieland songs on his fiftieth birthday. *Legwork* is sending your assistant out to find such a group.

Lovework is knowing all the things you want in a summer house so everyone in your family will be happy. *Legwork* is listing them for your assistant and having her call the real estate agents in four different communities to bring back options to narrow the field.

Lovework is all the decisions and plans and creative leaps and sober assessments you make to nurture those you love in your inimitable style. *Legwork* is simply carrying through on the mechanics.

And finally:

6. Delegate to yourself a peaceful weekend.

The same executive who hired her sister used to have terrible weekends dreading what was in store for her at the office on Monday: the people she had to reprimand, or soothe, or finesse; the disagreements she had to referee, the crises she had to troubleshoot—and the sheer avalanche of work that always seemed more than the week could hold.

She finally decided to put a stop to all that. Now, every Friday, instead of having a two-hour lunch, she has a sandwich at her desk while she clears two hours of work that she'd slotted for the upcoming Monday. Next, she "puts all the anguish in one one-hour grid on her wall calendar": she makes a list of all the unpleasant early week phone calls and confrontations, puts it in a desk drawer, and writes a big reminding A (for Anguish) under 3–4 P.M. Tuesday. ("Bad news can always wait a day," she says, "and burying it in a midweek time slot, rather than having it stare at me first thing Monday morning, makes it far less threatening and, on Friday afternoon, immensely forgettable.") Finally, she types a list of everything she's left for herself to do on Monday. No dread, no anguish and two hours' less work than she'd expected.

She slips the list ("my valentine to myself") into her typewriter so it'll be the first thing she sees when she sits back down at her desk forty-eight hours later.

And when she leaves the office for the day, she really leaves.

"For years, I thought of my life as a series of crises with small intermissions," this woman says. "I thought it had to be that way. Now I know it doesn't."

INTERINDEPENDENCE ON THE WORK FRONT FOR COMERS

Career help for Comers means one of two things: (1.) getting that job promotion that finally includes help (in the form of an assistant or secretary) so that you can more quickly and effectively prove yourself creatively; and/or (2.) developing a skills or time or favor exchange with another Comer, so that you can both get what you want, and get where you want to be, much faster and better than if you each had to do everything alone.

I call the first form of negotiated help Pushing Upward; the second, Teaming up and Pushing Outward.

1. Pushing Upward

Jill was an assistant to a man who owned a small, independent printing press catering to the Los Angeles film community. She wanted to stop doing the man's administrivia and to start doing the creative work along with him: going out into the client community, bringing in new customers, creating new projects.

The man was a controlling type with a big ego. The press was his baby, his alone. He was owner-executive; the printers were the faceless technicians. In between him and the printers, and nearly as faceless, was Jill, whose day was tied up doing invoices, checking production, doing typing, making sure orders were picked up and delivered.

How to move herself up and rearrange the deck on her boss's tight ship?

"What does your boss love the most?" I asked Jill.

"Making money and being in charge," she replied.

"All right," I said. "Your interindependent plan has to appeal to both of those loves; it has to allow him to maximize both of those things."

"While I'm also helping myself get ahead?" she asked, baffled at the seeming contradiction.

"It can be done," I assured her. "Let's start with the first of his loves."

a. Calculate how much money your boss is throwing away by not hiring you a secretary.

At my suggestion, Jill logged her day on a two-column sheet of paper. Under the heading PROFITABLE TIME, she listed those things she did that brought money into the business and the time she spent on these. Under UNPROFITABLE TIME, she listed her sheer maintenance tasks (typing, Xeroxing, etc.) and the times taken on these.

She called several office temp agencies and found the going rate for a secretary to be six dollars an hour. She calculated that by hiring a temporary secretary for twenty hours a week, her boss would be freeing her up to do the business-soliciting work that could well add thousands of dollars to the company's yearly intake.

b. Determine the form of your pitch and incorporate your boss's need for control and power into your own aims.

Jill was much more comfortable writing out her ideas than she was with presenting an argument orally. Her boss had a very different style. He was impatient with reading anything longer than two sentences. Besides, written communication denied him the showman's power he loved to display. He liked to lean back in his swivel chair and lace his fingers behind his neck and listen, then expound on what he heard. "I really want to avoid having to deal with his ego trip," Jill said. "It'll just throw me off balance. I'm going to write him a memo; that way, I'll stay in control."

"You won't stay in control that way," I corrected her. "Poverty Mentality is thinking that your way is the only way to do something. And one negotiating mistake I see working women make again and again is thinking that they can gain power by trying to combat or neutralize a man's form of power. That approach doesn't work. Instead of taking the defensive, incorporate his need for power into your strategy. Compromise. Write the memo, which you do well, but walk into his office and speak from it, giving him what he prefers. That way, both of you will be negotiating from strength. He'll feel comfortable enough to listen to what you're proposing without feeling he's giving something up or being asked to."

That would be the form of Jill's pitch for help. But she also needed to include two other things: (1.) substantiation of her immediate ability to move beyond administrivial work; and (2.) a creative idea for expanding her role in the company—and expanding her boss's business as well. Taking the first step first:

c. Get crash-course experience with the work you want to undertake. Don't make your pitch for help until you're ready.

It was all well and good for Jill to see how much money her boss could make if she were free to go out and bring business in. But did she know enough to bring that business in effectively? "I can't learn until I go out there and start," she said to me. "Not good enough," I replied. "If you're convincing your boss that it's going to be worthwhile to him to hire you help, you have to be able to make good on your end immediately. You make your plan less attractive to him if he has to wait for results after he's invested in the secretary. Train yourself before you ask."

We worked out a strategy through which Jill would spend two months finding out what she needed to know in order to go out and be an effective business representative.

"Go right to the people who know," I told her. "The office managers of various production houses and studio departments. Do so on your own time." She did. Over lunch, in person, and over the phone, she found out what she needed to know. And in the process of that research, she also found out enough to be able to:

d. Formulate a creative, lucrative, business-expanding idea that will justify your promotion.

Independent printers who catered to the movie and TV industry were basically anonymous outside jobbers. By printing scripts, production notes, budget reports, publicity packages and so forth, they were helping to put forth the glamour and visibility of the industry they served, but they had neither glamour nor visibility themselves.

Jill and I came up with the idea of putting out a monthly newsletter—called *Indiprint* (a play on the term "indieprod," which is the industry nickname for "independent producer")—which would call the industry's attention to new printing styles and innovations, spotlight the various printers and their specialties and generally heighten the visibility and image of companies like her boss's. And his financing and production of the project would guarantee his company the premiere place in the clients' minds.

She worked up a sample first issue, brought it in with her memo, which she presented as we discussed. She listed herself as the editor of the newsletter and her boss as publisher. And she gave over half the first page to a picture of and a letter from him.

He loved the newsletter; was easily convinced to hire Jill a secretary and to expand her job. She is now no longer an administrivial anything but the clear second in command, making 30 percent more than she had before. Meanwhile, his business has shot up and he feels important.

Now that's successful interindependence.

2. Teaming Up: Negotiate to Help One Another Through the Foundation of an Interindependent Partnership

You can negotiate for help not just vertically (from someone above you) but laterally: from a friend or a peer. I'm not just talking about business partnerships (by which two people start a service, agency, store, etc.) or creative partnerships (by which two people compose, write or design together). It's also possible to form a limited interindependent partnership whereby the two of you strategize to help each other out with time, childcare, household care, career contacts or administrivia according to a mutually useful, jointly tailored map of needs.

For example: Comer A, divorced with a five-year-old child and living in a two-bedroom house, needs three days a week of after-school-through-dinnertime childcare in order to leverage her market research career. Comer B, single with no child, living with a roommate in a small apartment, needs a quiet place to work on her novel. They come together and make a deal: Comer B will have the use of Comer A's house to work in five days a week (while Comer A is at work and her daughter is at kindergarten) in exchange for picking the child up from kindergarten Monday, Wednesday and Friday and caring for her until her mother comes home.

Another example: Comer C is returning to her acting career after the birth of her second child. She is taking a select acting class and going to highly competitive auditions. She doesn't have time to do this and to also do everything she has to do around the house. Her friend Comer D is single, has no children and is eager to move up in the large theatrical agency where she is an assistant. She is also a very good cook. They come together and make a deal: Comer C will bring Comer D along with her to auditions and to classes, so Comer D can get an inside track on new acting talent to sign up for the agency. In exchange, Comer D will do Comer C's shopping for the week, and will prepare three ready-to-freeze entrees for four which Comer C will pick up every Sunday, stick in her freezer and defrost for her family during the week.

For whatever kind of help you need, another Comer you know probably needs a complementary kind of help. With goodwill, clear goals, flexibility and trust, the two of you can make an ingenious and smoothly tailored trade of skills, services, space, time and introductions.

NEGOTIATING FOR HELP THROUGH INTERINDEPENDENCE ON THE CAREER FRONT FOR HAVERS

"I wish I could get a truly terrific staffer who could just take the ball and run with it, instead of the people I have now, whose work I have to do, on top of my own!"

"Loyalty and service from my secretary? That's a joke. But, now, if I were a man, I'd get an entirely different kind of treatment from her."

These are two complaints I hear again and again from Haver

women. Both can be eliminated: the first, by adapting to work the principles of living with your delegations that we discussed, as they pertained to the home front, a moment ago; the second, by providing (and making clear, up front, that you will be providing) humanistic and career-leveraging perks in place of whatever airs of sexual electricity and power by association your secretary believes she is getting from a male boss and cannot get from you.

Both solutions are interindependent ones. Your staff and secretary benefit at the same time that you get the quantity, and quality, of help that you need. Everyone gives and feels given to at once.

Here are three main points to the solution:

1. Don't rob your staff of their creativity. Stimulate each staffer's independent judgment. Let her confidence flourish and her responsibility increase, and everyone will be the better for it.

The ironic thing is, we hire a person for her judgment, yet by constantly peering over her shoulder—by refusing to let go of what we've delegated—we turn her into an anxious creature loath to make an independent move for fear of displeasing her boss. (And resentful, of course, of that stultification, that fear.) So instead of growing into greater responsibility, the staffer shrinks into less; instead of being freed from administrivia, the boss assumes more. Instead of two people bringing their different skills and strengths to a situation, one person (the staffer) is constantly asked to try to duplicate the other's (the boss's), at the expense of her own. And instead of getting a unique product or a new and creative solution, you just get more of the same thing that the boss would have come up with on her own.

Most of us don't let go of control enough to let our staffers grow into the kind of self-sufficiency and creativity that will make them happy, free us up and make for a unique product. Try to let go, and it will pay off.

2. Let your subordinates know you want them to rise along with you, that you care about their goals and will help them move toward them.

One of the most successful women I know, a retail executive, always begins an interview with a promising prospective staffer with the question, "Supposing you could do anything, what would it be?" They tell her their dreams. If they're hired, she tells them that she will try, whenever possible, to make sure their duties include elements of their aspired-to specialty. And she follows through on that promise.

Anyone joining this woman's staff has heard the stories about the artistically inclined secretary she hired who is now an assistant art director in the store, and the merchandise inventory checker who is now on his way up in the accounting department. Her staff knows that she cares about their future; in return, they put special care into the work they do for her. People will rise up to the trust, dignity and concern conferred upon them. It's as simple as that.

3. Celebrate with your staff.

The young co-owner of a thriving advertising agency has champagne and balloons and streamers let loose in the office whenever a big account is landed. And on the first day of spring, staffers arrive at work to find daisy bouquets on their desks. The Monday morning after the close of a harrowing campaign, everyone who was involved gets a handwritten note from her, explicitly thanking him or her for their individual contributions. And sometimes, on drizzly, draggy midweek afternoons, she treats everybody to pizza.

"What's the point of working with people," this woman asks, "if not for the chance to be spontaneous, to feel connected and to celebrate?"

Indeed, this is true not just for work but for all of life. Which brings us to Part V of this book, and to the words that, of all of the words I've written here, are probably those closest to my heart.

V

BEYOND MONEY

CHAPTER 14

Toward a Life of Expansive Abundance

"I've been rich, and I've been poor, and rich is better."

At the very beginning of this book, I told you that by the time we finished here together you would understand the deceptively simple truth of that phrase. I think that now you do. *It is just as easy to be rich as to be poor.* It is no "big deal" to go for, and achieve, abundance. There are no complicated secrets to spend a lifetime decoding; there is no morally suspect lunge required of you that leaves ruined or compromised lives in the wake.

Rather, abundance is a choice—just as its opposite, the Poverty Mentality, is a choice. You can elect to remain stuck in denial and deprivation, or you can elect to break out of them. The one decision takes no more time or energy or sacrifice than the other. What it takes is a different state of mind.

We have spoken in detail of that different state of mind: the feelings, attitudes and behaviors it consists of; the strategies it points to; and the negotiations with the people and tasks and time and resources of your life that can help you put it into an action that yields results. You have learned that there are responsibilities involved in breaking out of the Poverty Mentality—responsibilities to your capabilities, your goals, your dreams.

But beyond these responsibilities lie other ones. These are spiritual and ethical responsibilities. And they are the ones that matter most. For once you have "made it"—once you have achieved your Haver status, or consolidated that status, or know clearly all the things you must do to become a Haver—you see that, yes, you have slain that dragon; but what do you have in the dead dragon's place? You begin to face the yearning for internal richness which your lack of external richness had for years obscured from your sight. And that kind of richness, you begin to understand, is something that no amount of money or power can buy.

I could spend a lot of time trying to make these following statements sound thoroughly original and not a bit corny, but in their shopwornness, and under their unfortunate varnish of cliché, lie their truth:

- Fulfillment comes from the inside out. It is a feeling, an extremely personal, unquantifiable and sometimes inexpressible warmth that has nothing to do with the glories you have gained or the objects you have bought to surround you.

- I have met many, many very successful men and women, and none of them have been truly filled up by anything but their relationships—the love that they give and receive.

- I have never met anyone with money but with no generosity from the heart who has been happy.

Money, as we have seen, brings us the freedom to explore options, to accomplish, to perfect. Having money, as we discussed in Chapter 10, is like *not* having a toothache. It's the absence of preoccupying pain, the thing you get out of the way so that everything else can be clearly visible, enjoyable, embraceable. It is very important, as we have learned, to get past all those barriers and hesitations that we've invented or inherited, and to master money, to go for money, to shamelessly and aggressively and creatively leverage our money.

But once we are doing this, we must step back and seek a balance. We must keep up our vigilance but drop our obsession. We must expand our attention, and our hearts, to what is beyond money. If we do not do so—if we remain tunnel-visioned—then we keep feeling the toothache despite the fact that the toothache has been lavishly cured. People in this state graduate to the Poverty Mentality in its most ironic and pathetic form. "But he (or she) had everything!" we often say, in shock, of the suicides and drug overdoses of the rich and famous. Yes. The person had everything and nothing.

All of life may be arithmetic, but life only counts in the fullest once you have stopped counting.

What lies beyond money is an ethic, a life principle, that I call *expansive abundance*. It is an attitude of joyful, openhearted giving and getting; a self-regenerating, often infectious appetite for life. Expansive abundance magnetizes people to you and empowers those to whom you come in contact, creating a kind of great chain of giving—a ripple effect that keeps widening and widening, person to person, life to life to life, all around this planet.

People who operate out of the state of expansive abundance never worry that there won't be enough—enough love, support, influence, help, expertise, positions, status, energy—left for them after they have given to others. Yet these people aren't naïfs or Polyannas or saints. Rather, they are savvy people who, for all their spontaneity and inner harmony, know that they have clear duties—responsibilities that go beyond self-advancement and self-improvement and into life enrichment, and not just for their own individual or their immediate loved ones' lives.

People who operate out of the state of expansive abundance are the truly rich people in this world. We know them when we meet them. They radiate. They seem to have some "secret of life." Yet, though the aura they give off is luminous, it is not elusive. And though the source of their fulfillment is intangible, it is not unlearnable.

I have been lucky to have known three of these people, so far, in my life. As different as they are, one from the other, I see now that they all have had something in common. Each of them knew, and practiced, the three responsibilities that comprise the ethic of expansive abundance: (1.) the Responsibility to Optimism, (2.) the Responsibility to Others and (3.) the Responsibility to Delight.

I will tell you about each of these people in a minute, but first let me describe the qualities that they took as duties, as first premises of their lives.

THE RESPONSIBILITY TO OPTIMISM

Not long ago, I had the privilege of meeting a remarkable man, Robert Muller, the assistant secretary-general of the United Nations. He is not a young man, and his years of work with this world organization have placed him in the eye of the hurricanes of famine, bloodshed, seemingly implacable strife.

Yet he understands that sinking to despair solves nothing. "I have long known that I can join the ranks of the pessimists," he told me. "I can look at the war, the pestilence, the hunger, and let myself see little else. Or I can look at the distance we have come in some areas, in stopping cholera, in wiping out poisonous medications, in working toward population zero growth. I choose the latter so I can go on living and working purposefully."

In our own lives, we have the same choice. We can describe the glass as half empty or half full. The former view keeps us angry, bitter, cynical, blaming and inert. The latter allows us to take our realistic hope—not Vacant Hope or naïve hope, but measured, considered, informed hope, based on a genuine study of the probability and options and a desire to make the best of things—and to shrewdly act.

We can look at the lot of women in this country in the last ten years and see the backlash against feminism in many court decisions and elections, the intransigent (and in some cases worsening) wage gap between the sexes, the return to conservative social values. And then we can give up.

Or we can measure the gains—the really considerable gains, certainly in awareness, if you think back twenty years; analyze the mistakes; understand the growing pains (of the women's movement and the postwar American middle class); place everything in the context of history; and, separately and together, plot the next move. Some doors are half opened, some tightly closed. And we can concentrate on that which holds the most promise of good results. When the half-open door is pushed all the way open—with a strong, unfrustrated hand—alternative routes to what lies behind the closed door have a way of turning up.

I say to women who despair of "the way things still are" separately and in organizations: "Take all the time and energy and emotion you've been putting into trying to change the man in your life and the men at your job *out* of that effort—and use it, instead, to learn about leveraging your own life and to leverage your money." If every woman would do that, things would change fast.

Being responsible to optimism means staying on your course even when some would try to push you off it. Recently, I met a powerful businessman who, in the course of talk that had until that moment been positive, suddenly leaned in, said, "I'll do you a favor by telling you this"—and proceeded to make a statement that, however well meant, constituted a grave attack on my work.

Several things this man had said led me to see that he was coming from an emotional state of scarcity, not one of abundance; that he had recently suffered a setback at work; that he had a destructive negotiating style. Still, his words stung.

But before I was willing to allow self-doubt to enter my thinking, I realized my responsibility to my own optimism. It is at this challenged time that you must pull out all your internal resources and listen to your best self. That is what I did.

Pushing aside pride, I took the man up on the offer he had made to introduce me to an important business group. In the course of the next weeks, I made, through the man, some very valuable and positive contacts. And the man himself admitted his insecurities and his unhappiness with his offputting style. He wanted my professional help toward changing all that.

I took the initial adversity the afternoon with the man presented and looked at it as a kind of gift. Instead of running away from it, I moved toward it. When we adopt this kind of active optimism, we can all win.

THE RESPONSIBILITY TO OTHERS

This man came from the classic, defensive position of scarcity: We're all competitors after the same rare prize. If you get ahead in any way, then I'm all that much closer to failing. So I'm not going to help you without throwing in some whammy to throw you off balance. After all, how can I operate otherwise when there isn't enough to go around?

There's another position a person can come from: that of abundance. When you come from a position of abundance, you understand that your giving to or rejoicing for another not only takes nothing away from you but, in fact, adds something. You know that help and goodwill begets more of the same, that what goes around comes around, that you can only be empowered by empowering someone else. You see abundance not as the private, competitive accretion of things (tangible or intangible) but as a vital, living flow —of empathy, energy, concern, support, contacts, skills, reliances, from human to human to human. What is being shared and passed on, in that flow, doesn't dry up from use but is, instead, replenished by it.

I was lucky to have been raised by two parents who, though they had little money, both came from a state of abundance. My dear, wonderful mother (who to this day tucks dimes away in the freezer!) always kept a *knipple* (Yiddish for nest egg) so that I could buy that special book, that doll. She knew that it was important to plant tiny little surprise oases of plenty in our otherwise tightly budgeted life. In some small way, she wanted our material life to echo the emotional philosophy that she and my father lived by: There's always enough to go around; there's always more coming . . . and more, and more.

The sense of responsibility to others that grows from that philosophy of abundance can take many forms. I have become active in Physicians for Social Responsibility because I want to give back what I have been given, and I can't think of a more powerful or meaningful way than to try to save the people on this planet from a nuclear extinction. If you are a Haver, there is no excuse not to exercise your responsibility to others in whatever form you choose. Surely you have something—time, power, savvy, money, energy, influence, skills—of value left over to give. If you can't reach beyond yourself you will probably always feel empty, and you will certainly never feel rich.

If you are a Comer, you may feel you have little time and energy to give to social causes. For you, the responsibility to others takes a different form: that of mutual empowerment with your peers. The favors, advice and contacts you share with your co-Comer friends will create a circle of reciprocity through which you, in turn, will be given to. And all of this will bolster the general strength of your community of peers: as one of you succeeds with the other's help, it makes it easier for the next to succeed—and the next, and the next, and the next. I stress again, as I've shown through this book: in collaboration, in interindependence, lies the greatest, and most gratifying, power.

THE RESPONSIBILITY TO DELIGHT

It may seem a contradiction in terms to call joy a duty, but think about it a bit. The capacity to exult and to celebrate sanctifies and elevates the ordinary, foments good fellow feeling, spreads cheer like rain.

Close your eyes and picture the supporters of a candidate jumping up and down and hugging one another when victory has been announced . . . the face of the honored guest (and everyone else in the room) at a successful surprise party . . . the laughter of parents when their toddler has just come out with a remarkably funny new phrase. Such moments of spontaneous elation drive home to us, with a force not found elsewhere, the fact that the best things in life are emotional and interpersonal, not material; that people, together, can create a glory, a glow.

That's such an important fact, yet so many of us forget it. So many of us neglect our capacity to delight. Comers are too caught up in survival to make time to delight, and Havers have forgotten how to. "How sad and ironic," says my friend Marilyn Wood (who, as a professional celebration artist, actually makes a life's work out of spreading this neglected skill to others), "that our society tells people at sixty-five: 'Great, you're retiring! Now go out and enjoy life!' when, all along, it has never nurtured their ability to do that enjoying, so when they're finally given the time to do so, they don't know how!"

On the other hand, there are people like the New York couple I heard of who decided to marry after years of living together. They dutifully went off to buy a weekend country house (though both of them were city-lovers) and planned a dignified, appropriately small wedding. But the houses the real estate agent was showing them gave them no joy. On the other hand, their decision to marry —and the long, bumpy, but in retrospect beautiful road they traveled to their deeply felt commitment—did give them joy, and pride.

They chucked the idea of the country house and, instead, used the money to plan a jubilant, lavish, twenty-four-hour wedding celebration for all of their friends. They wanted to create an exhilaration, to spread a delight, that matched their own. They wanted to give the people they loved the most glorious day of their life.

They did just that. Was it impractical? By traditional standards, perhaps. But the expansively abundant approach to life they were getting in those twenty-four hours was an investment in the marriage as great as, if not greater than, that afforded by any house.

THE THREE TRULY RICH PEOPLE I HAVE KNOWN

To have all the three responsibilities that are the elements of expansive abundance in place gives a person a richness of mind, body and spirit that circumstance can't quite intrude on, can't dampen. Truly rich people are strong from within. They have a great appetite for life, but they never seem greedy at the table. They have a mastery of life, yet it seems so offhand, so evolved from the inside out as to be utterly uncalculated. Such people have a worldliness, a deep and comfortable fluency with people with all walks and levels and cultures of life, that no number of first-class plane tickets or Ph.D.s can buy. They are wise without wearing their wisdom like badges. You can learn from these people, yet they never preach.

The first of the three truly rich people I have learned from is Marilyn Wood, a dancer and celebration artist who travels the world working with other dancers and with musicians, singers, architects and others using buildings and rivers and mountains and shrines to create aesthetic joy. One month she'll create celebrations for the thousand-year anniversary of a Buddhist Temple in Hong Kong; the next, she'll do the same in the Atrium of New York's modern Seagram Building. She is a citizen of the world and, in a sense, of the centuries. She has a wealth of experience beyond belief. She is as much at home riding with the chickens in a fourth-class train in Mexico as she is mingling with French heads of state at a reception at the Louvre.

"I chose, a long time ago, to live my life as richly and as fully as possible," she has told me. "I'm happiest when I'm collaborating—with other people, with the environment, with history and land." Making a living as a dancer and an artist is not easy. Nor is traveling when you have, as she has, three children. But none of this has daunted Marilyn. "If your efforts come from the path of the heart, then people understand. You can give, and they'll receive. You can ask, and they'll grant you.

"Years ago, when my twins were very young and I was dancing in the Merce Cunningham company, Merce asked me: 'But how can you travel with two young children at home?' I just smiled and said: 'I'm not their only parent.' My whole family supports what I do. I have people that I love, work that I'm intensely connected to, with my heart, my body and my intellect. I have three meals a day. Even though I don't have all that much money, how can I ever feel *any* kind of impoverishment?"

The second rich person I have known is a woman with the marvelous name Elizabeth Addis Dickey-Pellett. She was the social studies consultant for the Los Angeles Public School System when I was working on the State of California's Curriculum Commission. Her job involved making sure that minorities and women were equitably portrayed in schoolbooks. But this was just one of the ways she gave to others.

Betty, as we called her, was a brilliant woman, immensely committed to humanity, always involved with the plight of people, whether Chicanos, Native Americans or Jews. Despite her fairly modest middle-class income, her ostensibly bureaucratic job and her unpartnered state, she lived one of the most abundant, sophisticated and unlonely lives I have ever known.

She was always taking in stray people who needed emergency support and lodging (stray animals, too), and she built an apartment over her garage for them. When these hapless friends and acquaintances weren't her houseguests, the apartment was turned over, free of charge, to foreign students, whom she fed and mentored. She felt it was her responsibility as a citizen of the world to take care of these students, who would then take back—and spread in—their homelands in Africa and the Far East the education and the values she had made it easier for them to obtain. She never felt she was giving more than she was getting from this act.

Besides, Betty knew that if she ever got into financial trouble, she could move into the garage apartment and rent out her main house. Thus, she gave heartfully and smartly. She was never a bit of a martyr in attitude or deed. She took care of others and of herself with the elegant economy that characterized her life.

Betty loved beauty as well as service. Her house was full of art and flowers. She collected ceramic eggs from Russia and Mexican folk pieces from artists who became her friends (and who became, through her work, positive exemplars to thousands of Hispanic California children). Making every meal a celebration, she set the table for the simplest lunches and breakfasts with her fine silver and sparkling imported crystal, and with the orchids she raised in her backyard greenhouse. I used to kid her that she was the only person I knew who bought expensive pitted cherries. ("Why should I put my guests to the bother of removing the pits?" she replied.)

And she had such a disciplined eye for beauty that in a room full of tapestries, while everyone else ambled from one to the next, not sure of what he or she was looking to appreciate, she moved swiftly and surely to the one six-inch square on the *one* tapestry that was the most special of all. To be that focused and that expansive; that welcoming *and* that discriminating; that committed and that aesthetic; and to be so instinctively a part of the whole world community—that's a rare wholeness. That's richness to me.

The third rich person I have known was my father. Like my grandfather, whom I told you about in Chapter 7, Dad made the conscious decision not to become a gladiator. He was a cost accountant by profession, but, oh, was that man rich! When he died, at age seventy-six, hundreds of people came to his funeral: rich people, poor people, they all wanted to say goodbye to a man who, by society's standards, had no wealth or power or status but who knew how to relish the human connection.

When I think of my father, I think of a man taking the family car (an old one, which we finally got, after years of riding the bus) out for a ten-minute errand—and come back home three hours later, beaming from ear to ear. "Where have you been? We've all been worried!" my mother would say (though by now she knew better). And Dad would tell about the couple he saw by the side of the freeway whose car had gone out on them and how he'd towed them to the gas station and then driven them the fifty-six miles to their home. "They loved me, kid!" he'd say, like a stock trader who'd just gotten a windfall. "They loved me!"

Like Marilyn and like Betty, Dad was never exploited or taken advantage of for his adventurous altruism. He was never robbed; he was never ripped off; he was never held up. I don't think this is an accident. And, also just like those other two, he was never jealous of others. "You just won the lottery?" he'd say to a friend. "Hot damn!" And he meant it.

Dad died with three things in his pocket that said so much about his life: twelve cents; peppermint-stick candy that he used to pass out to the kids at temple; and dozens of folded receipts from the temple for the donations that accompanied his constant prayers—

prayers he said for all the people he cared for: Baptist, Catholic, whatever.

Two days before he had that unexpected, fatal heart attack, we were sitting together, talking. In that offhand but significant tone people use when they alone know, for no "reason," that it's time to think about such things, he remarked: "You know, I've had a wonderful life."

"How can you say that?" I countered. "You've worked so hard. You've had sickness, you've had debts, you've had surgery . . ."

"I've had everything, Tessa," he corrected. "Look at your mother! And you! And Harriet and Ted! [My sister and brother.] Tell me." He laughed confidently. "What more could I ask?"

It's taken me years to know how right he was—to learn, in my own, more complex way, what he knew all along in his heart. But I don't for a moment regret my parallel, more circuitous search. It has given me this book. And, with it, I hope I have given something to you—because we will *all* be the richer for that.

I hope that all of you with whom I've shared these pages will be passionate for having, while able to ease up on your passion for getting. I hope you will take to your own lives the words of Robert Muller*: "I have decided to love my life—to throw in the gauntlet for it, to believe in it, to find it exalting in every respect, at every moment from the beginning to the end."

I hope that you will learn the lesson so eloquently and effectively provided by Lester Levenson and Virginia Lloyd's Sedona Method, that the only feeling we can really feel in a phenomenal way is loving. And I hope that you will make the opportunity to practice that truth, and that you will do so fearlessly.

I say "fearlessly" because you need give nothing up in the process. Once you're self-aware, once you're armed with the basic material (and I hope this book has given you that), you can trust yourself to let go. Having, finally, is as much achieved by releasing as it is by acquiring and holding. I'm reminded now of the way they catch monkeys in India. They take a bell-shaped jar with a narrow neck and fill it to capacity with nuts. The monkey comes, sticks his hand in, grabs a fistful of nuts—and is trapped.

All he had to do to have his freedom was to let go: relax his muscles, unclench his fist, let fall the nuts and smoothly draw his

* From *Most of All, They Taught Me Happiness*, Doubleday, 1978.

hand out of the jar. What a very simple act. What a very available choice.

And so it is with breaking out of the Poverty Mentality. Abundance—financial, emotional, professional, and spiritual abundance —takes no more effort than does deprivation.

Which is better?

Rich is better . . . after all.

INDEX

RESILIENCY

Resiliency
HOW TO BOUNCE BACK

STRONGER · SMARTER · FASTER · SMARTER · STRONGER · FASTER · FASTER · STRONGER

TESSA ALBERT
WARSCHAW, PED.
DEE BARLOW, M.D.

MASTERMEDIA

Resiliency: How to Bounce Back Faster, Stronger, Smarter is packed with practical techniques and insights on solving old problems in new ways. It shows readers how to become more resilient in their personal and professional lives and teaches the skills for bouncing back from everyday stresses to surviving disastrous multiple losses. Written by Tessa Warschaw, Ph.D. psychotherapist and specialist in personal and corporate negotiation strategies and author of the groundbreaking *Winning by Negotiation*, and Dee Barlow, Ph.D. a major contributor to two-best selling books on marriage and family and in private practice for 15 year, **Resiliency** will teach you to enthusiastically embrace life!

($21.95, Hardbound, ISBN 1-57101-021-1, October)

To Order call 1-800-334-8232 or 1-800-395-5599
📖 Just say "Resiliency" when ordering the book through any of our 800 #s and get $2.00 off! 📖
or if you wish to order by mail, please send in the form below

----

Please send me *Resiliency: how to Bounce Back Faster, Stronger, Smarter*
Book Order

_____ copies of *Resiliency* at $21.95 = $_____

NY residents please add 7.25% sales tax = $_____
Shipping/Handling

$2.50 for first copy

$2.50 + $_____   = $_____

Total Cost [Book(s) + Shipping] = _____

To Order Toll-Free Using Visa or MasterCard Call 1-800-334-8232
Or, If You Wish To Pre-pay By Check, Please Mail To:
MasterMedia Limited, 17 East 89th Street, Suite 7D, New York, NY 10128

Your Shipping Address

Name: _____

Address1: _____

City/State/Zip: _____

Phone: (_____)_____

Announcing The Heritage I

Chris Burke

Johnny Cash

Bill Cosby

Elizabeth Dole

Billy Graham

Jackie Joyner-Kersee

Colin Powell

Dave Thomas

Elie Wiesel

Oprah Winfrey

and more

American Heroes: Their Lives. Their Values. Their Beliefs.

Dr. Robert B. Pamplin, Jr., with Gary K. Eisler.

Courage. Integrity. Compassion. The qualities of the hero still live in American men and women today—even in a world which can appear disillusioned. Share their stories of outstanding achievements. Discover the values that guide their lives and give courage to all of us. And learn some startling facts about what Americans really think of today's heroes, as revealed in a pioneering coast-to-coast survey.

Dr. Robert B. Pamplin, Jr. is a member of the Forbes 400, has been awarded numerous honorary degrees and has written twelve books.

[$18.95, *American Heroes: Their Lives. Their Values. Their Beliefs.* Hardbound ISBN 1-57101-010-6, late June.]

Will be available at bookstores
or call 1-800-334-8232
or fax 212-546-7638.
Available through Spring Arbor:
phone 1-800-395-5599
or fax 1-800-395-2682.
Also through Ingram and Baker & Ta

MASTERMEDIA

MasterMedia launches The Heritage Imprint—books that speak of courage, integrity and bouncing back from defeat. For the millions of Americans seeking greater purpose and meaning in their lives in difficult times, here are volumes of inspiration, solace and spiritual support.

The Heritage Imprint books will be supported by MasterMedia's full-service speakers' bureau, authors' media and lecture tours, syndicated radio interviews, national and co-op advertising and publicity.

Heritage: The Making of an American Family

Dr. Robert B. Pamplin, Jr., with Gary K. Eisler, Jeff Sengstack and John Domini. Foreword by Dr. Norman Vincent Peale.

Fascinating saga of the Pamplin family, which has built one of the largest private fortunes in America. From the Crusades to today's multimillion-dollar corporation run by the author and his father, longtime head of the Georgia-Pacific Corporation.

[$12.95, *Heritage: The Making of an American Family.* Paperbound ISBN 1-57101-041-6, June.]

Resiliency: How to Bounce Back Faster, Stronger, Smarter

Tessa Albert Warschaw, Ph.D. and Dee Barlow, Ph.D.

Resiliency is packed with practical techniques and insights on solving old problems in new ways. It also shows readers how to become more resilient in their personal and professional lives and teaches the skills for bouncing back from everyday stresses to surviving disastrous multiple losses. You will learn to enthusiastically embrace life.

[$21.95, *Resiliency: How to Bounce Back Faster, Stronger, Smarter.* Hardbound ISBN 1-57101-021-1, October.]

The Ethical Edge: Tales of Organizations That Have Faced Moral Crises

Dawn-Marie Driscoll, W. Michael Hoffman, Ph.D., Edward S. Petry, Ph.D., associated with The Center for Business Ethics at Bentley College.

The authors link the current search for meaning and values in life with stories of corporate turnarounds. Now read about organizations that have *recovered* from moral crises—the tough lessons they've learned, ethical structures they've put in place to ensure a solid future. If every employee followed the mission of the book, America's companies would clearly have not only a moral edge, but a competitive edge.

[$24.95, *The Ethical Edge: Tales of Organizations That Have Faced Moral Crises.* Hardbound ISBN 1-57101-051-3, February.]

Journey Toward Forgiveness: Finding Your Way Home

BettyClare Moffatt, M.A., bestselling author of *Soulwork* and many other books.

Discover the difference forgiveness makes in your world. Learn to overcome anger, fear and resentment and live "in ever-increasing joy and satisfaction and wonder." Step-by-step guidelines to forgiveness, meditation and prayer, action, healing and change.

[$11.95, *Journey to Forgiveness: Finding Your Way Home.* Paperbound ISBN 1-57101-050-5, October.]

Prelude to Surrender: The Pamplin Family and the Siege of Petersburg

Dr. Robert Pamplin, Jr., with Gary K. Eisler, Jeff Sengsteck and John Domini.

"The special value of the family saga portrayed [here] lies not only in its engrossing tale of the remarkable Boisseau clan, but also in the insights shared when individual tales intersect with larger events."—Noah Andre Trudeau, Civil War Historian. The author's ancestral home was taken over by the Confederacy for use as a hospital and as a defensive position. It is now the Pamplin Park Civil War Site.

[$10.95, *Prelude to Surrender.* Hardbound ISBN 1-57101-049-1, September.]

"The best guide I know of for professional and amateur negotiators." -- Irving "Swifty" Lazar

Dr. Warschaw takes the fear out of negotiating and the adversary confrontation out of conflict. She shows how to identify and deal with the six negotiating styles: the Jungle Fighter, the Dictator, the Silhouette, the Big Daddy and Big Mamma, the Soother, and the Win-Win Negotiator. Winning By Negotiation maximizes achievement and minimizes abuse and put-down of others. It proves that negotiating through a series of collaborations rather than a sequence of power plays helps everyone succeed in the business of everyday life.

WINNING BY NEGOTIATION

HOW to get what you want from your Spouse, Lover, Parents, Children, Friends, Employer, Lawyer, Doctor, Agent, as well as Headwaiters, Salespersons, and Landlords—and make them love you in the process.

Tessa Albert Warschaw, Ph.D.

✂ — — ✂ — — ✂ — — ✂ — — ✂ — — ✂ —

Please send me
# of copies

_____	Rich Is Better @ $ 13.95
_____	Winning By Negotiation @ $ 11.95
$ 3.00	Shipping/Handling
$ _____	TOTAL.

Please print
NAME: _____
ADDRESS: _____
                    street   including apt or P.O. Box #
_____
        city   state   zip cod.

Please send check or money order payable to: T.W.G. Publishing, Box 307, Coventry, CT 06238.
Allow four weeks for delivery. Thank you.

ASK YOURSELF....

HAVE I RECOGNIZED THE STYLE OF MY COLLEAGUES, CLIENTS, CUSTOMERS, TEAM MEMBERS, BUSINESS PARTNERS OR FAMILY MEMBERS?

AM I AWARE OF THE IMPACT OF MY OWN STYLE UPON OTHERS?

DO I KNOW HOW TO CREATE WIN-WIN OUTCOMES?

HAVE I CREATED, IGNORED, AVOIDED, OR DIFFUSED CONFLICT IN MY DAY-TO-DAY NEGOTIATIONS?

CAN I SPEAK THE LANGUAGE OF NEGOTIATION AND USE *APPROPRIATE* TOOLS, TACTICS, AND STRATEGIES?

AM I READY AND RESILIENT <u>ENOUGH</u> FOR THE 21st CENTURY?

IF YOU HAVE ANSWERED "NO" TO ANY OF THE QUESTIONS ABOVE...THIS SEMINAR IS FOR YOU!

NEGOTIATING IN AN ATMOSPHERE OF CHANGE

A SEMINAR WITH
DR. TESSA ALBERT WARSCHAW
CONTACT THE WARSCHAW GROUP
EAST COAST: 212-717-4160   WEST COAST: 310-472-5114

SEMINARS FOR THE SERIOUS NEGOTIATOR

PRESENTED BY DR. TESSA ALBERT WARSCHAW
CONTACT THE WARSCHAW GROUP FOR INFORMATION

EAST COAST:212-717-4160   WEST COAST:310-472-5114

NEGOTIATING IN AN ATMOSPHERE OF CHANGE

OPTIONS AND OPPORTUNITIES FOR THE 21ST CENTURY

QUANTUM LEAP: HOW TO TAKE THE NEXT STEP INTO THE 21st CENTURY

TODAY'S LEADERSHIP PROCESS: CREATING A VISION TOWARD THE YEAR 2000

CORPORATE CONFLICTS: RECOGNIZING, UNDERSTANDING, PREDICTING AND RESOLVING

MANAGERIAL STRATEGIES FOR BUILDING A TEAM THAT CREATES, WORKS, AND THINKS ABOUT THE BOTTOM LINE

RESILIENCY: HOW TO BOUNCE BACK FASTER, STRONGER, SMARTER

IGNITING CREATIVITY - ACCESSING UNTAPPED POTENTIAL